GLOUCESTERSHIRE
AND NORTH BRISTOL
SOLDIERS ON THE SOMME

GLOUCESTERSHIRE
AND NORTH BRISTOL
SOLDIERS ON THE SOMME

NICK THORNICROFT

TEMPUS

First published 2007

Tempus Publishing Limited
The Mill, Brimscombe Port,
Stroud, Gloucestershire, GL5 2QG
www.tempus-publishing.com

British Library Cataloguing in Publication Data.
A catalogue record for this book is available from the British Library.

ISBN 978 07524 4325 6

Typesetting and origination by Tempus Publishing Limited
Printed in Great Britain

CONTENTS

LIST OF PLATES

(Copyright remains with individual/organisation in italics)

Capt. W.G. Warden (*Gloucester Citizen.*) N.B.: The original image was virtually in silhouette, and I am very grateful to Stuart Mann, of Sunesis Imaging in High Wycombe, for retrieving partial features of the officer

MAPS:

Lt C.W. Winterbotham (*Cheltenham Chronicle & Gloucestershire Graphic*)

2nd Lt D.H.H. Logan (*Wellington College Archives*)

Somerset Light Infantry in training (*private collection*)

Somersets & Dorsets at their camp (*private collection*)

An aerial view of a front-line trench (*private collection*)

British troops on the march (*private collection*)

Marching to the trenches (*private collection*)

Soldiers of the 8th SLI (*private collection*)

German machine gunners (*private collection*)

The 'Leaning Virgin' of Albert (*private collection*)

A church at Hebuterne (*private collection*)

A gas alarm bell at Habuterne (*Gloucester Record Office D3549*)

Lt G.H.S. Musgrove (*Cheltenham Chronicle & Gloucestershire Graphic*)

Capt. Neville of the 8th Battalion, East Surrey Regiment, provided his men with four footballs on the morning of 1 July 1916 (*courtesy of the Surrey Regt Museum*)

One of the balls used by Capt. Neville (*courtesy of the Surrey Regt Museum*)

The Devonshire Cemetery at Mametz (*Devon and Dorsets Regimental Museum*)

T/Lt W.N. Hodgson, MC (*Durham University*)

Officers of the 8th SLI (*private collection*)

Capt. A.B. Hatt, MC (*Dean Close School, Cheltenham*)

L/Cpl A. Parker (*Western Daily Press*)

Pte J.G. Eamer (*Western Daily Press*)

L/Cpl (later Sgt) L. Tizzard, MM (*Western Daily Press*)

2nd Lt F.A. Golding (*Bristol Times & Mirror*)

Maj. A.G. Niven (*Graham Stewart*)

Lt-Col A.J.E. Sunderland (*private collection*)

E.M.B. Cambie (*Dean Close School, Cheltenham*)

Lt-Col P.W. Machell, CMG (*Kevin Johnstone*)

Capt. R.V. Kestell-Cornish, MC & Bar (*Sherborne School Archives*)

Capt. E.J. Millin (*Cheltenham Chronicle & Gloucestershire Graphic*)

Pte M.P.H. Blumer (*Dean Close School, Cheltenham*)

Brig.-Gen. C.B. Prowse, DSO (*private collection*)

The original grave of Brig.-Gen. C.B. Prowse, DSO (*Somerset Record Office/SLI Museum DD/SLI/15/18/11*)

2nd Lt A.V.C. Leche (*John & Beverley Whalley* – www.silentcities.co.uk)

Pte F.C. Freebury (*Chelt. Chronicle & Glos. Graphic*)

Lt H. Jones (*Wycliffe College*)

Pte A. Morgan (*J & B Whalley* – www.silentcities.co.uk)

Capt. K. Herne (*Wycliffe College, Stonehouse*)

Sapper T.R. Lane (*Chelt. Chronicle & Glos. Graphic*)

A. Hurley (*Gloucestershire Echo*)

2nd Lt A. Beacall (*Gloucester Citizen*)

Looking towards Hebuterne from Serre in 1920 (*Glos. Record Office D3549*)

Original front line trenches, 2006 (*private collection*)

'Y' Ravine pictured in 2006 (*private collection*)

2nd Lt A.M. Herapath (*Dean Close School*)

Ruins in Foncquevillers (*Glos. Record Office D3549*)

'The Road Through Ovillers' (*Glos. Record Office D3549*)

Lochnagar Crater, 1936 (*Glos. Record Office D3549*)

The original grave of Capt. L.W. Crouch (*Glos. Record Office D3549*)

Wounded soldiers at Cheltenham's VAD Hospital (*Cheltenham Chronicle & Glos. Graphic*)

The Lochnagar Crater at 7.30 a.m. of 1 July 2006 (*private collection*)

Mash Valley, 2006 (*private collection*)

British Cemetery at Serre, 2006 (*Terry Carter*)

Ovillers Military Cemetery (*private collection*)

Fricourt British Cemetery (*private collection*)

ABBREVIATIONS

FM/Fd Marsh.	Field Marshal
Gen.	General
Lt-Gen.	Lieutenant-General
Maj.-Gen.	Major-General
Brig.-Gen.	Brigadier-General
Col	Colonel
Lt-Col	Lieutenant-Colonel
Maj.	Major
Capt.	Captain
Lt	Lieutenant
2nd Lt or 2nd-Lt	Second Lieutenant
T/… or Temp/…	Temporary rank
CO	Commanding Officer
NCO	Non Commissioned Officer
RSM	Regimental Sergeant Major
CSM	Company Sergeant Major
RQMS	Regimental Quarter Master Sergeant
Sgt	Sergeant
L/Sgt	Lance Sergeant
Cpl	Corporal
L/Cpl	Lance Corporal
A/…	Acting rank
Pte	Private
Gnr	Gunner (Artillery)
Spr	Sapper (Engineers)
Tpr	Trooper (Cavalry)
RFA	Royal Field Artillery
RHA	Royal Horse Artillery
RGA	Royal Garrison Artillery
RE	Royal Engineers
R.A.M.C.	Royal Army Medical Corps
RFC	Royal Flying Corps
SLI	Somerset Light Infantry
DCM	Distinguished Conduct Medal
DSO	Distinguished Service Order
MC	Military Cross
MM	Military Medal
VC	Victoria Cross
CMG	Commander of the Order of St Michael & St George
KBE	Knight Commander of the Order of the British Empire
SDGW	'Soldiers Died In The Great War' CD-Rom (Naval & Military Press)
ODGW	'Officers Died In The Great War'
CWGC	Commonwealth War Graves Commission
OR	Other Rank (i.e. not an officer)
POW	Prisoner of War
VAD	Voluntary Aid Detachment

ACKNOWLEDGEMENTS

I am extremely grateful to the following individuals and organisations for their help and advice during the course of writing this book: for giving their permission to use photographs: Kevin Johnstone; Graham Stewart; Dean Close School, Cheltenham; Sherborne School; Surrey Regiment Museum; Durham University; John & Beverley Whalley; Terry Carter; Devon & Dorset's Regiment Museum and Wellington College. For their permission to use original text and photographs: the staff at Gloucestershire Records Office; the staff at Somerset Record Office/SLI Museum; Wycliffe College; Stonehouse and Bristol Grammar Schools. The Editors of the following newspapers for the same (Copyright remains with the newspaper): Bristol Evening Post & Press Ltd (*Western Daily Press*); *Gloucestershire Gazette* (*Dursley Gazette*); *Stroud News & Journal*; *The Mercury* (*Dean Forest Mercury*); *Gloucester Citizen*; *Wiltshire & Gloucestershire Standard*; *Gloucestershire Echo* and the *Stratford Herald*. Also, The War Research Society; Frances Daniels (Bath); Liz Carter (Cambridge); Anne Powell & Anna Barrington-Ward (for the poem *The Cross of Wood*), the libraries at Gloucester, Stroud, Cheltenham, Bristol, Cirencester & Cinderford; Sunesis Imaging, High Wycombe; the National Archives; Clifton College; The Naval & Military Press; Customised Mapping, Barnstaple; and to my family for their unceasing support and practical assistance. Apologies to anyone omitted. A special mention must go to Mr C. Campbell, my English teacher and initial inspiration for this book way back in 1980 (see Introduction.) Sadly, Mr Campbell passed away before publication. I hope he would have approved of its content.

'I WANT TO SEE MY BOYS ADVANCING'

Capt. W.G Warden.

These words were spoken by Gloucester-born Captain Walter Warden (*above*), of the 8th Somerset Light Infantry, as he lay dying on the Somme battlefield on the morning of 1 July 1916, after leading his battalion into action. His sentiments encapsulate the sense of duty, honour and courage shown by the British army on the bloodiest day in its history.

MAPS

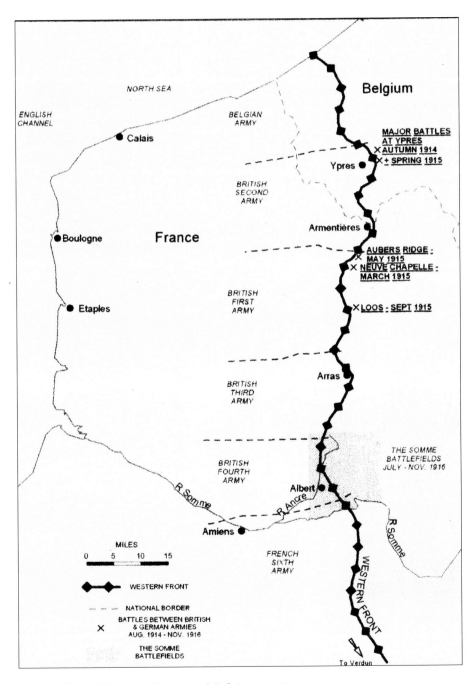

NORTH SEA

ENGLISH
CHANNEL

BELGIAN
ARMY

Belgium

● Calais

BELGIAN
ARMY

**MAJOR BATTLES
AT YPRES**
X **AUTUMN 1914**
X + **SPRING 1915**

Ypres ●

BRITISH
SECOND
ARMY

Armentières ●

**AUBERS RIDGE :
MAY 1915**
X **NEUVE CHAPELLE -
MARCH 1915**

● Boulogne

France

BRITISH
FIRST
ARMY

X **LOOS - SEPT 1915**

● Etaples

BRITISH
THIRD
ARMY

Arras

*THE SOMME
BATTLEFIELDS
JULY - NOV. 1916*

BRITISH
FOURTH
ARMY

R Somme

Albert ●

R Ancre

R Somme

Amiens ●

MILES

0   5   10   15

◆—◆ WESTERN FRONT

- - - - NATIONAL BORDER

X   BATTLES BETWEEN BRITISH
       & GERMAN ARMIES
       AUG. 1914 - NOV. 1916

       THE SOMME
       BATTLEFIELDS

FRENCH
SIXTH
ARMY

WESTERN FRONT

To Verdun

Western Front, Northern France and Belgium, 1916.

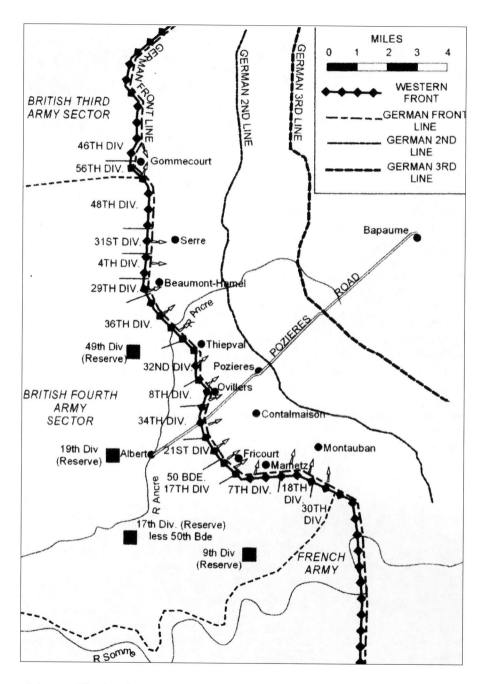

1 July 1916. The Attack.

(Maps compiled by Customised Mapping, Barnstaple)

PREFACE

Much has been written about the loss of youth, innocence and a significant percentage of an entire generation during the First World War, and this is personified in the two individuals included on this page. The death of Bristol-born 2nd Lt David Logan, of the 2nd Border Regiment, on 1 July 1916, was all the more tragic due to his tender years. On his seventeenth birthday – 4 August 1914 – war was declared on Germany, and he soon enlisted into the army, proceeding to France in May 1916. His conduct in battle was noted by his Platoon Sergeant, who later wrote to the officer's father:

> Your son was very young, the youngest in the battalion. We all liked him, he was a good and brave young officer, cool and collected under fire. The day before he was shot, he and some of his men were buried by the explosion of a 5.9 shell. On the morning of the attack, I said to him, 'Shall I stand near you, sir?' He said, 'Your place is on the left of the platoon, mine is on the right'. Your son would not allow any one to go in front of him, but went first into the [German] dug-outs.

The Wellington College Archives, which very kindly supplied the above information and photograph (next page) added: 'He was killed as the regiment was advancing from the first to the second line.'

On 27 August 1916, Lt Cyril Winterbotham was one of four officers and a number of men in the ranks of the 1/5th Glosters to lose their lives during a 'successful' raid on German trenches. The twenty-nine-year-old officer, a native of Cheltenham, also had links with Stroud, and had previously written a poem entitled 'The Cross of Wood', the third and fourth verses of which are published overleaf, along with an image of Lt Winterbotham himself. After studying Law at Oxford, he was commissioned in September 1914, and died near Mouquet Farm, Ovillers-la-Boisselle, less than halfway through the Somme Offensive.

'The Cross of Wood' was first published privately in 1917, in a book entitled simply *Poems*, and was later included in *The Fierce Light: The Battle of the Somme, July – November 1916* (edited and introduced by Anne Powell: republished by Suttons, October 2006.) It was even read by Sir Harry Secombe on the television programme *Songs of Praise*, and the 'cross of bronze' referred to is the Victoria Cross, the world's most distinguished gallantry medal. By coincidence, it was reported that Gloucester-born Pte Charles Bird, who was killed in the attack, would have been recommended for a VC had any witnesses survived, as it was believed he had acted with immense bravery. A sketch of the 'Cross of Wood', which marked the final resting place of these men from the 1/5th Glosters, later appeared in the *Cheltenham Chronicle* and *Gloucestershire Graphic* – the ultimate irony considering Lt Winterbotham's prose:

Lt C.W. Winterbotham.

2nd Lt D.H.H. Logan.

Not now for you the glorious return
To steep Stroud valleys, to the Severn leas
By Tewkesbury and Gloucester, or the trees
Of Cheltenham under high Cotswold stem

For you no medals such as others wear
A cross of bronze for those approved brave
To you is given, above a shallow grave,
The Wooden Cross that marks you resting there

INTRODUCTION

I can never quite pinpoint when my fascination with – and horror of – the First World War began, but it must have been during my time at Minchinhampton Primary School, near Stroud, in the 1970s. I would wait for the bus next to the War Memorial in the Market Square, and how I wish I had made the effort to visit veterans of that dreadful conflict, who no doubt lived in the town or nearby, asking them questions for an educational project or the like. Moving on to secondary education in Stroud, my interest in military history had not diminished, even if my enthusiasm for sitting behind a desk had waned considerably. One such event still sticks in my mind: on a gloomy November day, when the slightly eccentric but highly likeable English teacher, Mr Campbell, decided to set aside the normal curriculum to tell us all about the first day of the Battle of the Somme – 1 July 1916. He possessed a powerful and dramatic voice, coupled with a knack of story-telling which was put to a variety of uses during his career, and he managed to draw the attention of even the most committed rebels, who had previously been slumped at the back of the classroom gazing out of the window.

Mr Campbell implored us to recall the recently taken school photograph, which recorded for posterity the 800 or so teachers and pupils who were present on one particular day during 1980. This initially raised a few smirks, as some in the room had partaken in the usual mischief of disrupting the supposedly solemn occasion by throwing pieces of paper in the air at the moment of being blinked into permanence, as well as adopting bizarre hairstyles, teenage snarls and general non-conformity. The frivolity was duly noted. We were then told, in solemn tones, how 20,000 young men had lost their lives in just one day of a war which lasted over four years. The smirking stopped. Seeming close to tears, Mr Campbell suggested we imagined the 800 individuals of the photo dressed in army uniforms, waiting to receive orders to be sent abroad to the Front. He reminded us of the Pals battalions of 1914 – made up of approximately 800 men each – youngsters who had grown up together, gone to school together, played in the same football teams and joined up so patriotically when war was declared. These same men trained as one, went off to fight, and in a few horrific hours on the morning of 1 July 1916, went 'over the top' together and were slaughtered in their thousands.

I do not think I have ever been so stunned by a piece of history before or since. There was silence in that classroom. Sixty-six years earlier pupils and former pupils of the same school had no doubt been stirred into enlisting by impassioned speeches about their King and Country, fighting for freedom and moral right. (One would receive the coveted Victoria Cross as the Somme campaign reached its bloody conclusion. Cainscross-born Capt. Paul Bennett, of the Worcestershire Regiment, led his small party of men through a devastating fire and consolidated the position at Le Transloy on 5 November 1916, despite being wounded. He was christened in his local church on 1 July 1892, exactly twenty-four years before the British Army's blackest day.)

One of the most well-documented and tragic stories of the opening day of the Somme Offensive was the fate of the Accrington Pals from that close-knit Lancashire town. Yet in its officer ranks was a native of Gloucestershire, whose father was the headmaster of a county school. It has to be wondered whether the latter was asked to rally *his* local residents by standing up in public and calling for volunteers to join Kitchener's Army, accompanied by the famous 'Your Country Needs You' recruiting posters: this was a call which led thousands of young men to enlist nationwide.

Mr Campbell's spellbinding oratory transcended the years, but we had the awful truth of hindsight on our side. Would *we* have enlisted so enthusiastically, knowing what we know now? It is an impossible question to answer, but one which plagued us all as we trooped off to another lesson – an insignificant, instantly forgettable destination which did not matter one jot on that peculiar day in November 1980. So why do I remember it so vividly? How many of my contemporaries can recall its impact, if indeed there was any impact for them at all? Maybe, subconsciously, I resolved to do something about it when the opportunity arose, to tell a story – a *true* story – focusing upon the individuals from place-names I know well. I would hold them up not as deities, but as normal human beings who were thrust by time, fate and circumstance into lining up in the front line trenches in one place, on one day, of one month, of one year.

RESEARCHING GLOUCESTERSHIRE'S FALLEN

In July 1916, as the Somme Offensive raged across the English Channel, the *Dean Forest Guardian* published the following article:

> Who are these men who are doing such wondrous exploits, who are thus immortalising themselves? Not seasoned and hardened veterans, not men who have long experienced the exactions of military life, or taken an active part in military operations. On the contrary, less than two years since many of them, perhaps most of them, had scarcely ever handled a rifle or fixed a bayonet…They were in name and in fact civilians… Less than two years ago they were teachers in elementary or secondary schools, or clerks in commercial or other offices, or working on the railways, or in the mines or factories, or on the land. They had little or no knowledge of a soldier's life…

It has to be remembered that on 1 July 1916 there was not one conscript in a British uniform – all had joined up voluntarily. One wounded officer who took part in the initial attack spoke to the Press upon his arrival back in the UK, and the *Gloucester Citizen* was one of the newspapers which published his words:

> There never has been a finer spirit shown. I don't speak of my battalion only. Ask any officer. Every one I have spoken to had exactly the same experience. Our men are not bullet-proof. When they enter a zone of living fire they get hit. But till they get knocked out they baulk at nothing – no prospect can check them. They are as brave as mortal men can be, their morale is perfect, and the level of their spirit could not possibly be better.

When I first compiled the list of the men from Gloucestershire who fell on 1 July 1916, it was necessary to establish the southern boundary and address the question of whether North Bristol should be included. The urban conglomeration of today is very much an entity in itself – the City and County of Bristol – yet in the 1880s and 1890s, when the vast majority of the soldiers included in this book were born, much of the region which has now been swallowed up by the sprawl of Bristol was, in fact, very much part of rural Gloucestershire. Therefore, I decided to use the river Avon – which cuts through the city centre – as the 'dividing line' where Somerset begins, and I hope I do not offend too many staunch Bristolians by referring to residents living to the north of the Avon as hailing from Gloucestershire! The rest of the county borders have barely changed in hundreds of years, apart from the occasional village which has been claimed by one of its neighbouring regions over the centuries.

In 1921 the War Office published a monumental piece of research listing all of the 703,000 officers and men of the British army who died on active service between 4 August 1914 and 1921. (Beyond the Armistice of 11 November 1918, British servicemen were still required for duties in Russia supporting the anti-Bolsheviks, or with the Army of Occupation in the Rhineland.) The eighty-one printed volumes were catalogued alphabetically, by regiment, and a search for one individual whose unit was not known became a virtual impossibility until *The Naval & Military Press* produced the hugely impressive *Soldiers Died In The Great War* (SDGW) CD-Rom in the computer age, enabling a wealth of information to become available in a matter of seconds. If all of the data is present for a casualty who was not an officer (invariably seen in War Diaries as Other Rank – OR), then the following detail can be ascertained: surname, Christian name(s), rank, service number, regiment, battalion, place of birth, enlistment and residence at the time of joining up, date of death, nature of death (killed in action, died of wounds, etc.), Theatre of War (Balkans, Gallipoli, etc.), and the provision for supplementary notes such as previous regiment, gallantry award, etc. It is therefore possible to type in a specific date of death – 1 July 1916 in the case of this book – and bring up all of the individuals who died on this day in the Theatre of War sub-titled 'France & Flanders' (Western Front). All of the fallen soldiers who had a birth or residential connection with Gloucestershire or North Bristol were then collated, and it is interesting to note that even some of those who were born in the heart of Bristol – in areas such as St Paul's or Clifton – sometimes had the suffix 'Glos.' next to their entry.

The *Officers Died In The Great War* (ODGW) is on the same CD-Rom, but contains no personal background references along the lines of birthplace or an address which specifies a connection to a particular county. This category proved the more challenging, as it was then necessary to consult the Commonwealth War Graves Commission's (CWGC) Debt of Honour Register, which lists the site of burial or commemoration for each one of the British and Empire soldiers, sailors and airmen who lost their lives during the conflict. Some of those listed are accompanied by details of an individual's next of kin, but another factor to be considered here is that this data was compiled during the 1920s, and therefore refers to locations relevant to several years *after* the end of the conflict rather than when an individual actually died. A number of war widows had remarried when the CWGC contacted them, whilst some had relocated to other parts of the country, as had other family members. A proportion of servicemen who are to be found within the CWGC have no genealogical or geographical references, which leads to the assumption that, in the case of officers, a few whose links to Gloucestershire were not established during the research of local newspapers, schools, colleges or in the CWGC, have been inevitably – and regrettably – omitted.

It is also prudent to mention that the first Casualty Rolls – ODGW, SDGW and CWGC – were compiled by hand, in ink, from official military records which varied widely in legibility, and therefore some of the data is erroneous, despite the best efforts of all concerned. As we shall see, in the week leading up to the 1 July attack a number of casualties were possibly (or definitely) attributed dates of death which did not tally with the Battalion War Diaries – accounts which were written by eyewitnesses 'in the field' as events unfolded and are thus more reliable – and the general spelling of names and places of origin on enlistment forms is also open to interpretation.

The National Archives in Kew contain millions of original documents from the First World War, and these were an invaluable source to consult. Only a small proportion (25–30 per cent) of service papers relating to men in the ranks who served between 1914 and 1918 survived the Blitz in 1940, when the factory which housed them received a direct hit. Officers' equivalents fared a little better (and usually contain more information than the ORs'), so along with the Battalion

War Diaries (mentioned previously), local newspaper archives and the vast amount of information on the Internet, it slowly became possible to build up a true and accurate picture of the fate of men from Gloucestershire and North Bristol between 24 June and 1 July 1916. It became quite an emotional journey, and I felt a strange connection with their plight, experiencing a kind of historical foreboding as each life story unravelled before my eyes, knowing where, for most of them, that journey would end. In mid-July 1916, the *Stroud News* commented:

> In the Stroud district many homes are in mourning. In such a war as this it is inevitable that death should reap a great harvest. But in every home – in every house and every cottage from which a brave man has gone never to return – there is the same brave recognition of the necessity of the sacrifice, and the same unwavering faith in the cause for which these gallant men have yielded their lives.

Just how great that sacrifice would be could not have been known at the time, and reports like these have given the event an added poignancy that has lasted throughout the twentieth century and beyond.

1

THE WESTERN FRONT (AUGUST 1914–JUNE 1916)

With the assassination of Archduke Franz Ferdinand in Sarajevo at the end of June 1914, a series of long-standing treaties, alliances, feuds and rivalries brought much of Europe to the brink of conflict. The Germans had set their sights on capturing the French capital, Paris, and to do so they invaded neutral Belgium to bypass the strong defences on the Franco-German border. This act, at the beginning of August, led to Britain and her Empire declaring war on Kaiser Wilhelm – Queen Victoria's grandson – soon afterwards. Plans were swiftly put in place for the deployment of the British Expeditionary Force. Compared to the millions on the march across mainland Europe, the BEF was small, numbering about 100,000, yet it was thoroughly professional, well disciplined and trained to a very high standard. Most county regiments consisted of two battalions, with one based in the UK and the other generally overseas; the latter were recalled at once, although some took several weeks to reach Britain. Amongst those that were ready to go immediately was the 1st Battalion of the Gloucestershire Regiment and the 1st Somerset Light Infantry, crossing the Channel in mid-August to be received with great jubilation by the French people.

The BEF moved up into Belgium and engaged the enemy in strength on 23 August, but the Germans' superior numbers pushed the British, French and Belgian armies back towards Paris until, in September, the Allies finally checked the advance before successfully driving the invaders back northwards. A 'Race for the Sea' then ensued, with each side trying to outflank the other in order to secure the vital Channel ports, and a major battle was fought at Ypres in Belgium throughout October and into November, with the British bearing the brunt of the assault, which was only held back by some desperate fighting combined with outstanding bravery. As winter closed in and a stalemate began, the soldiers dug trenches to sit out the freezing months before hostilities could resume again in earnest the following spring. Thus a chilling line of fortifications soon stretched from the North Sea to the border of Switzerland, cutting through Belgium and vast acres of France to become known as the Western Front. Most significantly, the Germans held the higher ground almost everywhere, allowing them to establish tactically superior observation posts for their artillery as well as creating intricate systems of defences. From hastily crafted holes in the ground during the autumn of 1914 which offered scant protection from enemy bullets and bombs, the trenches became an elaborate art form in their own right, and images of soldiers suffering in their squalor are among the most enduring of the First World War. An anonymous former pupil of Wycliffe College in Stonehouse sent the following description to the college magazine as the conflict was unfolding:

> Do you realise what a trench is like? It is a little lane just broad enough to walk along. On each side a wall of earth some seven or eight feet high, overhead a narrow view of the sky,

and under foot – mud. Just greasy, sticky mud. Not the kind that you get at home on a wet day. In the trenches it develops into a species that I cannot describe to you. It pulls the boots from the feet. It tears the ankles. Five minutes' walk in the open takes an hour in a trench like this.[1]

By Christmas 1914 the BEF had virtually been wiped out, with a large percentage killed, wounded or taken prisoner, leading to an urgent recruitment drive back in the UK. Many had stepped forward as soon as war was declared, and the volunteers swamped the enlistment offices as the months went on. The county regiments expanded to accommodate the new arrivals, setting up training camps across the country, and the *Stroud News* revealed:

> Letters which relatives of recruits in the new army are receiving go to prove that the spirits of the men are excellent, and that they are generally enjoying their military experience. One and all speak of the long hours of arduous drilling day after day, but they seldom make a word of complaint… They could make a joke of sleeping on the floors of huts into which the rain had a vicious habit of invariably invading, of drilling on sodden ground ankle-deep in honest British mud. It was, perhaps, the best preparation for their coming acquaintance with the mud of Flanders, but it searched the stamina of many. And every man was eager to get through his training and join the fighting army across the Channel.

Yet the war was going badly for the Allies, and plans to break the deadlock when the weather improved in 1915 were established. The distance between the two opposing front lines varied enormously, but sometimes it was possible for a group of men in one to hear their opposite numbers talking or moving about in the other. Trenches were guarded by sandbags and endless barbed wire to prevent surprise enemy sorties across No Man's Land, although there had to be carefully hidden gaps in the defences to enable the swift emergence and withdrawal of a similar expedition from their own positions. Sentries were posted at regular intervals, and

Somerset Light Infantry in training, *c.*1915. Many British troops trained at home before leaving for the front. The 8th Battalion, for example, was based at Witley Camp in Surrey during August 1915, before embarking for France the following month.

Somersets and Dorsets at their camp, *c.*1915. Almost all of them were Kitchener's Men – new recruits who joined up at the outbreak of war. Both battalions suffered heavily on the Somme.

snipers fired at anyone reckless enough to raise his head above the parapet. The trenches themselves zig-zagged rather than follow a straight course. This was intended to negate the effects of a bomb-blast; dug-outs, latrines, cooking stations and ammunition dumps had to be squeezed in wherever possible, and communication passageways snaked back towards the second and third lines which marked relative safety. Although trench mortars and artillery shells came over intermittently, the soldiers could, at least, take some measure of shelter from the bombardments. But the action feared by all was going 'over the top' in broad daylight. In a sector which was relatively static, the gruesome remains of fallen men lying in No Man's Land often stayed out in the open for months, suffering the further indignities of the effects of exploding bombs, and it is little wonder so many individuals could not be recognised when their pitiful corpses were finally brought in for a proper interment. This grim fact was emphasised in a letter to the *Bristol Times & Mirror* written by Lt G.H. Gibbs of the South Midland Royal Engineers, and a former pupil of Clifton College:

> It is difficult to describe the state of things in the trenches and I feel sure the average person at home has no idea of what trench warfare is like. Graves and bodies are scattered all over the place. Men are buried in the trenches themselves, and along my mile of front there are dozens of known graves. You can see a little cross, built of timber resembling bad firewood, with the inscription 'Here lies an unknown soldier. R.I.P.' An old cap, torn and muddy, and as likely as not covered with mildew, or perhaps a bayonet, has been placed on the mound, and occasionally a flower.

Life in the trenches was marked by long periods of monotony followed by several moments of sheer terror. Each man, in his own way, tried to adapt to this new, almost primeval lifestyle, punctuated by all the horrors modern warfare could launch at them. J. Percy Marshall, an Old Wycliffian (OW) who served in the Royal Artillery, recalled:

> …the hissing whistle which a trench shell makes in its ride through space comes as a warning, and after a little practice one can tell approximately whereabouts the shell will fall, and when it is coming…[2]

Above: An aerial view of a front line trench. The ground is covered with shell craters.

Below: British troops on the march. New recruits were trained in military ways by officers and experienced NCOs.

Marching to the trenches; 'One felt their presence…always the steady tramp-*tramp*, tramp-*tramp* as they shouldered by, and they were always whistling.'

Lt Rex Bird, another OW, who joined the 12th Glosters as a Private before receiving a commission with the Wiltshires, wrote down his impressions of an artillery duel and sent them to his college magazine:

> I was suddenly awakened by [British] shells screaming overhead. It was a real bombardment, and the Hun took it as such, for in three minutes his shells arrived, in five he was going strong, and in seven or eight the heavies joined in. I didn't stay outside long, but sat in the opening (how can I call it a doorway?) of my dug-out, watching the fire caps of exploding shells bounding over, and the flying dirt and smoke. Suddenly, on the other side of the crater, a flash, a cloud of black smoke, and I lean behind the wall of sandbags as a blast of air hurls itself through the opening, fairly whistling through my hair, and a shower of earth follows it. Three times we had this little game…About 5:15 I went out, as only occasional shells came over, intending to go round the machine guns. As I was going round the crater, three whizz-bangs (so called because they whizz suddenly and then bang, unless they get very close, in which case they only bang – the first intimation of their arrival) came over…[3]

The British fought battles at Neuve Chapelle in March 1915, Ypres again in April and May, Aubers Ridge, and other skirmishes, but no breakthrough was forthcoming. In September a major offensive was launched at Loos, engaging many of the so-called 'New Armies' which comprised men who had joined up in the late summer and autumn of 1914, but it was another slaughter. Despite initial gains, when troops including those of the 10th Glosters punched a hole in the German lines, reserves were too far to the rear to be brought up in any significant number, and the isolated parties were pushed back or annihilated. Loos was a costly failure, with the casualty figures rising by tens of thousands, and the War Office statistics for 1915 reveal that over 280,000 British servicemen were officially classed as dead, wounded, missing or taken prisoner on the Western Front in that one year alone.

Soldiers of the 8th Battalion, Somerset Light Infantry. When it was formed in Taunton during October 1914 many local men joined its ranks. Colston Hall in Bristol was also a recruiting office, leading to a significant number of Bristolians enlisting from both sides of the river Avon.

The *Stroud News* revealed in October 1915 that:

> Evidence of the inevitable wane of the voluntary recruiting boom was forthcoming when, after a largely attended recruiting meeting held outside the George Hotel, Stroud, at which the Band of the 1st Gloucesters played selections of music, one man – an old soldier – stepped out of the crowd and offered himself amid cheers.

The same month saw the introduction of Lord Derby's scheme, whereby men of military age (eighteen to forty-one) were compelled to register themselves for compulsory service in the armed forces should they be called forward. This was the first step towards conscription, which became law in March 1916, yet none of these individuals would be in the ranks in time for 1 July 1916. As the new year dawned, it was proposed that a mighty Franco-British assault on the Western Front would obliterate the Germans once and for all, so new plans were drawn up accordingly. After the failure at Loos, Gen. Sir John French was removed from his position as Commander-in-Chief of the BEF and replaced by Gen. Sir Douglas Haig. But his plan to methodically build up to an all-out attack in the summer of 1916 was dashed almost immediately when the Germans launched their own offensive on the French at Verdun in February 1916, pouring thousands of men into the fray. The ancient walled city was defended with equal fanaticism and became a symbol of Gallic pride, leading to horrendous losses on both sides. Haig was informed that Verdun could not hold out indefinitely, and a strike at the Germans elsewhere on the Western Front would relieve the pressure considerably for those upon whose soil the battles were being fought.

Haig was in a dilemma. Mindful of the psychological and military consequences of the French capitulating at Verdun, he was keen to assist in the most positive of manners. But at the same time he knew that his own armies, consisting mainly of untried and relatively untested troops, could not achieve the hammer blow he had originally forecast. The British had recently taken over a new sector of the line, almost due south of Ypres, well inside French territory with the town of Albert its new Headquarters. This area was bisected by the river Ancre, but it was only a tributary of a major waterway which never actually flowed through the allotted district of the BEF, although its name will forever be associated with carnage and suffering on an apocalyptic scale. That river was called the Somme.

THE PLAN

The main thrust of the attack was to fall into the hands of the recently formed British Fourth Army, under Gen. Sir Henry Rawlinson, who would send his massed infantry forward on either side of the Albert Bapaume Road, capturing vital German positions, stores and strong-points which had not budged for nearly two years. To the right of the Fourth Army, the French would advance simultaneously, although it would be on a much reduced scale due to the endeavours and manpower being concentrated at Verdun. Further to the north of the British front, beyond the Ancre, smaller objectives and gains were to be consolidated in support of the primary assault, whilst a 'diversion' was intended for Gommecourt, which was the responsibility of the Third Army. Here, the line 'bulged' outwards towards the British into No Man's Land, and had been heavily fortified by the Germans as a consequence. By engaging the enemy and hopefully taking the position, it was intended as a useful method of preventing the Kaiser's men from being sent south to assist their comrades battling to resist the onslaught around Albert.

At Verdun, the Germans had pounded French front line trenches with artillery shells before the infantry rushed to occupy them; this had proved a largely successful ploy. Rawlinson decided he would do the same on the Somme, setting specific targets of taking one line of the defences at a time before moving on to the next one, believing that his gunners could destroy everything in the path of the assault troops, who would simply have to walk across No Man's Land and take the positions virtually unopposed. Cavalrymen were to be held in reserve, ready to exploit any gains along the Front. Yet one of the key failures of the 1 July advance was that of the Royal Artillery, and this will be focused upon shortly.

With the French on their knees at Verdun, the date of the British attack was set for 29 June, and even the hour of the initial advance was established – 7.30 a.m., a full three hours after dawn. This was at the request of the French, who believed artillery observation would be hampered by early morning mists, and they even asked for a later time, but Rawlinson would not concede. It is to be wondered how many of those in the know harboured grave doubts about this particular stipulation.

So, throughout the spring and into the early summer of 1916, thousands of British troops began arriving in the Somme sector. Their movements could not be screened from the Germans, who strengthened their own already formidable defences accordingly. *The Official History of the Gloucestershire Regiment* records how some of these were 'extraordinarily powerful', and that they possessed a strong second line system which was an average of between 3,000 and 5,000 yards behind the Front. There were often several stretches of deep trenches punctuated by bomb-proof shelters and numerous well-protected communication alleyways for the purposes of withdrawal. No Man's Land was guarded by impenetrable wire entanglements, many of them consisting of two belts up to forty yards broad, interlaced with barbed coils 'almost as thick as a man's finger'. A salient in the forward-most positions turned into a self-contained fort in the event of an attack, and these themselves were often backed up by mine fields and concrete gun emplacements, so designed as to be able to direct fire upon their own trenches should the enemy succeed in getting that far. All-round clear observation was essential, and the entire network was described as 'one composite system of enormous depth and strength'. It was also noted that, between the Somme and the Ancre, the British positions were below the enemy's, so the configuration of the German movements behind their own front could only be carried out by the Royal Flying Corps or through precarious and rudimentary balloons.

Most of the British soldiers, however, were unaware of the sheer scale of the daunting task which confronted them. Capt. Lyndon Moore, of the RFA, told his former teachers at Wycliffe College early in 1916, 'All are looking forward to the Spring and to the big offensive which is coming some day.' One of his contemporaries, Lt Leslie Bomford, added, 'Everybody here is confident that the push will fairly wipe out the Huns.' Lt J.P. Lakeman, a fellow OW, commented, 'This country reminds me very much of Stonehouse, being hilly and wooded to a great extent. In fact it would be a delightful place to live if it was not for the perpetual thunderstorm in its midst.'[4]

Many servicemen drew a parallel between whichever part of the UK they came from and the fields of northern France, but the Somme countryside had a few subtle differences which would bring about tragic consequences. Beneath the soil on which the soldiers trod was a layer of chalk – a welcome substance from the clammy clay of Flanders which did not drain – but trenches dug in this composition left tell-tale white heaps wherever it was disturbed, and with the German observation posts on the slightly higher ground, the upturn in manual work could not go un-noticed.

Between the villages, the landscape was open apart from the clumps of trees or larger woods which would soon become hideous burial grounds for thousands of Allied troops, and the chalk elements ensured the ground rolled gently with few sharp contours. Hedges were non-existent, allowing agriculture to flourish. Yet from the point of view of a military preparing to repel an offensive, there was one over-riding factor which stood out above all others – the German machine-guns had numerous positions which possessed almost uninterrupted views of the assault which was about to be launched towards them, and the men who would inflict such grievous casualties on 1 July and beyond are worth focusing upon in a little more detail.

Each gunner went through extensive training before joining a machine-gun (M.G.) crew, and schools were set up in Germany during 1915. The individuals were taught how to service, dismantle and repair a variety of weapons – including those captured from the enemy – as well as range-finding and reloading. Sights on the barrel enabled the operator to track targets at considerable distance, and with a maximum range of 4,400 yards plus a rate of fire between 400 and 500 rounds per minute, it is little wonder British losses were so horrendous on the Somme. There were 250 rounds to each belt of ammunition, and fresh water was added to cool the mechanics of the gun after every fourth belt had been expended. M.G. officers located their emplacements to allow a maximum scope of fire, as well as ensuring that each position was heavily fortified, but in the event of an overwhelming attack, arrangements were put in

German machine gunners, *c.*1914. Germany's war preparations were far more thorough than those of the British. These teams of men were trained to become ruthless and efficient in combat, and would prove themselves with deadly accuracy on the Somme.

Right: The 'Leaning Virgin' of Albert. Religious buildings on the Somme were not immune from the destruction of war. This was a familiar sight to the thousands of British troops who marched their way through Albert on their way to the Front.

Below: The church at Hebuterne. This was in the British Third Army sector close to the village of Gommecourt, which was attacked on 1 July 1916 in a 'diversionary' assault to the main thrust further south.

place to relocate to another site if the original was in danger of being over-run. These carefully laid-down plans would soon pay huge dividends.

In the early months of the war, a reporter from the *Bristol Times & Mirror* asked Lord Roberts, VC, the veteran warrior of over sixty years' experience, 'What is the supreme virtue of a soldier?' – 'Courage!' replied the eighty-two-year-old Field Marshall. Lord Roberts had spent much of his childhood in Clifton and received his Victoria Cross way back in 1858 during the Indian Mutiny. By 1914, he was full of praise for his successors: 'The British soldiers of today are showing themselves in that respect the equals of the British soldiers of the days of old.' Just weeks later, after reviewing his troops on the Western Front, he passed away, prompting universal mourning both in Flanders and around the British Empire. Roberts was revered by his men, the professionals of the BEF who were under such severe pressure on the battlefield, and they felt his loss most keenly. As the next generation of British soldiers assembled on the Somme, Lord Kitchener – the man who had done so much for recruitment in the initial stages of the conflict – was on board the armoured cruiser *Hampshire* bound for Russia when the vessel was sunk by a German mine close to the Orkneys on 5 June 1916. The Earl and many hundreds were drowned. The New Armies he had helped to create proudly called themselves 'Kitchener's Men', and it was another high profile death which the authorities could ill afford. It was not a good omen for the forthcoming assault.

A look through the many regiments which were making their final preparations for the attack on the Somme reveals just how heavily regional the UK and Ireland forces were. The Devons, Dorsets, Wiltshires, Warwickshires, London battalions, Lancashire men, Tynesiders, Scots and Ulstermen were widely represented, and as it turned out, there was only one entire unit lining up on the morning of 1 July which did not originate from the British Isles – the 1st Newfoundlanders from North America. There were no Guards either (Coldstream, Grenadier, Scots, Irish or Welsh) and no Empire troops from countries such as Australia, New Zealand, India or South Africa were to advance – their introduction into the Somme battles did not occur until later. The largest concentration of Gloucestershire and North Bristol men in one regiment was in the 1st and 8th battalions of the Somerset Light Infantry, and the majority of these were Bristolians. Those who had been born in the West Country and then moved away often joined units local to their new address, whilst others who relocated to the area around the river Severn sometimes favoured the cap badges which revealed their place of origin. The spread of regiments is, however, quite wide, and includes the Artillery and Engineers, whilst the officers mentioned in this text also cover a variety of famous fighting forces. Very often, if an individual was commissioned from the ranks, he would be sent to a battalion which required new officers, regardless of county affiliations, and the factor of family links to a particular regiment in which a father or grandfather served also bore relevance to the final destination of a new recruit.

As the third week of June passed, over half a million troops were assembling in the relatively small sector of the line around the town of Albert. (A well-known landmark here was the golden statue of the Virgin Mary, which stood on top of the basilica and could be seen for many miles around. Subsequently, the position was used by Allied observers, and in January 1915 a German shell partly dislodged this icon and caused it to hang precariously over the square below.) The British army was divided into Corps, Divisions and Brigades consisting of Regular, Territorial and New battalions, with the breakdown as follows:

> British Fourth Army – III Corps, VIII Corps, X Corps, XIII Corps, XV Corps.
> British Third Army – VII Corps

Each Corps contained between two and four Divisions, with each Division comprising three Brigades (of four battalions each) plus a further battalion of Pioneers. The Regulars only made up a small percentage of the overall strength, and very few of the originals who crossed to France back in August 1914 were still on the Western Front, leaving the bulk of the ranks to be swelled by Territorials ('Terriers') and the New Armies ('Kitchener's Men'.) Some of the former had seen limited combat, but the vast majority of the latter were completely inexperienced in the ways of warfare, and a number of Divisions about to go into the attack were made up entirely of N.A. battalions.

The *Stroud News* declared proudly during 1915 that:

> We may conclude that those earlier recruits from the district will very soon be in the firing line. It is probable that some of them are already there, for every one of the earlier contingents will have been adequately trained by this time. How vividly do we all recall those first recruits' prompt answer to their country's urgent call: from Stroud, Nailsworth, Painswick, Amberley, Minchinhampton, Chalford, Stonehouse, Bisley, Woodchester, Brimscombe, and every parish in the neighbourhood?

In June of the following year, the *Dursley Gazette* obtained these comments from Berkeley's Pte Watkins, serving at the Front:

> The Germans sent some gas over the other day, but we soon put our gas helmets on. All our boys are very well and happy but we shall all be glad when we can get back to the homeland...

Many thousands would not get that chance.

2

THE FINAL SEVEN DAYS

In the weeks leading up to the attack, the mammoth endeavour of transporting the big guns of the Royal Artillery to their positions all along the Somme Front took place. Once established, the gunners could begin the crucial task of range-finding, aided by observation balloons as well as the Royal Flying Corps. On 24 June, a gigantic hurricane of fire was opened up on the German lines. This operation continued for eighty minutes non-stop each morning followed by intermittent but regular barrages throughout daylight hours. At night, half the larger weapons fell silent, but British machine-gunners were brought into action to harass the communication and rear lines of the enemy, thus establishing a round-the-clock pounding of the entire German defensive system.

The 1st Gloucestershire Battery (3/1st South Midland Brigade, 48th Division), Royal Artillery, was situated close to the Gommecourt salient, and was part of the northern most Division of the Fourth Army, with the 56th (London) Division of the Third Army to their left. (Of the three Batteries affiliated to Gloucestershire, two were stationed in Bristol and one in Gloucester when war was declared in August 1914.) Its War Diary for 24 June 1916 reveals that:

> Bombardment began 5 a.m. A and B Batteries carried out wire cutting operations on German third and second lines respectively, 1,000 yards north of Serre. Bombed suspected O.Ps. [Observation Points] and M.G. [machine-gun] emplacements in same area. [Also] trench junctions and communication trenches. 18 pounders [fired] 125 rounds per gun. 4.5[in] howitzers - 120 rounds per gun. 'A' Battery had one man killed and one man wounded…[1]

The dead soldier was possibly Gunner Bernard Drury Jenkins (service No.2868), who was born in Warwickshire and enlisted in Bristol. Aged just seventeen, he should not even have been at the Front because of his tender years (combat troops had to be nineteen or over.) He was the son of Mr and Mrs F. Jenkins, from Birmingham. Both the SDGW and CWGC give the individual's date of death as 26 June, but the diary entry for this day simply reveals, 'Gas discharged from British lines'. Jenkins is the only fatality mentioned in the week prior to the infantry assault, so it is likely that he fell two days prior to the official Casualty Rolls. Gnr Jenkins, who was probably hit by a retaliatory German shell, lies buried at the Hebuterne Military Cemetery, in grave number I.N.15.

Further north at Fonquevillers, in the sector allotted to the 46th (North Midland) Division – the extreme left flank of the Somme Offensive positioned opposite Gommecourt – the 46th Trench Mortar Battery was in the front line. On 25 June it delivered its contribution to the overall British barrage which now stretched southwards for many miles until it reached the banks of the river Somme. The War Diary states, 'Z46 Battery [in the] left position, containing

A gas alarm bell at Hebuterne. Gas was a constant hazard to both sides.

two guns, was destroyed by shell fire. Three O.R.s being killed, Lieut Sudlow and four O.R.s being wounded.'[2]

On this occasion, one casualty can be positively identified as Gnr Frank Williams (No.66342), listed as serving with Z46 Battery by the CWGC. Their information concurs with the SDGW that he lost his life on 25 June. Born at St Jude's in Bristol and enlisting in his home city, Gnr Williams' name can be found on the Special Memorial No.2 in Fonquevillers Military Cemetery. (Two days later, Z Battery's right position was also 'seriously damaged by shell-fire', but the survivors maintained their duties and provided support for the infantry up to and including 1 July.)

Also on the 25th, men of the 1st Battalion, Royal Warwickshire Regiment, were holding the front lines of the 4th Division, close to Beaumont Hamel. On the twenty-fourth, gas attacks were released upon the enemy, who retaliated with artillery shells causing some damage, and the scenario was repeated the following day. The War Diary reveals that at 10.30 p.m. one of the gas cylinders was damaged by a piece of shrapnel, causing the lethal substance to leak into the Warwickshires' trench. The Special Brigade (Royal Engineers), which was responsible for discharging the chemical, was badly affected, not only by the accidental spillage, but also by the previous release which was supposed to drift across No Man's Land towards the Germans, only for the lethal substance to roll back when the breeze changed direction. Chillingly, two of the RWR lost their lives, asphyxiated by their own side. The SDGW indicates that nine men of the 1st RWR were killed in action on 25 June – two are confirmed in the War Diary as being victims of gas, and it may be assumed that the rest were lost during the enemy bombardment. One of the nine was Cpl Percival Edgar Stockwell (No.1608), who had been born in Stonehouse and enlisted in Stroud (SDGW). His birth was registered in the Stroud District during 1892, and by the time of the 1901 Census he was eight years old, the youngest of five children of George and Mary, who were living at Clifton Terrace in nearby Rodborough. The place where the youngster was born is given as 'Cashes Green', which is situated between Stroud and Stonehouse. Cpl Stockwell's body was interred at the Auchonvillers Military Cemetery (II.B.9).

The 1st Somerset Light Infantry was also in the 4th Division, but whereas the 1st RWR was in the 10th Brigade, the Somersets were in the 11th. With a high proportion of Bristolians in the latter, the city which bore many of them took a keen interest in their progress throughout the war, from the heady days of recruiting at Colston Hall and elsewhere in the locality to the pending assault on the German positions which was widely expected back in the UK. On 24 June, the 1st SLI was visited by Brig.-Gen. C.B. Prowse, DSO (Distinguished Service Order), who spent time in conversation with the men. Prowse had a particular interest in the regiment, as he was born near Taunton and received his commission into the SLI during the early 1890s. A career soldier of immense ability, Prowse was a fearless officer who had gained rapid promotion since the beginning of the First World War, leading by example to eventually take command of the 11th Brigade. He was held in very high regard by his troops, but even his exalted rank would not exempt him from facing mortal danger on 1 July.

The night following the Brigadier-General's visit, gas was discharged in the direction of the German lines, prompting the latter to unleash an artillery barrage upon the British assembly trenches. 'No one there,'[3] curtly records the Somersets' War Diary. The next day it was said that three enemy observation balloons had been brought down (possibly by the Royal Flying Corps), and a 'very heavy battery' kept up a rate of fire behind the SLI throughout the hours of darkness. The movement of troops into the forward positions began on 26 June, ready for the assault which was still set for the 29th. On the night of 26/27 June the weather was 'showery', trenches were 'very wet', and a shell burst one of the water pipes. The War Diary records, '6 casualties during night (1 killed & 5 wounded).'[4] L/Cpl George Bond (7702) of the 1st SLI is listed as being killed in action on the 26th, and he is probably the fatality mentioned in the War Diary. He could well have lost his life before midnight, even though the entry was written on the 27th. Born in the St Phillip's district of Bristol, he also enlisted in his home city, and he lies buried in the Sucrerie Military Cemetery at Colincamps (I.F.27.) This was the site of a small sugar beet factory, and the soldiers making their way from their billets towards the front lines had only recently passed this very spot, where wide trenches had just been dug. These pits turned out to be mass graves and L/Cpl Bond would not be the only soldier of the Somerset Light Infantry to be interred here.

With the British bombardment now well underway, the senior commanders were keen to establish just how much damage had been caused to the German forward positions. Regular raids were sent out under the cover of darkness with this end in mind, but the conflicting stories which came back are graphically illustrated in the 1st SLI's War Diary for both 28 and 29 June. The entry for the former records, '2nd-Lt Winstanley reconnoitred the enemy's wire last night and reports that it is completely cut,' and it was also noted that, 'German fire seems very subdued.'[5] However, the following insertion was much more worrying for the potential success of the entire operation:

> 2nd-Lt Armstrong & 2nd-Lt Dunn with party left our trench…at 1.10 A.M. The party reached the German line just before 1.30 A.M. having great difficulty in getting through the German wire; when about five yards away Germans opened fire from an apparently little damaged parapet. 2nd-Lt Armstrong was hit with 3 other men (one of whom is missing.) 2nd-Lt Dunn then ordered party to retire; he brought 2nd-Lt Armstrong in himself. The Germans then sent up several rockets and flares and a barrage started at once…The German retaliation was very prompt…[6]

This alarming state of affairs proved many points. Firstly, the wire in front of the German lines was largely intact, and it had done its job of slowing down an attack. Secondly, the parapet behind it was also still *in situ*, and was able to shield a group of Germans from view. Thirdly, these defenders were not only alive, but were able to resist the sortie to the extent of compelling an immediate retirement after inflicting casualties. Fourthly, the counter-fire on the British positions from where the raid had originated was accurate and swiftly executed.

These close-quarter observations were carried out along the entire stretch of the line, and inevitably reports were mixed. Some declared that the German trenches were, indeed, completely obliterated and devoid of occupation, as had been promised all along. Others brought back demoralised and dazed prisoners who appeared relieved their torment was finally over. A fair number, however, delivered grim news, such as the one recorded in the Somersets' War Diary. Unbelievably though, it seems that the most negative communications – those which spoke of unbroken wire, raids repulsed and deaths in No Man's Land – were ignored.

Returning to the line at Gommecourt, the 37th Division – which would be in reserve on 1 July – was assisting the 46th Division at Bienvillers-au-Bois. One of its combat units was the 112th Company of the Machine Gun Corps. On 25 June enemy targets were focused upon, and the following day an impressive 10,500 rounds were fired accordingly. A machine-gun emplacement received a direct hit during the 27 June, although the War Diary was keen to point out that the weapon and tripod were undamaged. It would seem that one of its operators was not so lucky, and this was most likely to have been Pte Wallace R. Martin (No.6075), who died of his wounds on 28 June, aged twenty-four. Born at 'Dowding, Glos', according to the SDGW, this is possibly a misinterpretation of Downend in North Bristol, as the new recruit enlisted in the latter city and his parents – Henry and Mercy – are listed as living in Bristol in the 1920s by the CWGC. Pte Martin, who was formerly in the Glosters, was buried at the Bienvillers Military Cemetery (V.B.I.). (A measure of the ferocity of the continuing fire levelled upon the Germans in the days leading up to the Somme Offensive is forcefully illustrated in the 112th Company's War Diary on the same day Pte Martin succumbed to his injuries. Fourteen machine-guns co-operated with trench mortars, launching 12,200 rounds of ammunition into Monchy, and 7,000 towards Essarts.)

This destructive power unleashed by such weapons of war could not be ignored, and Lt Max Hastings, a former pupil at Wycliffe College in Stonehouse then serving with a Canadian Infantry battalion, summed up his surroundings:

> Our abode is amongst the roots of a once beautiful wood. The beeches and elms are hopelessly mutilated, and the beheaded pines are gradually suffocating to death. Their amputated limbs are everywhere, trunks are riven from head to foot, even the ground itself is twisted and torn.

A fellow OW, Arthur Blanch of the Royal Engineers noted:

> The road to Beaucourt [near Beaumont Hamel] was turned into hills and valleys by huge shells, and down a ravine on the right, looking like the lake in Woodchester Park from Selsley Woods,* lay the silver Ancre, every now and then made dark and stormy as a shell pitched the water into a huge mountain of spray.[7]

(*Near Stroud)

As the final preparations were made to move thousands of troops up into the front lines in readiness for the 29 June deadline, sorties across No Man's Land were continued by soldiers who were already as far forward as they could get. In the 48th (South Midland) Division front trenches, the 1/5th Royal Warwickshire Regiment sent out raiding parties at 10.30 p.m. on the night of 26 June and again at 2 a.m. a few hours later, but neither was successful, resulting in two officers and thirty-four ORs returning 'wounded'. There is no indication of any deaths, but the SDGW reveals Pte Victor Henry Rugman (No.201406) lost his life in action on 28 June. The 1/5th RWR War Diary does not contain a reference to a fatality on this date, so it is possible that the nineteen-year-old was actually lost on one of the two patrols mentioned previously, although it was not realised at the time. The teenager was the son of Henry and Rose, who lived at Lake Cottage, Huntley, near Gloucester, and this village is given as the serviceman's residence on the SDGW, even though he enlisted in Birmingham. His native town is not given, but he is almost certainly the same individual whose birth was registered in the Thornbury district of south Gloucestershire in 1897. The fact that Pte Rugman has no known grave and is commemorated on the Thiepval Memorial to the Missing of the Somme lends weight to the theory that he was killed out in No Man's Land, and therefore that his body could not be recovered. The Royal Warwickshire Regiment has three 'panels' at Thiepval which contain the names of all of those who suffered a similar fate to Pte Rugman and have no recognised final resting place. These panels are numbered 9A, 9B and 10B.

The recovery of the fallen was a difficult matter in wartime. One officer of the 31st Division, opposite Serre, was killed out in front of his own trenches, and orders were issued to rescue his body. Men of the 10th East Yorkshires – 'Hull Commercials' – twice went out under fire to attempt the recovery, but twice were forced back after suffering casualties. The dead man was said to be the son of a well-known Hull dignitary, yet when it was demanded that a third attempt be made, the CO of the 10th EY – Dan Burges – refused, and was immediately relieved of his command. Burges and his family had strong links with Bristol going back several centuries, with many of their forebears holding civic posts in the city. Burges himself was a former soldier with the Glosters, having served with them throughout the Boer War, and was severely wounded at Ypres on 9 May 1915 whilst a Company Commander with the 2nd Battalion. Placed in command of the 7th South Wales Borderers in the Balkans during 1917, the following year he received a Victoria Cross for leading his men to their objective through a devastating enemy barrage before being rendered unconscious, which led to his leg being amputated. The abrupt withdrawal of his senior status with the Hull Commercials on 30 June 1916 was clearly the result of a compassionate frame of mind towards his own men, who he felt were needlessly risking their lives out in No Man's Land where so many bodies already lay. Lt-Col Burges died in Bristol during 1946.

Instructions were now being issued to the men who would be carrying out the main assault – the infantrymen:

> Any stranger in uniform must be detained and sent under escort to Battalion H.Q. There will probably be many cases of Germans dressed in English uniforms of private soldiers.[8]

Although it was impressed upon all of those soon to be going 'over the top' that there would be little or no opposition from the Germans, some notes of caution were raised:

> Each successive wave passing over the German trenches should be on the look-out for Germans getting up to fire from their trenches into the backs of the men in front. Men should be ready to shoot down into each trench as they reach it if necessary.[9]

As if to act as an incentive, the soldiers were told, 'Rum will be issued to all ranks actually in the trenches and engaged in the attack. No indiscriminate use will be allowed, and issues must be made in the presence of an officer.'[10]

The need for consolidation was a vital part of the plan:

> The word RETIRE is not to be used under any circumstances, and no man will be justified in letting go a forward position once he has obtained same.[11]

It was also stressed that an objective must be held 'at all costs', as there would be, 'masses of troops in the rear who will be pressing forward'.

With regard to casualties, officers were informed that reports of the dead and injured should be compiled as accurately as possible before sending the results to each respective Battalion H.Q. The War Diary of the 6th Northants., in the 18th (Eastern) Division, makes the cursory observation, '55th FA [Field Ambulance] will collect all the wounded…'[12] But it seems to attach more importance to the information regarding the collection of enemy documents in captured trenches. This was to be carried out by men carrying sacks with a red, white and blue bullseye on each side. Soldiers were also told that they must not, in any eventuality, stop to assist a fallen comrade, as the medics would be following up behind. This, of course, went against the basic spirit of humanity and camaraderie built up between servicemen, especially those of the Pals battalions who had often known each other since childhood.

But there was no room for sentiment in the wider picture. This was the opportunity for the major breakthrough all had hoped for since the early days of the war. Although different battalions were allotted varying tasks for the opening day of the offensive, the general 'fighting order' worn by each infantryman weighed roughly sixty-six pounds, which consisted of: standard issue steel helmet and entrenching tool, rolled ground sheet, water-bottle and haversack (the latter containing mess tin, towel, shaving kit, extra socks, message book, unconsumed rations), gas helmets and goggles, wire cutters, field dressings, iodine, 220 rounds of ammunition, sand bags and two Mills grenades. This cumbersome and awkward array of items meant that a swift charge towards the enemy was virtually impossible, and any quick evasive action to avoid machine-gunners or snipers would prove especially difficult. Once on the ground, movement would also be restricted, so the Royal Artillery bombardment on the German forward trenches really would have to be complete in its destruction and unequivocal in its message.

In early July, Mr Caddy, the Headmaster of Coaley School near Dursley, received a letter from one of his former students, Gunner C.P. Brown, of the Royal Artillery, who informed him:

Dear Sir, -

Being one of your old scholars, I think it is my duty to drop you a few lines as regards some of my last experiences. I am now sitting down in a little 'dug-out' somewhere in France, writing this, and while I am doing so the shells are flying over to the German lines from a Battery just to the rear of us. No doubt you would like to know in [which] part of France I am, but as you know, we are forbidden to mention names of any places. We think ourselves pretty lucky so long as no German shells happen to drop anywhere near us…[but] you may be sure for every one they send over to us our boys reply with about half a dozen.[13]

Cutting the seemingly impenetrable coils of barbed wire which guarded the German front lines was the responsibility of shrapnel shells, which burst in mid-air sending razor-sharp projectiles over the immediate area. This bludgeoning procedure actually required delicate precision, as the fuses needed to detonate at exactly the right moment for their impact to be successful, otherwise the explosion would be relatively harmless. Deep in their dug-outs, the Germans most feared the force of the British 'heavies' which could cause the roof to collapse with catastrophic results, yet the military hardware required to launch these missiles was not present in any great strength on the Somme Front. Finally, and perhaps most crucially, a percentage of bombs were 'duds' and did not even explode – a fact later verified by a British POW who, having been taken into captivity during the final week of June, was marched to the rear through many complete shells in the same state as when they had been fired. However, the Germans undoubtedly were suffering casualties, and the endless battering must have driven some survivors insane. Food, arms and supplies still had to be brought up to the forward lines, yet as the British fatally discovered on 1 July, there were still significant numbers of defenders who had survived the artillery onslaught and were ready to tackle whatever was thrown at them, however strongly it came. Deep in their bunkers, they grimly held on for the opportunity to exact what would turn out to be an appalling retribution.

Two British Commanding Officers are known to have expressed their concerns about the uncut wire before the attack began. Lt-Col E.T.F. Sandys, DSO, of the 2nd Middlesex, was convinced that the barbed entanglements confronting his men near La Boisselle had barely been touched, and he passed his fears on to his superiors. Close by, Lt-Col Cordeaux of the 10th Lincolns ('Grimsby Chums') believed that a large number of Germans were sheltering below ground and were there in sufficient strength to put up a heavy resistance once the British assault was underway. Neither viewpoint held any sway.

On 28 June, the 8th Battalion of the Somerset Light Infantry, part of the 21st Division situated to the south of La Boisselle, began its march to the fighting zone. But with so many men packed into such limited space, a German aerial bombardment did not need pinpoint precision to inflict casualties. The War Diary reported that, 'In the evening we took over from the 4th Middlesex…Lost 1 Corporal and 6 men in the relief.'[14]

The NCO was Bedminster-born William Henry King (No.11690), of 'A' Company, whose parents – Alfred and Emma – were living at Chatterton Square in Bristol's Redcliffe area by 1916. A former employee of the Great Western Railway, Cpl King was eighteen years old when he was killed in action, and the circumstances of his death were passed on to his mother by 2nd Lt Fred Oldham in a letter which was later published in the *Western Daily Press*:

Dear Mrs King,

I am very sorry to inform you that your son was killed in action on June 28th, whilst we were preparing for the offensive. He was killed by a shell and died instantaneously. We all miss him very much, as he was one of the pluckiest and cleanest boys. Please accept my deepest sympathy with you in your great loss.

Another of the casualties was Pte James Crook (No.9838), a native of Bristol's St Phillip's district and the son of William and Mary, who later lived close to Stapleton Road in the city. Both soldiers lie buried in the Norfolk Cemetery at Becordel-Becourt, to the east of Albert (grave numbers I.C.69 and I.A.80 respectively). The CWGC and SDGW are in agreement that the two men lost their lives on 29 June, but with the contradictory evidence from the War Diary and 2nd Lt Oldham's letter, it is prudent to rely upon the information contained in the latter. The War Diary itself reveals on the 28th that, '…the attack [has] been put off for 48 hours.'[15]

The reason for the delay was a series of heavy rain-storms which had swept across parts of the Somme, flooding roads, trenches and the battlefield, so it was decided not to risk the assault potentially floundering in the heavy conditions before it had even begun. This readjustment inevitably caused huge logistical problems, as the carefully staged timetable of bringing numerous battalions up from their billets into the assembly trenches and then forward to the front lines had to be halted, in addition to the difficult position the artillery Batteries now found themselves in, having to make their barrage last for a further two days on limited supplies of shells. Their rate of fire was reduced, but the cavalcade was maintained both day and night.

In the early hours of 29 June – the now postponed date of the original offensive – four officers and seventy other ranks of the 13th King's Royal Rifle Corps, situated in the front trenches close to Gommecourt, were preparing for a raid. Over the previous two weeks they had been trained under the supervision of Temporary Major Charles Francis Simonds, the Second-in-Command of the battalion. He proceeded to control operations via telephone from the 13th's lines whilst the patrol went out into No Man's Land behind a smoke screen. The War Diary states that:

…many Germans were killed by bomb, bayonet and bullet. Unfortunately, the [position] in which Maj. Simonds and an artillery officer were directing the proceedings was blown in soon after 4.30 a.m., and all the occupants lost their lives. This was a great loss to the battalion. Maj. Simonds was the first officer to join the battalion and he was loved and respected by [all ranks].[16]

At 8.30 p.m. on 30 June, the Major's body was borne by senior officers for a burial service in the Church Hut, and his grave is now to be found in the Berles-Au-Bois Churchyard Extension (G.5).

The General Officer Commanding the 37th Division wired his appreciation to the 13th KRRC for their '…successful raid this morning, and my congratulations to all concerned. Also my deep regret at the death of Major Simonds.'[17]

The Major's wife, Evelyn, received a telegram on 1 July at the couple's marital home in Reading, informing her that her husband had been killed in action. They had been married in Kensington during 1907, and were the parents of two sons. There is no indication that Major Simonds had any personal links to Gloucestershire, as his parents – Mr and Mrs James Simonds – were also residents of Reading, and their son had served with the Royal Berkshire Regiment throughout the Boer War. However, when the CWGC compiled its Debt of Honour Register in the 1920s, Evelyn had moved to Strattonend in Cirencester, and here lies a strange coincidence. The Commanding Officer of the 13th KRRC, and Major Simonds' immediate superior, was Lt-Col R.C. Chester-Master, DSO & Bar, who was a native of Cirencester, and lived at Querns Lane House in the town. He was also the Chief Constable of his home county, and he lost his life in action during the Passchendaele Offensive of 1917, at the age of forty-seven. The Lieutenant-Colonel is commemorated on the War Memorials at Cirencester and Cheltenham.

The day prior to Major Simonds' death – 28 June – a patrol of the 6th Royal Berkshires at Carnoy, in the south of the line covered by the 18th (Eastern) Division, found that the German wire opposite had been 'badly cut' by British artillery. Close by, below the village of Montauban, the 2nd Wiltshires also sent out a sortie which reached a point known as 'Loop Sap', and although the men were heartened to find the remains of the barbed coils in a similar state of destruction, they were suddenly attacked by grenade-throwing Germans who were found to be 'holding [the] front strongly.'[18] One of the 2nd Wiltshires was injured, and the War Diary indicates that his comrades experienced 'great difficulty in bringing in the wounded member of the patrol'.[19]

The following day, at Carnoy, men of the 6th Royal Berkshires had to take cover from an enemy bombardment which killed one of their number and wounded three more. The dead man was almost certainly twenty-three-year-old Pte Zachariah Bartley Davenport (No.13022), born at Northleach near Cirencester, and the son of George and Alice. Pte Davenport was married to Annie, and his wife as well as his parents are all listed as living in Swindon by the CWGC. The soldier's grave is to be found at Carnoy Military Cemetery (Q.13).

On 30 June, Pte Walter John Dyer (No.8960), of the 2nd Wiltshires, died of his wounds, and it is a fair assumption that he was the individual incapacitated on the raid at 'Loop Sap' two days previously. Born in Berkshire and enlisting in Swindon, his residence in the SDGW is given as 'Bristol', with the CWGC revealing that his father, Frederick, was a citizen of Victoria Road in the city's Kingswood district by the 1920s. Pte Dyer lies buried at the Daours Communal Cemetery Extension (II.A.5).

During the same day, but further up the line in the 4th Division, the War Diary for the 1st Somerset Light Infantry records: 'No rain yesterday. Today fine. Cpl Knowlson H. was killed and four men wounded by a shell which burst in front of their dug-out.'[20] Herbert Knowlson (No.9797) was born at St Jude's in Bristol, and enlisted in the city. The SDGW gives his date of death as 29 June, but this does not concur with the War Diary. Even though the Corporal died in his own trenches, his name is carved at Thiepval (2A), suggesting there was nothing left of him after the explosion.

As time ticked by, there was now no question of the attack being postponed for a second time. The appointed hour was 7.30 on the morning of 1 July 1916, and final preparations were put in place to this end. The 1st SLI was to be one of the first battalions to go 'over the top', and its War Diary continues on the thirtieth:

> 2nd-Lt Winstanley again reconnoitred the enemy's wire last night and states that it is cut, but that he could not get near the 'quadrilateral' [a formidable German strong-point].
> Last night 2nd-Lt Treasure took a fatigue party with 39 buckets to bale trenches…10 P.M. Battalion marched out to take up position…[21]

The men who were about to form the attack were left with their own thoughts as midnight passed. The jumble and congestion of troops and supplies trying to reach the front line was finally sorted out, and now all they could do was wait. Undoubtedly thoughts of family and home were in the minds of most, if not all, at some stage during the eerie hours of darkness. Yet this was no time for minds to wander, as the Germans still kept launching reminders of their scope for defence and retaliation by sending over artillery shells on a regular basis. 2nd Lt Sidney Garlick, an Old Wycliffian and former Bristol University student serving in the King's Royal Rifle Corps, noted: 'The whole battalion are going over the parapet [soon]…It is really hell here; nobody can realise it that has not been through it…Today is the darkest hour before the dawn. Tomorrow the sun may have risen….'[22] The officer only had two weeks more to live.

Expectation and a sense of history were weighing heavily upon the minds of men from all ranks. The *Wiltshire & Gloucestershire Standard* would declare a week after the offensive began that: 'The opening days of July are destined to stand out boldly in the chronology of war, marking the end of an historic period of enforced waiting, and the beginning of a great offensive by the Allies.' A week later it made the bold assertion that:

> …the broad outlines of the picture, which will some day be elaborated in a despatch that will be treasured in every corner of the United Kingdom, already bear their plain testimony to the magnificent deeds of our New Armies…Our fine old British sports and past-times have taught them to 'play the game', and to 'play for the side'.

Opposite Gommecourt, where the 46th (North Midland) Division was waiting to take part in the 'diversionary' assault on the salient, Lt Horace Jones, of the 1/6th North Staffordshires, and a former pupil of Wycliffe College in Stonehouse, was putting the final touches to a letter he hoped his family would never read:

> What I am going to write is intended for you all, and I am not writing to you individually because it is too hard. I am leaving this behind to be posted in the event of my not being here to write or see you again. A big attack is coming off – in fact, we are on the eve of it – and they have honoured me by selecting me and my platoon to lead the attack, so far as my Company is concerned. I have a grand lot of boys and am certain we shall succeed – nothing will stop us – but of course we must pay the price of victory, and many of us will not answer the roll. I do not want you to think I am going in with a faint heart – on the [contrary], I go in with every confidence – but realising that I might fall, I cannot do so without expressing my gratitude to you all. I thank you all from the bottom of my heart for the wonderful kindness and love you have always shown me.[23]

3

HOW THE NEWSPAPERS
REPORTED THE ATTACK

Before moving on to focus upon the progress of the attack on 1 July 1916, it is worth looking at how the media in Gloucestershire and Bristol reported the initial stages of the dreadful events unfolding on the Somme. Despite the newspapers having correspondents at the Front, inevitably they were not in the firing line, and therefore they could only rely upon the official communications from the War Office which, as we shall see, varied from wildly optimistic to completely inaccurate. It should also be remembered, however, that even if the offensive was going badly, it was not in the interests of the military to pass on this negative news to a public already reeling from mounting casualty lists and the looming threat of conscription. Therefore, the propaganda value of any success in the field was seized upon and elaborated for the benefit of a readership eager to hear how the Germans were apparently falling back in disarray. The following piece of descriptive journalism from a reporter working for Bristol's *Western Daily Press* is a deeply evocative account of the final hours before the offensive and its opening salvoes; it represents the complete, unexpurgated facts as he saw them before this most historic of dates:

At six o'clock this morning I stood upon the brow of a ridge overlooking the much 'strafed' town of Albert. The sun had not yet risen high enough to eat up the dawn mists which hung on the slopes and valleys…What I beheld was the slow settling away of a dense fog of vapour, which, like a waterfall, was always receding without ever growing less. At moments, a slit would open in it and dimly reveal the spire of Albert Cathedral with its drooping Virgin…[Then] the sun drew off the morning haze. July was being ushered in with true summer tenderness; a deep azure sky, delicately mottled with fleecy traceries, and a soft, warm breeze coming from the west. Even as I stood there, with the lark singing overhead and the cattle browsing in the foreground unconcernedly as if nothing else on earth mattered, the desultory crackling of the guns began to make a more rapid and deeper note. With [increasing] rapidity the devastating chorus swelled, for the time-table of the momentous day had now been reached, until from horizon to horizon, the uproar rolled in a ceaseless [crescendo] of thunder. Several times I tried to count the pulsations of the inferno, but it was a hopeless task. I do not think I exaggerate in the least when I state that the shell bursts often reached 500 to one minute… The concentration of artillery was literally appalling; every species of weapon from the gigantic 18in howitzers to the quick rattling of the trench mortars, poured thunderous avalanches upon the enemy positions… After about one hour and a half the fury of the bombardment appreciably slackened. I knew the range of our fire had been lifted, and that our infantry were getting to death grips with the foe.

On 3 July, the *Gloucester Citizen* published the official report it had received from the War Office forty-eight hours previously:

BRITISH OFFENSIVE OPENED. German Defences Broken Into. Attacks launched near the River Somme this morning at 7:30, in conjunction with the French. British troops have broken into German forward systems on a front of 16 miles. Fighting is continuing… The assault was preceded by a terrific bombardment lasting about an hour and a half. It is too early as yet to give anything but the barest particulars… The public must await with patience, albeit with confidence, the full development of a movement which, as yet, cannot be in more than its earliest stages.

The next day a typical headline blared, 'EARLY SUCCESSES FOLLOWED UP. OVER 12,000 PRISONERS TAKEN.' Local newspapers maintained the positive theme. The *Bristol Times & Mirror* announced, 'FEARLESS ADVANCE INTO A BATH OF LEAD', whilst the *Dursley Gazette* gave the story a local flavour: 'BERKELEY SOLDIERS IN THE BIG PUSH; OUR SMASHING BLOWS. ANGLO-FRENCH FORCES MAKE BRILLIANT PROGRESS. 16,000 PRISONERS TAKEN.' As the days passed, it seemed all was going well. 'GERMANY IN A VICE' declared the *Gloucestershire Echo*. 'VIGOROUS ATTACKS ON THE SOMME', 'WIDENING THE BREACH', 'BRITISH SUCCESSES' and 'FUTILE GERMAN COUNTER-ATTACKS' all pointed to the imminence of a stunning victory. Yet there were whispers of caution tucked away behind the bravado. 'WOUNDED ARRIVE' noticed the *Gloucester Citizen*, although it did try to place a positive spin on the announcement by transcribing the words of an injured Major who had been brought back to 'Blighty' along with many others:

> If the public see such a devil of a lot of us chaps coming back with our mud and blood and bandages and all that, they'll be apt to think the Boche has done wonderful things with us. You ought to explain things to them. They see a steady stream of us, but if they were out there they would see stacks and stacks of dead Boche – trenches full of them.

The *Bristol Times & Mirror* also broadcast, 'SECRET WELL KEPT. ENEMY CASUALTIES HEAVY. ALLIES' LOSSES SLIGHT'. There was no doubt that the Germans had known a heavy offensive was on its way, and, in parallel with their enemies, would emphasise the positives rather than reveal to their own public that their soldiers had suffered widespread losses. The *Western Daily Press* did obtain the views expressed in the *Cologne Gazette*, which intimated, 'Only within the next few days will it be possible to ascertain how far the general attack has brought the [British].' This brought a sharp retort from its Bristol counterpart: 'It intends, no doubt, to give comfort to its readers, but its words are salutary to ourselves.' As if to confirm the dominant position the British apparently found themselves in on the Somme, the *Western Daily Press* reiterated, 'CASUALTIES COMPARATIVELY LIGHT', and clarified this statement as follows:

> A Canadian M.O. [Medical Officer] just returned from France in charge of wounded gives reassuring news as to British casualties. 'We have had a comparatively slack time,' he says, 'by comparison with Loos [Sept./Oct. 1915] this has been child's play.'

The General Staff were also said to be 'satisfied' by the results, and predicted, '…the end will be won by the braver of our troops.'

On 8 July the *Gloucester Citizen* sounded a note of triumph: 'THE MIGHTY GERMAN EFFORT IS DYING AWAY.' The report went on to claim that:

> The game is going fast in favour of the Allies, and the ball is now being passed to us for the final rush.

But just twenty-four hours earlier, the same newspaper had published these three shocking headlines:

'BRITISH REGIMENTS PAY THE PRICE', 'FEARFUL TOLL EXACTED' and 'SUPERB GALLANTRY A NEGATIVE CONSOLATION'.

It has to be wondered if the Editor was censured for casting doubt on the supposedly sweeping successes of the Allied fighting machine on the Somme, even though, with hindsight, we know this trio of statements to be entirely accurate. Only when newspapers up and down the land began publishing endless names and photographs of those who were missing, wounded, taken prisoner, or known to be already dead, did the public at large finally come to realise that the offensive in France had not achieved the breakthrough everyone had anticipated. Moreover, the claims of 'CASUALTIES COMPARATIVELY LIGHT' took on a ghastly shroud of mis-information when compared to what *really* happened on 1 July 1916, and if ever there was a warning from history, this date must surely be coloured in the most vivid red.

GLOUCESTERSHIRE'S CASUALTIES

Using the criteria set out previously I will now detail, Division by Division, the men of Gloucestershire and North Bristol who fell on 1 July 1916. I will start in the south of the line near Montauban, where the British Fourth Army advanced alongside the French Sixth Army, who were on the right-hand flank of the former. The British soldiers who held this sector were still several miles from the banks of the river Somme, and each successive Division was positioned further away from the now infamous waterway than its nearest neighbour. Had it been an entirely British offensive, the engagement would probably have ended up being labelled as the Battle of the Ancre, but the Somme bisected the two Allied nationalities which went forward together, hence the title.

4

30TH DIVISION

Arthur Blanch, an Old Wycliffian and officer of the Royal Engineers, related his experience of the first day of the Somme Offensive to his former college. Although it is not known exactly where he was positioned at the time of the attack, the evidence suggests he was most likely in one of the 7th, 18th or 30th Divisions:

> [We heard] an avalanche of barks as the huge artillery barrage, prompt to time, opened on the enemy. 'They are over now,' we said to one another, and it was true, for at that moment our valorous men were hurling themselves through the bullets. In three minutes the wounded were coming back; those slightly wounded, walking, and those who were worse, supported by comrades…Three hours after the advance we went over as far as the second German line to find the notices already posted outside the dug-outs, stating that they were clear and clean…The big onward wave is over. The hostile land that we have so long seen before us is torn and dead, and another line of hostilities has been set up to bristle over the top of the hill in the distance.[1]

The 30th Division, due south of Montauban, contained three Pals battalions of the King's Liverpool Regiment – the 17th, 18th and 20th – plus one from the Manchesters – the 19th – in the front line. The breadth of the front allotted to the latter was measured between 250 and 300 yards, with its final destination being the enemy-held Glatz Redoubt. The War Diary reveals:

> After intense bombardment [the] 1st wave went over the parapet at 7:30 a.m., successive waves followed at about 100' intervals. British artillery barrage checked advance but objective reached at 8:35 a.m. 2 sections of support Companies used as reinforcements. The Lewis guns were not used in the actual advance. The clearers examined all trenches and dug-outs but found little opposition…'C' Company encountered small opposition – quickly overcome. [The] heaviest casualties [were] caused by machine guns on left flank. German guns and POWs taken. Smoke candles and flares lit in GLATZ REDOUBT. Saps dug and manned by Lewis guns. Rifles cleaned and water bottles filled. H.Q. moved up into new position, communication remained good. Smoke from shell fire interfered with visual signalling. All companies were in telephone communication with advanced HQ by afternoon on 1 July. 1 officer and 40 O.R. killed. 1 officer and 11 O.R. missing. 1 officer and 136 O.R. wounded. 1 O.R. died of wounds.[2]

Lance Corporal Albert Alfred Wollen (No.12476) was amongst the dead. Born in Bristol, he was the twenty-seven-year-old son of Albert and Emily, who later lived at Lawrence Grove, Henleaze, Westbury-on-Trym. However, the soldier himself was residing at Catherine Street,

Newtown, when he enlisted in Manchester. The *Western Daily Press* published a letter sent to the deceased's loved ones by an officer of the 19th Manchesters, who informed them, '…death was instantaneous and he suffered no pain. During the action I noticed that he displayed great coolness and courage, and his section had great confidence in him.' The newspaper added that the Lance Corporal was a former member of the Boys' Brigade at the Shaftesbury Institute, and also published an obituary from his '…mother, brothers and sister, and sweetheart. Barrow Road, Newtown.' L/Cpl Wollen is commemorated at Thiepval (13A & 14C). (His birth was registered in Barton Regis – central Bristol – during 1889.)

The progress of the 18th King's was similar to that of the 19th Manchesters, but the former were caught by enfilading machine-gun fire from Railway Valley, which also hit the 2nd Green Howards, following up behind. When a group of Germans emerged from a deep dug-out, they were bombed back by a section of grenade throwers, enabling the 18th King's to reach the Glatz Redoubt at the same time as the Manchester men. Second Lieutenant George Andrew Herdman, of the 18th King's Liverpool Regiment, had, by this stage of the action, lost his life at the age of twenty. Born in 1895, he was the son of Professor and Mrs W.A. Herdman of Liverpool, and attended Bristol's Clifton College between 1909 and 1914. Also a scholar of Trinity College, Cambridge, G.A. Herdman received his commission in January 1915, and proceeded to the Western Front the following August. His battalion suffered losses of 164 men from the ranks on 1 July 1916, whilst the War Diary estimated that two-thirds of the entire strength had become casualties (dead, wounded, missing or taken prisoner) by the end of the day. No chances were taken during the close-quarter fighting, as indicated by the fate of a German NCO who was shot after he appeared to be surrendering, even though he had '…one hand on the [machine] gun and one hand in the air'.[3]

The CO of the 18th King's was Lt-Col E.H. Trotter, DSO, who was related to the Gifford family on his mother's side. (Lord Edric Gifford, of the 24th Foot, received a Victoria Cross during the Ashanti Wars in the 1870s, and had spent much of his childhood at the family home – Ampney Park, near Cirencester. The Giffords were also linked with the ancient Berkeley clan, who had lived in the famous castle overlooking the river Severn for centuries.) Lt-Col Trotter, who was to die in action on 8 July 1916, wrote his own account of his battalion's actions on the momentous day of the offensive. As the assault reached a critical stage, he observed:

Our forward bombing parties had all been shot down by snipers, [when] 2nd-Lt G.A. Herdman, who had come forward to deal with the situation, was blown to pieces by an enemy shell. [This occurred at Train Alley, which ran eastwards towards Glatz Redoubt before it stretched north in the direction of Montauban. Lt Watkins attempted to go down and found the body of 2nd-Lt Herdman, and threw a bomb which failed to reach the enemy bombing guard.[4]

However, another well-aimed grenade thrown soon afterwards found its target, driving the Germans out of their bunkers and allowing the allies to capture the Glatz Redoubt, whereupon six officers and fourteen men in the ranks were singled out for 'gallantry and devotion to duty'. 2nd Lt Herdman is now remembered at Thiepval (1D, 8B & 8C). Even after his death, he appears to have been in the thick of the action which finally ended in success for the 18th King's.

The 18th Manchesters worked in support of the 19th Battalion, and were detailed to transport ammunition, equipment and bombs to their comrades in the vanguard of the attack. Their War Diary reveals:

All carrying parties had casualties on the way up…but showed admirable devotion to duty. The loads were very heavy due to combat stress and heat, [and] most men arrived exhausted, but continued making journeys, causing more casualties. 6 officers wounded & approx. 170 O.R.s killed, wounded or missing.[5]

One of the fatalities was Pte George Dauncey (No.10768.) Born in Bristol and enlisting in Manchester, the CWGC does not give any personal detail, although in the 1901 Census there is a George Dauncey. He is aged two, living at Gideon Place in Bristol's St Clements with his twenty-eight-year-old father, also called George, a 'mason's labourer', and his mother, Mary. If this is the same individual, then he would have been only seventeen at the time of his death, but as has been established previously, underage recruits were known to be at the Front in the firing line. Pte Dauncey is another whose name can be found at Thiepval (13A & 14C).

With the Somme campaign now underway, the *Bristol Times & Mirror* transcribed the details of a letter sent by a soldier of the Manchester Regiment (who used to play cricket for Clifton) to his brother who still lived in the city:

> On July 1 and 2 I learnt more about what war is than all the time since I joined the army. We did a good piece of work in taking a certain village. The village was a sight – not a house left standing…I fear we are up against big resistance, and that this is but the start. We shall need every man we can get hold of before the end. Above all, we can never win without SHELLS, and an endless supply of them. Infantry is helpless without the guns. If you see any munitions people, tell them to work like devils, because otherwise we will not win the war.

With the censor in operation, the village is not mentioned by name, but it is possible it was, indeed, Montauban, as the 30th Division seized all of its first day objectives with approximately 3,000 casualties. This number was counter-balanced by the capture of several field guns, many prisoners, and the morale-boosting rout of the enemy, who were seen retreating in large numbers beyond the ruined hamlet, across open fields and unscathed woodland. The Division had not been ordered to follow, so it set about consolidating its new gains and could only hope that the rest of the line was experiencing similar triumphs.

5

18TH (EASTERN) DIVISION

Situated to the north of Carnoy, the 18th Division was under the command of Maj.-Gen. Maxse, whilst the XIII Corps of which it formed a part was the responsibility of Lt-Gen. W.N. Congreve. Lt-Gen. Congreve was a Boer War Victoria Cross recipient whose son, Brevet-Major W. Congreve of the Rifle Brigade, would perform a series of gallant acts over a two-week period during July 1916, which led to him also receiving a VC. The award was, however, posthumous, as the Brevet-Major was killed by a sniper on 20 July. Some of his heroics took place around Montauban, and this village was one of the objectives of the Division's right flank on 1 July, which included the 8th East Surreys, 7th Queen's (West Surreys) and 7th Buffs (Royal East Kents.)

The War Diary of the 8th East Surreys contains the following tongue-in-cheek assessment of the forthcoming attack, and its tone may appear almost flippant. However, this was 'trench humour' at its sharpest, whilst at the same time the men to whom it applied were under no illusions as to the danger of the tasks which lay before them:

Bed Sitting Room. Shower Bath and louse kennel complete. 10 minutes from MONTAUBAN. 1 second from Hell. Gas and water laid on. The bus fare from CARNOY to MONTAUBAN has been reduced owing to the competition with the new express train service.

COME AND JOIN US IN THE GREAT
INTERNATIONAL FINAL
ENGLAND v GERMANY
KICK OFF. ---ZERO
NO REFEREE[1]

There then followed an example of the steely determination typical of those on the Front:

And when you take the Field just remember; we're the only East Surreys going over anywhere near here. Remember that we've got many more battle honours than any other Regiment, and we've got the best chance we'll ever have of winning now. Remember why you ever joined up at all. Remember eleven months of mud and ration carrying waiting to get at 'em, and now you've got the chance. Don't forget you owe 'em a bit for all your pals who had to go before your chance came. Remember we've got the best name in the best Brigade of the finest Division in the most wonderful Army in the World…And lastly, remember what Gen. Maxse says! It's lead in the Belly that'll win the War – and damned good luck.[2]

From midnight on 1 July, the Germans shelled the front lines of the 8th East Surreys, knocking in trenches, damaging dug-outs and causing thirteen casualties, three of whom were killed. At

5.30 a.m., all Companies reported that they were in position, and an hour later another enemy salvo came over. The battalion was about to take part in one of the most celebrated moments of the first day, as alluded to in the War Diary:

> At 7:27 a.m. 'B' Company started to move out to their wire, Captain Nevill strolling quietly ahead of them, giving an occasional order to keep the dressing square on to the line of the advance. This Company took four footballs out with them which they were seen to dribble forward into the smoke of our intense bombardment on the Hun front line. The first part of 'B' Company's advance was made with very few casualties, but when the barrage lifted to the second Hun trench, a very heavy rifle and machine gun fire started from our front and left, the latter coming apparently from the craters and the high ground immediately behind them.

> At 7:50 a.m. the Adjutant [who was observing the progress of the attack from one of the parapets] reported that the Battalion was in the German trenches. Hand to hand fighting went on for a long time…and news [was] received that Captains Flatau and Pearce had been killed and later it was known that Captain Nevill, Lieuts Soames, Musgrove, and 2/Lieuts Kelly and Evans had also been killed.[3]

Lt George Henry Stuart Musgrove was the twenty-seven-year-old son of William and Rebecca, but both of his parents had passed away by 1916. His step-mother was residing at Suffolk Parade in Cheltenham at the time of his death, whilst his sister lived in Fairfield Avenue close to the town's Leckhampton Road and there were close links to the area via his late father's position at Cheltenham College. The *Gloucestershire Echo* said William Musgrove would be remembered by '…thousands of Old Cheltonians whom he trained in the College Cadet Corps.' When the 1901 Census was taken, the Musgroves were living in Cheltenham's Naunton Park Terrace, with forty-eight-year-old William, a widower who was born in Westminster, listed as being a 'Drill Instructor' at the local College. His four children, of whom George was the youngest, had birthplaces ranging from Bermuda and Canada to Chatham, with twelve-year-old George having been born in Gibraltar. The latter, who worked in a Cheltenham counting house before moving to London, originally trained with the Artists' Rifles before receiving his commission with the 8th East Surreys. His step-mother received a telegram on 10 July informing her of the officer's death, and that his body had been interred at the Military Cemetery in Carnoy. (The modern-day grave reference is E.30.) The ceremony was described in the War Diary on 3 July:

> At 2 p.m. the burial took place in Carnoy Valley of Captains Pearce, Flatau and Nevill, Lieuts. Soames and Musgrove, 2/Lieuts Kelly and Evans, this being attended by Major Irwin and Captain Gimson, R.A.M.C. and 6 representatives from each Company, as although the whole Battalion wished to be present it was thought inadvisable to have any large number of men together as the enemy were still occasionally shelling the Valley. The service was read by the Revd Capt. Chester Masters, ★C.E.[4]

Following the reports of the fallen officers named, the 8th East Surreys' War Diary continues with its narrative for 1 July and indicates that the CO sent an urgent message to his opposite number in the 7th Buffs requesting reinforcements. By 9:21 a.m., news came back that Train Alley and Pommiers – two German positions – had been occupied by the Surreys, but that heavy fighting was ongoing. Maj. Irwin, who attended the burial service of his fellow officers on 3 July, was with the forward-most assault soldiers. Keeping in contact with HQ via telephone, he urged that more support troops be sent up as soon as possible. Just after mid-

★Almost certainly related to the Chester-Master family of Cirencester.

Lt G.H.S. Musgrove was one of Neville's officers who fell on 1 July 1916. Musgrove moved to Cheltenham as a child, where his father became a Sergeant Major with the town's College Cadet Corps.

day, the Major took command of all the men in his sector to the west of Montauban, and the whole Brigade objective was reached by 1.30 p.m. At this point, Lance Corporal Brame arrived with a bottle of champagne to be consumed at Montauban following its capture, and this was shared amongst '…all of the East Surrey Officers engaged in the attack who had not been killed or wounded.'[5] Lt Musgrove is not mentioned by name. The danger had not yet passed, however, as when the new Battalion HQ was being established, several German shells came over, and the position was rapidly relocated. In the evening, a party of Suffolks brought along twenty-five canvas buckets of water, which were 'extremely welcome'.[6]

The incident with the footballs was widely reported in the newspapers of the opposing countries, with the Germans deriding the whole affair as another example of reckless British eccentricity. In contrast the British Press championed the men who took part as personifying the spirit of those who 'played the game'. 'GLORIOUS EAST SURREYS' read one headline, while others took a more sober tone: 'A FOOTBALL MATCH WITH DEATH IN PICARDY'. Two of the footballs were found in the German trenches, and one is now proudly displayed as a trophy in the Regimental Museum back in Surrey. The 8th Battalion distinguished itself on 1 July, with Gen. Maxse expressing his '…greatest pride and admiration of the work done [by the 8th East Surreys].' He congratulated the Commanding Officer on creating an 'immortal name'[7] for the battalion, which was awarded two DSOs, two Military Crosses, two Distinguished Conduct Medals and nine Military Medals on this date alone.

The 7th Buffs provided support for the 8th East Surreys in the morning, and were later called upon to assist the 7th Queen's – which had also suffered heavy casualties – just after midday. Half of 'D' Company, 7th Buffs, under Temp./Capt. Gerald Tassell-Neame, was sent up

Capt. Neville of the 8th Battalion, East Surrey Regiment, provided his men with four footballs on the morning of 1 July 1916, and these were kicked into No Man's Land at the start of the attack.

to the Mametz–Montauban Road after the Queen's CO expressed his doubts over whether his left flank was strong enough to hold out, and the action was successful, allowing the British to advance and occupy Montauban Alley. Temp./Capt. Neame, however, lost his life during this crucial phase of the day's fighting. The officer had been born in Surrey during 1885, the son of Frank and Louisa, and was educated at Cheltenham College between May 1899 and Easter 1903. A member of the College Cadet Corps, he would undoubtedly have known Sergeant-Major Musgrove, who was his Drill Instructor at the time. (Fourteen individuals with the surname Neame attended Cheltenham College, including Phillip, who received a VC at Neuve Chapelle on 19 December 1914. Whilst serving with the Royal Engineers he had held off a ferocious German attack and rescued all of the wounded men whom it was possible to move. On 1 July 1916, Capt. Neame, VC, DSO, was a Brigade Major with the 56th (London) Division at Gommecourt. Not only did he survive the First World War, he lived to see the end of the Second, despite spending a period as a POW of the Italians.)

Captain G.T. Neame, who was commissioned in the autumn of 1914, had been injured in April 1916, when 'D' Company took a direct hit from an artillery shell. His body was originally interred to the north of Carnoy, and his wife, Phyllis, was informed of his death via telegram on 5 July. But the officer's final resting place was to be several miles to the north-west of Carnoy at the Delville Wood Cemetery, Longueval (XXIII.Q.9). After the war, several isolated burial grounds or singular interments which were difficult to access or maintain were 'amalgamated' to form larger, more manageable sites. The decision to transport Capt. Neame's body to a point some distance from where he fell is perhaps surprising, but this may have been the only cemetery 'available' for burials at the time, even though the more logical destinations would have been the Carnoy Military Cemetery, or the Dantzig Alley British Cemetery nearby.

Another officer of the 7th Buffs to lose his life was Lt Edouard Herbert Allan Goss. Pte J.H. Dow, who was hospitalised, made the following written testament: '…on 1 July, at Carnoy, Lieutenant Goss was blown up by a shell.'[8] Born at Rangoon in 1877, E.H.A. Goss was one of four brothers who attended Clifton College (in his case between 1889 and 1895), where he, '…gained his cap and also a place in the Gym VIII'.[9] Having served in Upper Burma, he was a former member of the Volunteer Rifles, and when the First World War broke out he intimated that he would like to join 'any Kentish unit',[10] presumably

One of the balls used by Capt. Neville on the morning of 1 July 1916 is now on display at the Regimental Museum.

due to the connections with family members who are known to have lived in the county. Receiving his commission in December 1914, Lt Goss and the 7th Buffs arrived in France during July 1915. Following his death, his body was interred in an isolated grave within a crater on the Carnoy–Montauban Road. In 1920 his Cambridge-based parents, Louis and Marie, were told by the War Office that their son's remains had been exhumed and re-interred at the Dantzig Alley British Cemetery (VIII.R.4). 'The re-burial has been carefully and reverently carried out',[11] the War Office assured them. An obituary for Lt Goss appeared in the *Bristol Times & Mirror*, which stated that he was 'formerly of Clifton.'

One aspect of the 1 July plans of which many of the assault troops were unaware until the day itself was the digging of tunnels in order to place mines under the German positions. Work of this nature had been going on beneath their feet for months, and by its very nature it was extremely dangerous. The left flank of the 18th Division, which included the 7th Bedfords in the front line, and 6th Northamptons in support, witnessed the spectacular but deadly endeavours of 183 Tunnelling Company, Royal Engineers, at 7.27 a.m., as revealed in the War Diary of the Bedfordshires:

> At 7:28 a.m. immediately after the blowing of mine at Kasino Point, Mr Rawes left our trenches with the first wave. The Berkshires on our right left their trenches in advance of us and at [the] time of the [explosion] their men were lying down in the open and some men [were] very close to Kasino Point. It must have caused them casualties [because] we in our front line trenches [and] were covered with falling debris.[12]

Sustaining heavy losses from machine-gun fire, the Bedfords and Berkshires pushed relentlessly onwards until they arrived within seventy yards of Pommiers Trench and 'went to earth' to avoid the withering bullets. A stretch of uncut wire was spotted and the survivors began crawling towards it, although artillery shells – thought to be British – were falling amongst the foremost troops, checking the advance. Meanwhile, close by, small groups of men had reached parts of the enemy wire which were still intact, and Capt. Bull, the eyewitness who wrote the official report in the War Diary, confessed:

…the half hour outside that trench will be a nightmare for years to come, and this was our expensive time…The way they [the Berkshires and Bedfords] cut the wire, just as if nothing was doing, was splendid…[13]

These gallant efforts allowed entry to the German lines, and bombers began their precarious journey along the maze of dugouts. Still, with reinforcements arriving all the while, sufficient numbers were available to maintain the momentum, taking Pommiers Trench and surrounding Pommiers Redoubt. Montauban Alley, the Division's second objective, was in British hands by the afternoon, and the most advanced patrols reached the edge of Caterpillar Wood, to the north-west of Montauban. Capt. Bull ended his account:

> The behaviour of the men under most trying circumstances was wonderful, and it is entirely by their own initiative and total disregard of danger that the Pommiers Trench was taken. Every man went over perfectly clear in his mind of his objective and full of determination to get there.[14]

The battalion contained a number of men with strong Bristol connections in its ranks. Acting Sergeant Bert Knapp (No.15028), was a native of Winterbourne, to the north of the city, and was the son of James and Edith, of Crossley Cottages in the town. Aged twenty-two when he died, he is commemorated at Thiepval (2C). Lance Corporal William Smail (No.13538) hailed from Edinburgh, but enlisted in Bristol from his home in the latter city. The CWGC does not elaborate as to the exact location or next of kin details, but it does reveal that the soldier lies buried at the Dantzig Alley British Cemetery (III.C.2).

The next two casualties of the 7th Bedfords are also buried at this same location. Pte William Mead (No.14823), who hailed from Woodborough, Wilts., lived in Bristol (again, no personal detail is given) – grave number II.D.5. Pte Ernest Stanley Palmer (No.14828) was also buried there; he was born and lived in 'Henbury, Glos.', the twenty-two-year-old son of William, who later resided at Worrall Road, Clifton (grave number – III.D.4). Bristolian Pte Thomas Richard Westlake (No.14940) was the holder of a Military Medal, and his mother, Mrs G.A.B. Westlake, was a resident of Wilder Street in St Paul's by the 1920s. (Thiepval 2C.)

The 6th Northamptons, part of the 54th Brigade which included the 7th Bedfords, had undergone a week's training prior to the assault, and moved up from Bronfay Farm at 11.30 p.m. on 30 June on their way to the Front. At 8.00 a.m., the battalion went forward in support of the 11th Royal Fusiliers and 7th Bedfords, advancing '…as steadily as if they were on a parade ground…'[15] despite the heavy barrage they were under. Reaching the German positions, they met fierce resistance at Pommiers Trench, but all strong points in the first objective had been captured by 10.15 a.m., even though 'D' Company had been 'almost wiped out'.[16] The War Diary went on:

> All Company Commanders carried out their orders correctly and handled their [men] with gallantry and skill. Platoons were well led by officers and NCOs. Casualties: Officers – wounded – 3. Other Ranks – killed – 29, wounded – 123, missing – 4.[17]

Amongst the dead was Pte Wilfred Robert(s) Savage (No.13484), whose service record[18] has survived at the National Archives. It reveals he was born at Patchway, Glos. (North Bristol), and was working as a taxi cab driver when he enlisted at Bristol's Recruiting Office No.2 on 3 September 1914, at the age of twenty-three years and one month. He had a dark complexion, brown eyes, dark brown hair, with a distinguishing 'scar on small of back'. The 7th Northamptons arrived in France during July 1915, and exactly twelve months later (on the 9th) Pte Savage was confirmed by the Officer Commanding his battalion as having been killed in action on 1 July 1916. The soldier's personal items were dispatched to his mother, Mrs Sarah Jane Savage, in March 1917, to her home at Redfield Road in Patchway. Pte Savage was interred at the Dantzig Alley British Cemetery (VII.C.4.)

The 6th Northamptons received the thanks of the Fourth Army's Commander, Gen. Rawlinson, its Corps Commander, Lt-Gen. Congreve, VC, and its Divisional Commander, Maj.-Gen. Maxse.

There was to be one more Gloucestershire fatality in the 18th Division sector on 1 July, this time behind the lines. No.3 Section of the 92nd Field Company, Royal Engineers, was loading trucks with railway material near Carnoy at 9.30 a.m. when a shell exploded amongst them, killing four men. One of them was Sapper Frank Stringer (No.112462), who was born and lived in Bristol (area unknown) but enlisted at Barry, Glamorgan. Sapper Stringer lies buried at the Carnoy Military Cemetery (G.34).

The success of the 30th and 18th Divisions – both part of the New Armies – had been achieved with many hours of daylight left. Along with the French to their right, the Allied advance had captured six miles of the German front lines. The enemy had suffered losses to their manpower, territory, equipment and guns, whilst the 18th Division's casualty list was estimated to be just over 3,000 men killed, wounded or missing. Survivors could now consolidate their positions and tend to the wounded, whilst the question of whether the cavalry should be sent in to exploit the gains was left to the General Staff.

6

7TH DIVISION

The main objective of the 7th Division was the fortified village of Mametz and its associated defensive systems. On the right of the line, the 22nd Manchesters '…moved forward to the assault at 7.30 a.m. in 4 lines',[1] reaching Bucket Trench and Danzig Alley with heavy casualties. Bombing parties began clearing the dug-outs and, in conjunction with the 2nd Queen's (Royal West Surreys), moved along Fritz Trench in the afternoon, with all positions secured by the evening. Although seventy-five POWs were taken, the 22nd Manchesters suffered heavily, recording losses of ten officers dead and eight wounded, with 120 ORs known to have been killed, 241 wounded, and a further 111 unaccounted for. Pte William Ernest Bruton (No.21390) was one of the fallen, born in Bristol and enlisting in Manchester. The 1901 Census reveals three young men between the age of sixteen and twenty of that name living in Bristol at that time – two to the north of the river and one to the south – so without any corroborating evidence from the CWGC, his identity remains, for now, unclear. (Thiepval (13A & 14C.)

The 2nd Queen's were informed that their first objective was Mametz – the village and high ground to the east along the Montauban – Mametz Road; the second was German positions described as 'strong and well-made trenches'[2] by the War Diary; whilst the third was further elevated territory to the south of Mametz Wood. At 8.00 a.m., the battalion occupied the forward lines recently vacated by the 22nd Manchesters and 1st South Staffordshires, before 'A' and 'C' Companies were deployed across No Man's Land at 9.50 a.m. 'B' and 'D' Companies joined them in the afternoon, assisting in the capture of prisoners who were guarded by small groups of British soldiers, and the War Diary notes:

> The [German] officer on seeing how superior in numbers his party was tried to get at his revolver but on being shot in the right shoulder he again threw up his hands.[3]

After reorganisation of the Companies in Danzig Alley, it was revealed that: 'Cpl Shaw had the satisfaction of training the German automatic rifle on the enemy whilst they were trying to escape from Fritz Trench.'[4] Another piece of heartening news reached the 2nd Queen's at 12.50 p.m: 'The enemy in full retreat and many prisoners taken…Montauban has fallen [to the 30th Division].'[5]

Six officers were dead and thirteen wounded (including T/Capt. E.C. Thorneycroft who had been '…struck by a rifle bullet which caused a wound of the scalp'[6]), whereas forty men in the ranks had been killed, 226 injured and forty-one were missing. (The SDGW gives the OR number of fatalities for 1 July as forty-eight.) Stroud-born Cpl Harry Richard Gething (L/9553) had lost his life; nevertheless his service record[7] is another which is still in existence at the National Archives. He enlisted in 1908 at the age of seventeen years ten months, giving up his previous occupation as a kitchen porter, and he was just over the minimum height requirement, standing at 5'3¾". The new recruit had brown hair and eyes, and his personal notes reveal that he had:

> …spent a long time before he entered the army in kitchen work. [He] had been successfully employed in this capacity at the Trocadera, London, where his father was at one time [the] chef. Is evidently well-versed in all kitchen work and intends to resume this employment in civilian life. Is a hard worker, honest, sober and trustworthy. [This testimony is dated 1913]

Having served his five years in the 'Soudan', Gibraltar, Bermuda, Somali and South Africa, it is almost certain that he was placed on the 'Reserve', and received his recall to the Colours at his home in Walworth, Surrey, during the summer of 1914. Cpl Gething never had the opportunity to return to his work in the restaurant trade, and is commemorated at the Thiepval Memorial (5D & 6D).

From a defensive perspective, the Somme campaign is perhaps most associated with one weapon – the machine-gun. One which was captured at Mametz was found to have fired 'a great quantity of rounds', and the following eyewitness account, printed in the *Western Daily Press*, was definitely from within the 7th Division's sector, but its eye-opening revelations could have been from any point along the front lines on 1 July:

> His machine-guns did the Boche priceless service. It was these, and not his infantry, that enabled him to hold our men at all. And never in my life have I seen anything finer than the way our successive waves of men marched singing and cheering into that bath of lead. The more casualties they saw in front of them the louder they cheered and sang, the harder they pressed forward into it. I've not heard one single case of shirking. They went into it as though it was a football scrum. When I got into the Boche front line below Mametz, I stumbled right into his machine-gun lodge. The trench was knocked flat, but that made no odds. Leading forward from his front line he has a tunnel going down into a dug-out over 20 feet deep, and splendidly shored-up and protected. That's the home of the gun and the section. From that…a flight of steps leads up to a small dug-out, out in front of the parapet, splendidly roofed…No shells in the world would hurt 'em in the big lower chambers.

The 20th Brigade, consisting of the 8th and 9th Battalions of the Devons, as well as the 2nd Battalions of the Border Regiment and Gordon Highlanders, had to brave this 'bath of lead' as they stormed towards Mametz, encountering one of the most notorious enemy gun emplacements, known as 'The Shrine', which was situated in a graveyard with a sweeping line of fire across the exposed ground below. The 2nd Gordon Highlanders launched their attack at 7.30 a.m., following an intense bombardment aimed at Mametz, with all four Companies – 'A', 'B', 'C' and 'D' – committed to the assault. Three lines of trenches plus thick barbed wire had to be crossed before the village was even reached, and 'B' Company lost all but one of its officers, whilst 'D' Company emerged at the end of the day with only one NCO and eighteen men (from an approximate strength of 120). Reinforcements were urgently requested as casualties were piling up before The Shrine, but Capt. A.N. Davidson rallied his men in the Sunken Road before attacking Mametz itself. Throughout the afternoon, bitter fighting went on, and the village finally fell to a mixture of British battalions, including those sent up in support. The Gordons' War Diary reports:

> The enemy had taken advantage of the high bank to make it an impregnable position [but] the result of the engagement was entirely successful.[8]

Just after 4.00 in the afternoon it was announced that 600 Germans had surrendered, and this morale-boosting incident was seized upon by the British Press. The *Bristol Times & Mirror* noted how the defenders had caved in 'after facing the music for a comparatively short time', and added: 'Their opinion of the "contemptible little army"* is of a character not altogether calculated to endear their regiment to the heart of the Kaiser.'

The *Western Daily Press* ran the feature under the headline 'THE RAGGED JOCK'S PARADE', and went on:

> The following story is told by an officer of the Gordons, and the village he mentions is M_____ [censored by the War Office, undoubtedly 'Mametz'], somewhere in France: – 'It was the finest thing I ever saw in my life', said the officer, 'we'd got the village by then, so the fire behind was nothing. It was six hours after I had been wounded. I saw six hundred Boches of all ranks marching in a column of route across the open, towards our rear. They were disarmed, of course, and what do you think they had for an escort? Three ragged Jocks – our battalion – all blood and dirt and rags…That was good enough for me. I brought up the rear, and that's how I got to a dressing station and had my arm dressed. I walked behind a 600 strong column of Boches but I couldn't equal the swagger of those three Jocks in the lead.'

The newspapers did not, however, reveal the cost to the 2nd Gordons of taking Mametz. Of the twenty-four officers and 783 men in the ranks who went into action, seven officers were killed and nine wounded, 119 ORs were dead, with 287 injured and thirty-nine missing. Captain Henry Brian Brooke, the son of Sir Harry Vesey Brooke, KBE, and Lady Brooke, of Aberdeen, had received three bullet wounds during the assault, with the last having entered his neck causing him to fall in the third German line. Brought back to a Field Dressing Station, Captain Brooke began the agonising process of being sent home to the UK, and he eventually arrived at the Empire Hospital in Vincent Square, London, where he finally succumbed to his injuries at 10.53 p.m. on 24 July 1916. His father had already been informed of the seriousness of the Captain's condition via telegram on 6 July, and he now made arrangements to bring his son's body back to Aberdeen for interment at the town's Springbank Cemetery (N.19.) Born in December 1889, Henry Brooke was educated at Clifton College between 1903 and 1905 before he took up a position as an Assistant General Manager with W. Graham and Co., coffee planters. Wounded in British East Africa at the start of the war, Capt. Brooke then proceeded to France, where he fell at the moment of victory during the storming of Mametz. (His brother, Lt J.A.O. Brooke, also of the 2nd Gordons, was awarded a Victoria Cross on 29 October 1914 in Belgium, where he regained a lost trench under heavy fire, preventing the enemy from breaking through the British lines, but was killed when he was bringing up support. In 1936, a private enquiry was sent to the War Office to ascertain whether both of the Brooke brothers – J.A.O. and H.B. – were in receipt of a VC, but it was established that only the former, who was posthumously promoted to Captain, was a holder of the medal.)

In the ranks of the 2nd Gordons on 1 July 1916 was Pte William R. Holborow (No.S11876), who lost his life whilst advancing with 'B' Company, one of the leading sections of the battalion. Aged twenty-one, he was the son of Daniel and A.E. Holborow, of Burden Court, Tresham, near Wotton-under-Edge, and his obituary appeared in the *Wilts & Glos Standard*, stating that he was attached to the Gordons from the Scots Greys. Born at Hawkesbury and enlisting in Bristol, his name is to be found upon the Special Memorial within the Gordon Cemetery near Mametz, which was the site of one the regiment's old trenches. There is a famous photograph of the Gordon Highlanders crossing the vast expanse of exposed No Man's Land during the initial assault, their silhouettes framed against the white chalk thrown up by trenches and shell-fire.

Another well-documented incident from 1 July relates to Captain D.L. Martin of the 9th Devons, who created a plasticine model of the ground across which his battalion, alongside

---

*The BEF of 1914 was referred to as Britain's 'contemptible little army' by Kaiser Wilhelm; the former defiantly responded by referring to themselves as the 'Old Contemptibles'.

the 2nd Gordons, would have to attack. But what started as a source of mild amusement to pass the time whilst on leave soon took on a frightening reality; the officer realised his men would have to walk up a small incline close to Mansel Copse before marching in full view towards The Shrine machine-gun, some 400 yards away. Capt. Martin forecast the Devons would suffer dreadfully from this spot onwards, and he expressed his fears to his superiors when he returned to the Front.

The 9th Devons were told to advance in four successive lines of four platoons each, and forty wire cutters were to be issued to the men who would go over first. Each soldier had to carry 'two tins of meat and eight hard biscuits, [plus] a canteen packed with emergency grocery rations'.[9] Arrangements were made to store their great-coats and haversacks, whilst items of value were to be left in their pockets, with the intention of bringing up all the equipment and clothing afterwards. 'All packs must be clearly marked'[10] was the unambiguous instruction.

At 7.27 a.m., the battalion left its trenches, crossed the temporary bridges and moved out into No Man's Land towards Mansel Copse. As the men reached the ridge and came into view of The Shrine, the machine-gun opened up on them and casualties were strewn across the battlefield. Captain Martin, who had predicted such a catastrophe, was one of many who fell dead, but the survivors pushed on towards Mametz, with the War Diary giving the merest indication of the mayhem:

> Our men behaved splendidly throughout in spite of the fact that all Company Officers except one, and all senior NCOs, had been killed or wounded. This speaks well for the individual training of the men, as the remains of the Companies and Platoons were led to the final objective by Lance Corporals, and, in some cases, Privates…[11]

Held up on the outskirts of Mametz, having taken some of their initial targets, the 9th Devons struggled to drive the enemy from the village, and requested reinforcements from their sister battalion, the 8th. Whilst some of its manpower was deployed in the original front lines, 'A' Company moved up to strengthen a gap which had appeared between the 9th Devons and the 2nd Borders. Lewis gun teams accompanied the advance and proved to be of 'great value in sweeping the enemy down in his trench and also caused him a good many casualties'.[12] Another factor was the high-standing corn which made it difficult to pinpoint the German positions, yet it also 'afforded good cover'.[13] With the surrender of the majority of defenders during late afternoon, reserves could be brought up relatively safely, and it was noted that 'no enemy counter-attacks developed through the night.'[14]

The two Devon battalions had paid a heavy price. All but one of the 9th's officers had either been killed or wounded, with the OR figures topping over 300, whilst the 8th recorded approximately 200 from all ranks either dead, injured or missing. Three officers from the 8th and 9th had links to Gloucestershire and North Bristol, and as it is not known precisely when each one fell, they are listed below in seniority of rank.

Captain Geoffrey Phillip Tregelles was the officer who led 'A' Company of the 8th Devons out into No Man's Land at 10.00 a.m., and the next mention of him is in the officer's own service record,[15] which contains the statement of a Pte Kidd, from the latter's hospital bed, who must have transcribed the following testimony to another as it is in the third person:

> He [Kidd] saw Capt. Tregellie [sic], who belonged to his Company, lying dead on the field. At the time they were going across the open country.

The Captain's body was originally interred at Mansel Copse, and the burial ground is now known as the Devonshire Cemetery (B.6), from where both battalions attacked on the morning of 1 July. It contains the deeply moving epitaph at its entrance: 'The Devonshires Held This Trench, and the Devonshires Hold It Still.'

The Devonshire Cemetery at Mametz. The village was captured by the 7th Division on 1 July 1916, but at a heavy cost. The 8th and 9th Devonshires left their forward trenches under heavy fire, and the position was later used to bury the dead of both battalions.

Born in Penzance during 1892, G.P. Tregelles was the son of George and M.S.* Tregelles, who later moved to Barnstaple in Devon. The young man was educated at Clifton College (1904–11) before becoming a scholar at Caius College, Cambridge, but as with so many undergraduates or graduates at the time, study and career was set aside for the sake of King and Country. Commissioned in August 1914, Captain Tregelles was an experienced officer when he fell leading his men into action.

Along with Captain Martin and his grimly accurate prediction of his own demise at Mansel Copse, another feted officer of the 9th Devons who was killed nearby was Temporary Lieutenant William Noel Hodgson, MC. Born at Thornbury, south Gloucestershire, during 1893, he was the son of the Reverend Henry Hodgson, DD (a future Bishop of Ipswich), and Penelope, and received his education at Durham School followed by Oxford University. Commissioned in the autumn of 1914, he was awarded a Military Cross at Loos on 25 September 1915, when he and a group of men held on to a captured trench for thirty-six hours without food or reinforcements. On 1 July 1916, some contemporary reports indicate Lt Hodgson was taking a supply of bombs up to his men in newly captured positions in Mametz when he lost his life, suggesting he had already made the perilous journey at least once, whilst others claim he fell after only advancing a few yards. His body was also interred at the Devonshire Cemetery (A.3), and the death was reported in *The Times*. On the eve of the Somme Offensive, the officer had written the poignant poem 'Before Action', and in addition he was the author of 'Verse and Prose in Peace and War.'

Temp. Second Lieutenant Raymond Boycott Holcroft was the last member of the trio. Described by the *Gloucestershire Echo* as working at Mr Guilding's Farm near Bushley when war was declared, he was 'well-known in Tewkesbury cricket circles'. Born in Staffordshire during August 1895, he was the son of Arthur and Ethel, attending 'The Wergs' Prep. and Warwick Schools

*His mother, Marion, was born in North Bristol.

Thornbury-born T/Lt W.N. Hodgson, MC, 9th Battalion, Devons, wrote a famous poem on the eve of his death.

before obtaining his commission. His address is given as 'Bushley Park, Tewkesbury'[16] at this time. The *Echo* also reveals that the officer had been wounded twice during 1916 before he was killed on 1 July. Pte F.C. Lock, of 'D' Co., 9th Devons, informed his superiors that 2nd Lt Holcroft had been hit in the leg close to 'Manselle Wood', and whilst he was in the act of stooping down to help a stricken Corporal, the officer was shot dead from the direction of Mametz. Pte Lock, who was also injured, saw the Second Lieutenant's body 'clearly', and Pte Morgan, of IX Platoon, 'C' Co., told his friend, Pte Jack Owen, at the end of the day, 'Holcroft is killed, Jack'.[17] The latter added, 'He was a good soldier and was bound to have been in the German front line',[18] and recalled that the officer was in charge of the battalion's Lewis Gun Section. One of the strict commands of the advance, reiterated in the War Diary, was that 'No one shall fall out to assist a wounded comrade.'[19] 2nd Lt Holcroft, expected to lead by example, was himself incapacitated when he tried to help one of his men, and it can be safely said that he did his duty. As with the interments of Capt. Tregelles and Lt Hodgson, 2nd Lt Holcroft's remains were taken to the Devonshire Cemetery (A.1). (After the war, the body of 2nd Lt Cecil P. Hirst, 8th Devons, was exhumed from its original place of burial and taken to Dantzig Alley British Cemetery (IV.J.4.). The officer's sister, Dorothy James, was informed of the reinterment at her home 'The Chalet' at Cleeve Hill near Cheltenham. This is the only known link with Gloucestershire, as the family hailed from Yorkshire.)

In the ranks, Pte Arthur William Bowles (No.16942), 9th Devons, was also one of the dead. The SDGW lists him as having been born in Cirencester, but the 1901 Census reveals an eight-year-old Arthur Bowles – a native of nearby Fairford – as living with his parents, Albert (a 'domestic gardener') and Elizabeth, along with his two sisters, at Cornwell St Peter near Chipping Norton in Oxfordshire. As the CWGC indicates, Pte Bowles was the son of Mrs E. Bowles, of 'Cornwell, Oxford', this is almost certainly the same person who now lies buried at the Devonshire Cemetery (A.5).

Pte Frank George Williams (No.12000), of the same battalion, had also fallen. Born in Bristol (he is possibly the same person whose birth was registered in the Barton Regis area of the city centre during the summer of 1889), the new recruit joined up in Exeter, and the CWGC notes he was the twenty-six-year-old son of Mrs Warbutton, who was living in Pontypridd by the 1920s. Pte Williams can be found in the same grave space as Pte Bowles.

The 2nd Border Regiment attacked alongside the left flank of the Devons, and fared better crossing No Man's Land than their West Country counterparts, reaching the German front line with comparatively few casualties. Small parties of enemy bombers were soon encountered, however, prompting one eyewitness to note in the War Diary:

> We proceeded to advance down a trench towards them, as a bombing section, and soon found ourselves in contact with them, and both parties started bombing. We [had] advanced 20 or 30 yards when bombs began to run short, and as there was no sign of anyone on our right flank or in support, the position seemed to be rather serious.[20]

When British artillery shells began falling perilously close, flares were lit to alert the gunners of the potential hazard. But this only served to draw more German fire upon the point of attack, although the arrival of fresh ammunition, plus reinforcements in the afternoon, enabled the assault to be pressed home successfully.

Second Lieutenant David Herbert Hosken Logan was one of three battalion officers who had fallen by the end of the day. Born at Rokeby Road in Bristol's Redland district during 1897, he was the son of a Royal Artillery Colonel who also served on the Staff. The service record[21] of the former reveals that he attended a school in Apsley Road, Clifton, between 1907 and 1911, was married in October 1915, and he desired to join the Border Regiment because of his family's Scottish 'ancestral claims'. Having only been at the Front since May, the body of the young officer – who was aged only nineteen – was eventually interred at the Citadel New Military Cemetery, Fricourt (II.D.12). (See Introduction.)

Mametz was in British hands, yet this was almost the furthest extent of the first-day objectives achieved by the Fourth and Third Armies, and the rest of the line was struggling against a ferocious defence which was cutting men down in their thousands for little or no territorial gain.

17TH (NORTHERN) DIVISION – 50TH BRIGADE

With the line now 'curving' round to the north, the orientation of the British Divisions was at this juncture facing roughly eastwards or north-eastwards. The main bulk of the 17th Division was kept in reserve on 1 July, close to the Ancre south of Albert, but four battalions of the 50th Brigade – 10th West Yorks., 7th East Yorks., 7th Green Howards (Yorkshire Regt) and 6th Dorsets – were sent to assist the 21st Division at Fricourt. The 'underbelly' of the village was the responsibility of the left flank of the 7th Division, whilst the 7th Green Howards, 7th East Yorks. and 10th West Yorks. would attack from west to east, yet all of the latter were to encounter tragedy. The 10th's War Diary reveals:

> At 7:30 a.m. the Battalion took part in the grand assault. The Battalion assaulted in 4 lines, 2 lines got through the German positions to the 4th line and were cut off, the attack on the left having failed. Casualties were very heavy caused by machine-guns which enfiladed our left flank and were so deadly that the 3rd and 4th lines failed to get across No Man's Land. Officer casualties★ were Lt-Col Dixon [Dickson] (commanding) and Major J. Knott, 2nd in command, both killed, and approx. 750 O.R.[1]

The 10th West Yorkshire Regiment recorded the highest number of dead, wounded and missing on 1 July, officially put at 710 out of around 800 men. One of the officers was Second Lieutenant Francis Joseph Hicking, who, in the ODGW, is listed as serving with the 13th Battalion, attached to the 1st. He was, however, with the 10th, as confirmed by the CWGC, which also revealed that he was the son of Joseph and Kate who were living at Halsey House in Cheltenham's Pittville by the 1920s. There is no indication that 2nd Lt Hicking had any personal links with Gloucestershire – he was born in Nottingham during 1896 and attended Uppingham School in Leicestershire – and is included here purely by virtue of his parents' later residence. The young man enlisted into the Honourable Artillery Company at the beginning of 1915 before obtaining his commission in the West Yorkshires, with whom he was serving when he was wounded by a gun shot to his right thigh later in the year. Aged just twenty, his body was interred at the Fricourt New Military Cemetery (C.4) amongst 158 of his comrades from the same battalion who fell on the same day. The cemetery is situated in No Man's Land, across which they advanced on the fateful day. The officer's father received the grim news on 8 July, at a time when he was also pondering the fate of his other son, George, who was a Lieutenant in the 8th York and Lancasters. George's regiment was destined to attack Ovillers with the 8th Division on 1 July, further north of Fricourt.

★There were twenty-two in total.

In support of the 10th West Yorks were the 7th Battalion of the Green Howards on the right flank, and the 7th East Yorkshires, following up to occupy the front lines once the 10th had gone over. The East Yorkshires' War Diary gives a summary of the day's events:

> 7:52 a.m. Major King reported C Co. all in Surrey Avenue.
> 8:26 a.m. C Co. in front line.
> 9:50 a.m. First batch of wounded brought down.
> 11:15 a.m. Guides say one Company went over without orders…This is only a rumour.
> 2:33 p.m. C and D Companies advanced to attack, but owing to heavy casualties from machine-gun fire it was impossible to reach enemy front line.
> 3:15 p.m. Have [estimated] probably 150 casualties of first six platoons going over.

(A reference is made to there being only one ladder with which the men could climb out of the trenches, therefore they could only 'go over' in single file.)

> 5 p.m. [Order to 'C' Co.]: You must get in touch with Battalion on your right.[2]

With only four small gaps in the enemy wire, it is little wonder no progress was made, and the few who reached Fricourt were either captured or killed almost immediately. Capt. John Bedell Rutledge was one of four officers from the 7th East Yorkshires reported to have fallen. He was the son of Revd L.W. and Alice Rutledge, and husband of Theodora, who, at some stage between the autumn of 1916 and the time when the CWGC Debt of Honour Register was compiled, moved to Cheltenham before passing away. The couple were married in 1910, and the officer's widow was residing in Kent in the October following his death. There are also addresses in Steeple Aston, Oxford, and Shepperton-on-Thames, as well as references to Argentina for the Irish-born Captain and his spouse, who became parents to Theodora Elizabeth during 1915. Aged thirty-three, Capt. Rutledge – who is mentioned here due to his wife's later connections with Gloucestershire – lies buried at the Fricourt New Military Cemetery (B.4).

The 7th Green Howards had a disastrous day. Referring back to the 11.15 a.m. entry of the 7th East Yorkshire's War Diary, one Company had, indeed, attacked in error at 7.45 a.m., but its men were actually from the Green Howards. Quite how or why this order was given is unclear, but it ended in carnage with the main force practically annihilated within a few paces. At just after 2.30 in the afternoon, the remaining three Companies were given their orders to advance in broad daylight with hardly any preliminary bombardment. Three minutes later, 351 men had become casualties before they had advanced fifty yards, and those who were able crawled back to their trenches.

Gloucester-born Lance Corporal Sydney John Norman (No.14597) was amongst the dead, although whether he fell during the erroneous assault in the morning, or the equally ill-fated and short-lived attack in the afternoon, is not known. Enlisting in his home city he was, nonetheless, a resident of London's Battersea at the time, and is remembered on the Special Memorial (D.5) within Fricourt British Cemetery, which contains many interments of men from the 7th Green Howards who were killed on the morning of 1 July. The 1901 Census does contain a possible match – one-year-old Sydney Norman, living with his parents, Thomas (a 'railway guard') and Agnes, in Gloucester's Clement Street. If this is the same person, then he would still have been aged only seventeen at the most in July 1916, but it is possible. 2nd Lt Harold Hornsby enlisted into the ranks of the 12th Glosters at Cheltenham during September 1914, and trained at Bristol before receiving a commission with the 7th Green Howards. This is the only known link with the county for the Yorkshireman who fell on 1 July.

Pioneer Harry Lionel St John (No.129813), of the 5th Battalion, Special Brigade, Royal Engineers, is included here because his grave is close to the 17th Division's reserve position. He died of his wounds on 2 July and lies buried at the La Neuville British Cemetery (I.A.29), several miles to the south-west of Albert, well behind the British lines. Born in Ceylon, he joined up in Westminster from his home at Thornbury, and served in the Middlesex Regiment before transferring to the 'Special Brigade' of the RE, which was responsible for the deployment of gas. The 5th Battalion was a Stokes Mortar Unit with several Companies deployed along the entire line, and the nature of the Pioneer's death is open to question, although it is likely he was caught in a retaliatory strike. The War Diary states for 1 July:

> All companies carried out smoke bombardments★ on the Third and Fourth Army Fronts.[3]

Two officers were killed and two wounded (two were attached from the Royal Field Artillery), whilst five men in the ranks lost their lives, a further sixty-five were injured, and two more were unaccounted for. The following day, one Company was at Fricourt, and the War Diary notes that the purpose of this barrage was to:

> …completely fill Fricourt village with smoke for thirty minutes. [This was] cancelled at the last moment as Fricourt village was found to be evacuated. 1 O.R. died of wounds.[4]

(The Germans withdrew during the early hours of 2 July, and the British sent cautious patrols into the ruins before it was secured later in the day.)

It is therefore likely that the casualty mentioned was Pioneer St John, although it cannot be confirmed. Lt Robert Hardman, of 'C' Company, lost his life in action on 1 July near Aveluy Wood, to the north of Albert, whilst another known fatality occurred at Gommecourt, in the Third Army sector. The compiler of the War Diary was in the village of Villers-Bocage – close to Amiens – when the attack began. Returning to Harry St John, his service record has not survived, but the documents belonging to Richard Lionel St John, who joined the 5th King's Royal Rifle Corps in 1917, are still in existence. He is almost certainly H. St John's brother, as when the former was discharged in February 1918, on health grounds, he requested a passage back to his home overseas, informing the War Office: 'I came over to England from Ceylon purposely to join the Colours.'[5] He had a temporary address near Cannon Street in the City of London, and it was probably from here that Harry St John made the short journey to Westminster when he enlisted.

Exactly a week after the offensive began, many British newspapers were still in a buoyant mood, convinced that it was only a matter of time before the German cause would be crushed. The *Western Daily Press* reported many 'Battle Cameos', such as the following from a wounded soldier:

> We are making no mistake this time. Everything possible seems to have been thought of beforehand, and for weeks we've been having rehearsals of every involvement. It was not a repetition of Loos [autumn 1915]. Our fellows hopped over our parapets and tore across the uneven ground to where the first lines of German trenches used to be. As a matter of fact, these trenches had ceased to exist as trenches. They were simply battered to bits, and here or there, where something like a broken crevice marked a line of a trench, we found nothing but dead Germans. I didn't see a shot fired from a German trench…

However, there were also notes of caution from the *Western Daily Press*:

> Among the places we have occupied and still have in our possession are the fortified villages of Mametz, Montauban and Fricourt. It is urged by those in a position to know that the public should not be carried away by the initial success.

These were wise words indeed.

★No chemical rounds were available at the time.

8

21ST DIVISION

The 63rd Brigade of the 21st Division, comprising the 4th Middlesex, 8th Somerset Light Infantry, 8th Lincolns and 10th York and Lancasters, went on the attack to the north of Fricourt. At 6.30 on the morning of 1 July, trench ladders and bridges were put into position as an intense British barrage was opened, and just under an hour later, the first waves of the Somersets' 'B' and 'C' Companies crawled out into No Man's Land. 'A' Company was in support, whilst 'D' Co. was to act as a carrying party, bringing up bombs, picks, shovels and stores. When the artillery bombardment was lifted, the 8th SLI '…advanced in quick time',[1] but were met by heavy machine-gun fire. 'Officers and men were being hit and falling everywhere, [yet] the advance went steadily on',[2] noted the War Diary, adding that a Brigade Major had called it 'magnificent'. Fifty per cent of the leading platoons had fallen before the enemy wire was reached, and the survivors were held up by concentrated artillery and machine-gun fire from the Germans which caused casualties in No Man's Land, the British front line and the support trenches. Dogged determination pushed the SLI onwards, however, and several enemy machine gunners were killed, allowing entry to the German forward positions, which were described as being '…battered out of all recognition', and 'a mass of craters'. A Stokes mortar team brought across was 'knocked out', but a Lewis gun section provided 'timely support', although the 'enemy's barrage of shrapnel prevented further advance'. Approximately one hundred men consolidated the newly taken positions in the afternoon and evening, repulsing a bombing attack from the direction of Fricourt, and reinforcements laden with rations came up at 8.00 a.m. the following morning. Two days later, in the early hours, the battalion was withdrawn.

The *Western Daily Press* inevitably devoted a fair amount of space to the progress of one of its local regiments under headlines such as: 'THE CHARGE OF THE SOMERSETS!', and 'GALLANT SOMERSETS!'. It went on:

> [The SLI] has a large percentage of Bristol lads in their ranks. In the early days of recruiting at Colston Hall, the Somersets were singularly popular…Now these young fellows are seasoned soldiers.

One of the latter told the *Western Daily Press* from his hospital bed: 'When the British artillery were raining shells on them [the Germans], they hid their machine-guns in concrete bunkers.' A Somersets' officer praised his men by declaring: 'They were splendid, and went for the enemy with a yell! Men dropped in all directions from machine-gun fire, but happily fatal wounds were not numerous.' An NCO added: 'One would like to know [the identity] of a heroic young officer, who encouraged his men with the cry "Stick it, Somersets!" He was not [yet] nineteen, the Sergeant said, but he, too, was of the stuff heroes are made…'

Officers of the 8th Battalion, SLI. The Chaplain (standing, right) and the officer sitting in front of him both wear the ribbon of the Military Cross.

But amongst the tales of bravery, there was inevitable sadness. As Bristolians waited anxiously to hear of news of their men in the Somersets (including those in the 1st Battalion, further up the line), the *Western Daily Press* revealed a 'Haunting Memory' of the sight of:

…several men, almost in a row, leaning forward in various motionless postures upon their rifles, the bayonet points of which were buried in the ground, and between two of them a seated terrier, with its drooping head, faithful unto death to its soldier master. One needed not to be told that it is the work of a slowly swinging machine gun…which had wrought this dreadful tableau.

The SDGW reveals that eight officers and 107 ORs of the 8th SLI were killed in action on 1 July. Captain Walter George Warden led his battalion 'over the top', and Sgt Freeman, of 'C' Co. revealed from his hospital bed ten days later that the Captain had been '…hit by a bullet from a machine gun [and] died from the effects.'[3] Pte Bradley, an orderly who was severely wounded, reported that the officer's words as he lay dying on the battlefield were: 'I want to see my boys advancing.'[4]

Born in Gloucester during August 1885, he was the son of George and Jane Warden, who were living in the city's Elmbridge Road by 1916. (The couple had moved to Gloucester from the Midlands in the years prior to Walter's birth, along with their elder daughter, Annie. George Warden was a District Locomotive Superintendent for the Midland Railway.) The *Gloucester Citizen* revealed that W.G. Warden was:

…extremely popular at school, and was a sportsman in the best sense of the word. When war broke out he came over with the first Canadian Contingent. He fought in the battles of La Bassee and Neuve Chapelle, and was then offered a commission in the Somerset Light Infantry, and came home in March 1915. In September he went out with the Somersets as Sec.-Lt and took part in the battle of Loos. For his fine work at Loos he was promoted to a captaincy on October 12th. In the great attack on 1 July the Somersets were the first to leave the trenches, and Captain Warden led the attack. He died like an officer and a gentleman, loved by his brother officers and men. In nearly all the men's letters after the action they spoke of their love for their Captain, and said that if he had been spared they would have gone twice as far as they did. A relative of Capt. Warden who was allowed to see his Colonel★ (now wounded in London) was told by him that 'Warden would never be one to spare himself; he thought so much of his duty always'. On August 4th he would have been 31 years old.

Capt. Warden had married Constance in Weston-super-Mare during November 1914 and his widow was still living in the town in the 1920s. The officer was originally reported to be 'missing' the day following the attack, but his wife only received definite news of his death at the end of the month. The interment was carried out by the Chaplain of the 8th Royal Berkshires, Arthur Longden, and the Captain's grave is now to be found in the Gordon Dump Cemetery (II.Q.2), Ovillers La Boisselle. It is almost certain that his remains were brought here after the war, as the position of the burial ground is within the neighbouring 34th Division's sector. There are, however, forty men of the Somerset Light Infantry buried here who fell in the vicinity during the Somme battles of 1916 and 1918.

Lt-Col Scott, the battalion's injured CO who was having to deal with so much death and suffering amongst his men, soon sent a letter to the Mayor of Bath, Alderman (later Sir) Harry Hatt, which appeared in the *Western Daily Press* shortly afterwards:

> The last I heard of your son was that he was badly hit, and the stretcher-bearers were trying to get him in. He was perfectly splendid, leading his company up to the first line of the German trenches, talking and smiling and saying: 'Come on, you fellows, we've got them now', just as quiet and ordinary as he always does. He is simply splendid at inspiring confidence into people and quieting anyone down. I only hope my information is incorrect, as I did not actually see your son, though I gather he was not far from me.

Captain Arthur Beach Hatt, MC, was born in Oxford and spent part of his education at Dean Close School in Cheltenham before finishing his schooling in Holland and Germany. Farming in Worcestershire when war broke out, the *Western Daily Press* reports that he joined the Somersets as a Private (his service record notes it was the 12th Royal Sussex Regiment), before receiving his commission with the SLI the following February. Awarded his Military Cross for 'conspicuous gallantry and determination' at Hill 70 during the Battle of Loos (September, 1915), when he and a handful of men held on to a forward position when practically everyone else in the vicinity had retired, he was slightly wounded early in 1916 before his death on 1 July. (The service record also differs by giving the official date of death as 2 July. As he was initially known to have been wounded, the exact time of his demise may not have been confirmed.) Part of 'A' Company, in support of 'B' and 'C' Companies, the twenty-seven-year-old Captain now lies interred at the Gordon Dump Cemetery (II.M.4), Ovillers La Boisselle, and his death was also reported in the *Bristol Times & Mirror*. (His brother, Edward, a Captain in the 7th SLI, fell in action on 26 August 1916, near Montauban.)

As the *Western Daily Press* rightly observed, the ranks of the 8th SLI contained a heavy Bristol bias, and soon telegrams were arriving on doorsteps across the city. Lance Corporal Ernest Archibald Parker (No.15998) is listed in the SDGW as being born in Bristol, but the 1901 Census reveals him, when aged five, to be living in Easton's Croydon Street and a native of 'Wells, Somerset'. This was also the birthplace of his father, Ernest senior, who was employed in a soap works at the time. The *Western Daily Press* reported that the twenty-year-old Lance Corporal was:

★Lt-Col J.W. Scott.

Capt. A.B. Hatt, MC, 8th Battalion,
SLI. He attended Dean Close School
in Cheltenham and fell on 1 July
1916.

…highly esteemed by his family, friends, and his school-master, Mr Francombe, of St Gabriel's, who intimated that the young soldier's name would be inscribed on the school's honours board in due course.

(His grave is another situated at the Gordon Dump Cemetery (IV.P.6).)

Pte Henry Davis (No.16401) was born in Bristol's St Phillip's district and enlisted in Taunton from his home in Weston-super-Mare. There are numerous 'possibles' in the 1901 Census, and in the absence of any personal data, his family details are not known. (Thiepval 2A). Pte Reginald Duckett (No.19248) hailed from the Somerset half of Bristol, but when the 1901 census was taken he was aged four and living in Kingswood, to the north of the river Avon, with his parents, James and Bertha. (Thiepval 2A.) Pte Joseph George Eamer (No.17057) grew up in his native hamlet of Hawkesbury Upton, south Gloucestershire, the youngest of five brothers. When war broke out, he was working at Mr Nicholls' Farm in Upper Chalkley, and joined up early in 1915. The *Dursley Gazette* noted, 'It is worthy of recalling that the gallant young lad and four others from the village who enlisted at the same time, were considered to be five of the smartest young men to pass [through] the recruiting depot at Bristol.' The quintet of Eamer siblings all served in the armed forces, and the twenty-year-old Private in the Somerset Light Infantry was originally reported to be 'missing' on 1 July, verified by his comrades who had not seen him since they went into action together. Letters addressed to him, written by his parents – Mr and Mrs Joseph Eamer – were returned, and by the end of July it was confirmed that Pte Eamer was, indeed, dead. With No Man's Land in British hands by nightfall, and considering the length of time it took to establish his fate, it is a reasonable assumption that the soldier had managed to advance some distance into the German lines before he fell. (Thiepval 2A.) Pte John Thomas Holloway (No.17537) was born in St Phillip's, Bristol, and enlisted in his home city. No other official information about him exists, so

L/Cpl E.A. Parker. 8th Battalion, SLI, was killed on 1 July 1916. He lived at Easton, North Bristol.

he may be the son of John Holloway (a chimney sweep from St Phillip's who was living near Brick Street, to the north of Temple Meads at the turn of the twentieth century), aged fourteen in 1901, which would have made him twenty-nine in 1916. There is also an individual with this name whose birth was registered in the Barton Regis district of Bristol at the end of 1880, and he is not to be found in the on-line 1901 Census database, which covers England and Wales only. (He may have been serving in the forces during the Boer War, or anywhere around the Empire, and there is the possibility that he had emigrated, or had since died.) To positively identify a particular person in the records can often pose a number of problems, and the only other piece of cast-iron data relating to Pte J.T. Holloway is that he is remembered at Thiepval (2A.) Pte James Steven Horler (No.19090) has more background detail than some of his contemporaries. A native of Farrington Gurney, Somerset, he was the twenty-year-old son of John and Hannah, who had moved to Vicarage Road in Hanham, Bristol, by the 1920s. The soldier lies buried at the Gordon Dump Cemetery (V.R.2).

Pte Thomas Joseph Milliner (No.21304) was born at 'Filton, Glos' (SDGW), and was a seven-year-old schoolboy when the 1901 Census was compiled. An indication of the rural nature of Filton prior to the First World War can be found in the occupations of his family: his father, Patchway-born Jacob (forty-seven), was a 'wheelwright'; his brother William worked in haulage; and his other male sibling, Herbert, was a farm worker. His sister, Lilian, was also of school age, and their residence was close to a farm, the spelling of which is somewhat obscured on the Census, but begins with 'C-O-N--'. Pte Milliner died of wounds on 2 July 1916, almost certainly from injuries received on the previous day, or the build-up to the Somme Offensive. His grave is situated at the Mericourt-L'Abbé Communal Cemetery Extension (I.C.14), to the south-east of Albert. Close by were a number of Field Ambulances, and the stricken soldier was undoubtedly being taken along the Casualty Clearing Chain set up before the assault. Pte Bert James Parsons (No.15991) was another who came from St Phillip's in Bristol, the nineteen-year-old son of Robert and Mary Ann, who resided in Bedford Street off the Stapleton Road after the war. (Thiepval 2A.) Pte Thomas Scriven (No.15993) was a native of Bristol's St George's, and his parents – Arthur and Harriet – later lived at Proctor Street, Russell Town Avenue. Aged twenty-one when he fell, Pte Scriven's name is also to be found at Thiepval (2A.) The birthplace of Pte Alfred Harry Smith (No.16938) is given simply as 'Bristol' (SDGW), and he joined up in Aberdare. The son of Alfred and Bertha, he was

Pte J.G. Eamer, 8th Battalion, SLI, perished on 1 July 1916. He hailed from Hawkesbury, south Gloucestershire.

aged thirty-two when he fell. The 1901 Census reveals a 'probable' match: sixteen-year-old Harry Smith, a 'weaver' living with his widowed mother, Bertha, and his siblings at Southey Road, off Ashley Hill in Bristol. If Pte A.H. Smith was known by his middle name, then this is almost certainly the future soldier who is now commemorated at Thiepval (2A). The 1901 Census however, produces too many matches to be certain when considering Pte Charles Williams (No.9634) from Easton in Bristol, who enlisted in the city but lived at Bridgwater. (Thiepval 2A.)

Later in July Mr Tizzard, who lived at the Industrial Buildings in Pit Road, Hanham, Bristol, received the following letter from Sgt Frankcom, stating that the son of the former, L/Cpl Lyndale Tizzard, had been awarded a Military Medal for gallantry on 1 July:

> He led two bombing parties against strong German [positions]. He also rescued a wounded man under heavy rifle and machine gun fire. We are all proud of him. He never sees any danger, and is always willing for the toughest job, however dangerous. He is a son to be proud of.[5]

Later promoted to Sergeant, Clifton-born L. Tizzard transferred to the 7th SLI, and died, mortally wounded, on 25 March 1918, following the massive spring offensive launched by the Germans four days earlier. He has no known grave and is remembered on the Pozieres Memorial.

To the left of the 8th SLI on 1 July, the 9th and 10th Battalions of the King's Own Yorkshire Light Infantry (64th Brigade) went forward at the same time, and its Brigade-Major was an officer of the Gloucestershire Regiment. Major Graham Bromhead Bosanquet was born near Hereford in November 1885, the son of Day – a future Knight of the Realm, Royal Navy Admiral and Governor of Australia – and Mary Bosanquet. Joining the Glosters as a Second Lieutenant during 1907, G.B.B. was promoted to Captain in October 1914, and suffered severe injuries whilst serving with the 1st Battalion at Festubert on 21 December 1914. (The *Official History* indicates the Glosters advanced 500 yards but suffered heavy losses.) After recuperating at Guy's Hospital, Captain Bosanquet returned to Flanders and was wounded again (by a gun shot to his right arm) at Aubers Ridge on 9 May 1915, when eleven officers and 253 other ranks were either killed, incapacitated or reported missing. Carrying out the duties of Adjutant of the 1st Glosters until January 1916, he was awarded a Military Cross (the announcement of which appeared in the *London Gazette* on 23 June 1916) and also became a Chevalier of the Legion of Honour. There is a difference of opinion as to how the Major met his death on 1 July, with one source indicating he was reconnoitring an advance towards Round Wood which was to be led by Brig.-Gen. H.R. Headlam, DSO (CO of the 64th Brigade), whilst another states that Major Bosanquet was himself leading the Brigade along the Fricourt-Contalmaison road when he was killed. His body was originally buried just over a mile to the north of Fricourt, but in 1919 it was exhumed and re-interred at the Gordon Dump Cemetery (IV.H.10). 'The re-burial has been carefully and reverently carried out',[6] his family was told. The Major, whose death was reported in the *Bristol Times & Mirror*, had married Flora in 1910, but his widow died at the beginning of 1918, and his father was living in Sussex by 1916. The family seat for over a century had been at Dingestow Court, Monmouthshire. Major Bosanquet was the only officer of the Glosters known to have lost his life on 1 July 1916.

The 9th and 10th Battalions of the KOYLI attacked side by side, with the War Diary of the former stating:

> Within ten minutes or quarter of an hour of the start, the whole Brigade was united, irrespective of battalions, and driving the enemy rapidly out of his support trenches…Of the twenty-four officers who left our trenches, only five succeeded in passing the German front trench…The battalion suffered heavily in NO MAN'S LAND [and was] greeted by a hail of m.g. and rifle fire.[7]

Thirteen of the 9th's officers, including the CO, Lt-Col C.W.D. Lynch, DSO, were dead, nine were wounded (two fatally), and 475 ORs had become casualties. In the 10th, nine officers had been killed, sixteen were injured (the CO, Lt-Col H.J. King, was one) and fifty men in the ranks had lost their lives; 292 required medical attention and a further 135 were unaccounted for. Second Lieutenant Frank Alf Golding, of the 9th KOYLI, was originally reported 'missing' in a telegram to his parents, Alfred and Gertrude, of Cranbrook Road in Bristol's Redland district. 'This does not necessarily mean either wounded or killed',[8] they were told, and their son's name was circulated amongst the organisations which sought details of prisoners of war. Eyewitness reports from men under his command, however, soon dashed all hopes that the officer was alive. L/Cpl Green stated:

> He was a Second Lieutenant in C Company [and] he wore specs. I saw his dead body in a shell hole on 1.7.16 in No Man's Land at Fricourt. I was right next to him in the shell hole and am quite certain that it was Mr Golding and that he was dead. He was the only officer of that name. This was between the first and second line of German trenches and we held them both but the shelling was very heavy and he must have been buried. He was a new officer…[9]

From his hospital bed in Sheffield, Pte Naylor concurred: '[2nd Lt Golding] was hit by shell fire in the head in the German lines. He died at once.'[10] Walter Ward, of XI Platoon, 'C' Co., added:

> [The officer] was lying dead in the open between our first line and the first line of the enemy.....at about 8 o'clock. He looked quite dead. We started out at 7:26 in the morning and took the German stronghold, altogether 3 lines of trenches, a road and a shelter. I did not think it possible [that] Germans took POWs as they were retreating very quickly and giving themselves up.[11]

Frank Golding was born at City Road, Bristol, and attended Bristol Grammar School (1909–14) before studying at the local university. He was commissioned into the KOYLI

Above left: L/Cpl (later Sgt) L. Tizzard, SLI. He was awarded a Military Medal for gallantry on 1 July 1916. Born and bred in north Bristol, he died from severe wounds in March 1918.

Above right: 2nd Lt F.A. Golding, 9th Battalion, KOYLI (below). A victim of 1 July 1916, he was a native of north Bristol and attended the city's Grammar School & University.

in November 1915, and lost his life the following July. His Regimental Chaplain wrote to Mr Alfred Golding soon afterwards, and the letter was published in the *Chronicle* of Bristol Grammar School:

> [2nd Lt Golding] was advancing with his platoon with the Sergeant beside him, when suddenly he said to the Sergeant, '…you had better go to the side of the platoon, and I will stay in the centre as I would not like the two of us to be killed together.' It was a most heroic and gallant thing to have done, for the centre was far more dangerous than the side. Then, alas! as Fate would have, scarcely had the Sergeant got to his place when a shell came and killed your son. Death was instantaneous. He was buried near Fricourt close to where he fell.

The officer, who would have turned nineteen the day after his death, now lies buried at the Gordon Dump Cemetery (II.N.4).

In the ranks of the 10th KOYLI was Acting Corporal William White (No.3/1519), born in 'Colford, Gloucester' (Coleford, in the Forest of Dean), according to the SDGW. When he enlisted in Pontefract, Yorkshire, he was married to Gertrude. Aged thirty-two at the time of his death, he is remembered at Thiepval (11C & 12A).

Some units on the left flank of the 21st Division were faced with a counter-offensive from the Germans, advancing from the direction of Contalmaison, and one of the British soldiers involved told the *Western Daily Press* afterwards: 'The last few minutes of that attack…I shall never forget. It was like fighting against a rising tide, but our fellows stood at their ground with extraordinary courage.'

34TH DIVISION

The Albert–Bapaume Road went straight through the 34th's sector, bisecting the strongly held, fortified German villages of La Boisselle (on the front line) and Pozieres, several miles further back. Bapaume itself lay in the distance, and the British attack was centred along this strategic axis. With this firmly in mind, the officer in charge of the Division, Maj.-Gen. Ingouville-Williams, boldly committed all of his Brigades into the main assault, intending to initially capture La Boisselle with a frontal advance, to be followed up by masses of reserves punching a huge hole in the German defences. On the flanks were two valleys known as 'Sausage' and 'Mash', with the former to the south of La Boisselle which 'funnelled' towards a formidable strong-point called 'Sausage Redoubt', exposing any attackers to a deadly fire from three sides before it was even reached. The onus which rested upon the Royal Artillery for total annihilation of the defenders was immense, and the four battalions of the 101st Brigade on the extreme right of the Division opposing 'Sausage Valley' – the 15th and 16th Royal Scots, 10th Lincolns ('Grimsby Chums') and 11th Suffolks – were about to find out if the bombardment had been successful.

At 7.28 a.m. on 1 July, the huge 'Lochnagar' Mine – packed with 60,000 pounds of explosives – blew up beneath the German positions on the edge of La Boisselle, virtually opposite the front line held by the Grimsby Chums. To their right, several platoons of the 15th Royal Scots were already out in No Man's Land when the general advance began, but almost immediately a number of German machine-guns poured a deadly fire from their elevated emplacements – one was pinpointed to be situated at the southern end of 'Boisselle', whilst another was believed to be '…higher up the Sausage Valley'[1] – a full 500 yards of exposed ground away. Despite heavy losses, the right of the 15th Royal Scots' line made steady progress, skirting round Sausage Redoubt and taking Scots Redoubt as well as Wood Alley before pressing on towards Birch Tree Wood. Here, the Scots met up with men from the 21st Division, forcing the former to re-adjust their own direction northwards. By now, however, their numbers had dwindled, and consolidation was extremely difficult.

The parties tasked with storming Sausage Redoubt, supported by the 16th Royal Scots, were in dire trouble, repelled by flame-throwers, machine-guns and bombs at every attempt they made. Many did not even get close to the position, and their bodies were strewn across the battlefield. The 15th Battalion suffered over 500 casualties on 1 July, including Pte Alfred Simmons (No.20097), who was born at 'Bristol, Glos' (SDGW) and enlisted in Manchester. This is likely to be Alfred S. Simmons, a native of Clifton and aged fifteen in 1901, living with his widowed mother, Sarah, in St Michael's Hill. He was working as a 'shipping clerk' at the time, and if this is the same person, he would have been thirty in 1916. (Thiepval 6D & 7D.)

The Grimsby Chums' CO, Lt-Col Cordeaux, had already expressed his doubts as to whether the German positions opposite his men had been blown to pieces, and when his soldiers went forward at 7.30 a.m., his worst fears were soon realised. The War Diary states:

[The men] were immediately exposed to a heavy shell fire, shrapnel and HE [high explosives] and the most intense enfilade machine gun fire from LA BOISELLE and HELIGOLAND Redoubt. [They advanced] with the utmost steadiness and courage, not to be surpassed by any troops in the world, yet the distance they were away from the German trench – 800 yards – and the intensity of the machine gun fire did not allow of the possibility of reaching and penetrating the enemy's line. Some few men were able to enter the German trench from the NEW CRATER ['Lochnagar' mine] and bombing their way up blocked it and helped to protect the right flank of the 102nd Brigade which attacked on our left…It is doubtful if troops have ever been subjected to a more intense machine gun fire than was experienced in this assault; a fire which made it absolutely impossible either to retire or reinforce units during daybreak…The battalion went into action with a total of 20 officers (of whom 4 were killed, 10 wounded and 1 missing) and 822 other ranks of whom 66* were killed, 259 wounded and 162 missing.[2]

Brig.-Gen. R.C. Gore, in command of the 101st Infantry Brigade, wrote the following communication to Lt-Col Cordeaux on 5 July:

Will you please express to your Battalion my admiration of their fearless conduct in the battle on 1 July. Having to start further back than the two right battalions [15th & 16th Royal Scots] they had to bear the brunt of the full force of the machine gun fire during their advance across the Sausage Valley…No troops could have done better and it was no fault of theirs that they did not reach their allotted objective.[3]

The service record[4] of Lance Sergeant Kenneth Robson Brotherton (No.1096), 10th Lincolns, is another to have survived the Blitz. Born at 'Stapleton, Glos' (SDGW), he and his family had moved to Sunderland – the birthplace of his mother, Jane – by 1901. His two younger brothers were natives of Bristol, but his elder sibling, Eric, hailed from the North-East. K.R.B. enlisted in Grimsby during November 1914, at the age of twenty-seven years and sixty-five days, and gave his previous occupation as 'optician'. Jane had passed away by this time, and there are various addresses given for her husband, Thomas, including Sunderland, Barton-on-Humber and Goxhill, Lincolnshire, as well as the residences of a number of aunts and uncles, some of whom lived in 'Priory Road, Bristol', although there are several thoroughfares with this name across the city. The Grimsby Chums went to France at the beginning of 1916, and the Stapleton-born soldier was promoted to Corporal in March followed by a further elevation to Lance Sergeant on 23 June. His documents note that he was 'killed in action – place not stated' on 1 July, and his name is to be found on the Special Memorial 14 at Ovillers Military Cemetery.

Another Gloucestershire man known to be serving with the Grimsby Chums on 1 July was Regimental Quarter Master Sergeant George Cowburn, who was born in Amberley, near Stroud, during 1890, the son of the headmaster of the village school. Later moving to Wakefield, he became an accountant's clerk, and enlisted a month before Kenneth Brotherton. Whether George Cowburn went forward with his battalion on 1 July or remained behind is unclear, but just seven days later he was a Corporal, became a Sergeant several weeks further on and was an Acting RQMS by August. Seventeen Lance Corporals and Corporals plus twelve Sergeants – including Kenneth Brotherton – fell on 1 July, leaving a huge deficit in experienced NCOs. RQMS Cowburn survived the rest of the Somme campaign, as well as the fierce battles at Arras the following April, only to be fatally wounded by a bomb dropped from a German aeroplane behind the British lines on 28 January 1918.

Following behind the Grimsby Chums was the 11th Battalion of the Suffolk Regiment, which recorded casualty figures of fifteen officers and 527 ORs by the end of the day. Temporary Lieutenant Robert Quilter Gilson was one of the dead, as testified to by Cpl

*The official number of dead in the SDGW is put at 161.

Hicks of 'C' Co., who stated: 'Lt. Gilson was killed by a shell at about 9 a.m. when they were advancing.'[5] Born at Harrow in London during 1893, R.Q. Gilson was the son of Thomas – a future Headmaster at King Edward's School, Birmingham – and Emily, and the grandson of Surgeon-Major Isaac Newton, who lived at 'Broadlands' near Cheltenham's Tivoli Road for many years. Commissioned in the autumn of 1914, 2nd Lt Gilson was a former student of Trinity College Cambridge, training to be an architect, and went to France in January 1916. His body now lies at the Becourt Military Cemetery (I.R.28), Becordel-Becourt, close to the reserve positions of the 34th Division.

In the ranks, Pte Richard Bissett (No.15345★) is something of a mystery. According to the SDGW, he was born in Gloucester and enlisted in Cambridge, with the CWGC indicating that he was the son of the late Richard and Jane, and husband of Emma. The latter lived in Nelson Street, Cambridge, and the soldier is remembered at Thiepval (1C & 2A). It is likely this is the same person as five year old Richard Bisset, born at 'Chepstowe, Gloucester', who lived with his Devon-born parents Richard and Jane in Sussex when the 1881 Census was taken. A Richard Bissett, 'labourer', first appears in a Cambridge Street Directory in 1913, living in Nelson Street, whilst ten years later, the entry has changed to 'Mrs R. Bissett'. Each Brigade was assigned a Company of the Machine Gun Corps, and the 101st's was in Becourt Wood on the morning of 1 July. Following the path of the assault battalions, the 101 MGC War Diary reveals:

> No one reached the intended objectives. Parts of Nos. 2, 3 and 4 Sections got into the German front line, but on the way came under heavy machine gun fire and nearly all became casualties. The remains of these sections were collected in the evening.[6]

At one stage during the day, ten survivors of No.1 Section were sent forward towards Scots Redoubt:

> ...unaware it was still in German hands. Of the 9 officers, 8 Sergeants, 8 Corporals and 106 men who went out in the morning, 7 officers, 6 Sergeants, 5 Corporals and 71 became casualties.[7]

Pte Arthur Clark (No.14993), a former soldier with the Glosters, was dead. Born at 'St Mark's, Glos', he enlisted in Bristol. (Thiepval 5C & 12C.) With numerous 'possibles' in the records, it is not prudent to list each one.

In support of the 101st Brigade came the 207th Field Company of the Royal Engineers, the War Diary of which noted that: '...heavy enemy fire hindered operations'.[8] At 11.00 p.m., a portion of its men were ordered to make contact with any isolated parties at Scots Redoubt, which at that time comprised of soldiers from the 15th and 16th Royal Scots, as well as the 4th Tyneside Irish of the 103rd Brigade. The 207th's War Diary continues, 'Lt Wilding wounded in the back, but after being dressed, he remained at duty. 10 O.R.s slightly wounded, 5 evacuated and 2 wounded (shell shock.)'[9]

Lt H.D. Wilding was living in Worcestershire when he received his commission, but his mother lived at Stowell House in Charlton Kings, near Cheltenham. ('Trefula House, Old Bath Road, Chelt.' is also mentioned in the officer's service record.) He was awarded a Military Cross during the conflict, and although the date of the deed is not given, it seems likely it occurred shortly after 1 July:

> For conspicuous gallantry during operations. With two Sappers he brought in a badly wounded man from No Man's Land. Later he laid out a line of trenches in No Man's Land. He also carried out a dangerous reconnaissance, during which he penetrated part of the enemy's front line. He had previously been wounded.[10]

★The service number suggests he joined up either September or October of 1914.

Maj. A.G. Niven (middle), Second-in-Command
of the 2nd Tyneside Scottish. His family once
lived in Cheltenham and his death on the first
day of the Somme Offensive was reported in a
Cirencester newspaper.

Lt Wilding was rendered unconscious by a head injury on 5 August 1916, and was incapacitated yet again just over a year later. The officer, who arrived in France during July 1915, survived the conflict, but suffered from 'tremors of hands', 'headache' and 'depression'.[11]

The attack of the Tyneside Scottish and Irish Brigades on La Boisselle is one of the most chilling of 1 July. The 21st Northumberland Fusiliers (2nd Tyneside Scottish) advanced in four lines, with 150–yard intervals, between Sausage Valley and the village itself, with the intention of capturing Pozieres, but only a handful even reached the far side of La Boisselle. Lt-Col F.C. Heneker, the CO, was one of twelve officers who were killed, as was his Second-in-Command, thirty-eight-year-old Major Allan Graham Niven. The Major's obituary was placed in the *Wilts & Glos Standard*, stating that he was the second son of Commander Oswald Niven, RN, and Rose, of Torquay, and the 'dearly loved husband' of Lucy Emma. (The couple married in London during 1909.) A native of Buckinghamshire, Allan Niven was a Boer War veteran, and there is a link with Gloucestershire as his sister, Florence, was born in Cheltenham in the 1870s, although it would seem the family did not live there long. The reason for his death notice appearing in a newspaper which covers the Cirencester/Malmesbury area is not revealed. Major Niven is remembered at Thiepval (10B, 11B & 12B). The fact that the Northumberland Fusiliers have three panels of names at Thiepval is indicative of just how many men the regiment lost on the Somme.

The 102nd Brigade comprised the 1st, 2nd, 3rd and 4th Battalions of the Tyneside Scottish, and their respective War Diaries tell a similar, grim tale of bloodshed and bravery. The 1st TS, for example, attacked along Mash Valley, to the north of La Boisselle, and its advance was '...carried out in a most gallant way in the face of a deadly machine-gun and artillery fire... Not a single officer who went forward escaped becoming a casualty.'[12] (Ten were killed, ten wounded, and seven missing.) The CO, C.C.A. Sillery, was amongst the dead, whilst 557 ORs were killed, wounded or unaccounted for. Temporary Lieutenant George Eric Cope was the son of George and Elizabeth, and was educated at Cheltenham College between 1911 and 1914. Originally enlisting in the 12th Glosters (Bristol's Own), he was given a commission in the Northumberland Fusiliers (the 'Fighting Fifth') the following May. His parents were living in Bristol's Horfield Road at the outbreak of war, and later moved to Upper Belgrave Road in Clifton, where they were residing when they heard the dreadful news about their son, who is commemorated at Thiepval (10B, 11B & 12B). Born in April 1898, Lt Cope had only just turned eighteen when he fell.

The War Diary of the 4th Tyneside Scottish also reveals the intensity of the machine-gun fire, which caused the most losses to all of the TS battalions as they crossed No Man's Land:

> It was here that the following officers lost their lives, namely, Lt Col W. Lyle, who was last seen alive with walking stick in hand, amongst his men about 200 yards from the German trenches. Major M. Burge who fell before he had gone many yards from our own lines. Capt. J.G. Todd commanding B. [Company], who fell immediately he reached our wire. Capt. J.B. Cubey commanding A Company was killed before he had gone 100 yards. [Five other named officers] also fell mortally wounded before reaching the German line. In addition Lt W.B. Tytler who was reported to have reached the German trenches and to have been seen there badly wounded, is now missing and believed killed. 2nd Lt R. MacDonald last seen wounded is now missing and believed killed. The German first line was taken and the second line was also reached but owing to the heavy casualties it was impossible to hold on to these lines.[13]

In fact, a strong German counter-attack pushed the Tyneside Scottish back out into the ground they had just fought so hard to gain, and the survivors were forced to lie out in the open until darkness fell, when they crawled back to the British lines in an 'exhausted condition'. The compiler of the Diary also stressed that there were 'many heroic deeds' performed during the day which would never come to light, and with the third highest recorded casualty figures (629 all ranks) across the entire line on 1 July, this is a sobering thought indeed.

Pte Harold McCarthy (No.23/962) provides another conundrum as to his early life. Born at 'Berkeley, Glos' according to the SDGW, he enlisted in Newcastle-upon-Tyne and was killed in action on 1 July. Searches through the usual documents and data provide no evidence for his having any links with Gloucestershire, and apart from the maritime link with Sharpness Docks on the river Severn and its much larger counterpart on Tyneside, proof of, or speculation regarding Harold McCarthy's West Country origins is sparse indeed. (Thiepval 10B, 11B & 12B.)

Small parties of the 3rd Tyneside Scottish were seen heading for the third German lines, but did not get much further. 'ALL RANKS greatly in need of water and very much fatigued',[14] revealed the War Diary in the evening. The 3rd Tyneside Scottish was another battalion to suffer more than 500 losses on the first day; among the fallen was Pte Frank Wilkey (No.22/1762), born in Bristol and joining up on Tyneside. This is likely to be the same individual who was aged fourteen in 1901, living at St Michael's Hill, North Bristol, as a 'ward' of John Knowles – a 'joiner/chapel keeper' – and his wife, Emily. F.W. himself was born in St Luke's, Bedminster, to the south of the river Avon. (Thiepval 10B, 11B & 12B.)

At 7.30 a.m., the War Diary for the 4th TS recorded: 'Each Company was played over into 'NO MAN'S LAND' by its piper who continued to play until either killed or wounded.'[15] An injured officer, possibly of the 2nd Middlesex, later told the *Western Daily Press*:

> The pluckiest thing I saw was a piper of the Tyneside Scottish playing his company over the parapet in the attack on the German trenches near Albert. The Tynesiders were on our right, and when their officers gave the signal to advance, I saw the piper – I think he was a pipe-major – jump out of the trench and march straight over No Man's Land towards the German lines. The tremendous rattle of the machine-gun and rifle fire which the enemy at once opened up on us completely drowned the sound of the pipes, but it was obvious that he was playing as though he would burst the bag, and just faintly through the din we

heard the mighty shout his comrades gave as they swarmed over after him. How he escaped death I can't understand, for the ground was literally ploughed up by the hail of bullets. But he seemed to bear a charmed life, and the last glimpse I had of him, as we, too, dashed out, showed him still marching [onwards], playing for pride and quite regardless of the flying bullets and of the men dropping all around him.

The man in question was almost certainly Pipe-Major John Wilson, who received a Military Medal for acting as a stretcher-bearer later in the day. His uncle, L/Cpl Fyfe, performed an identical role to the one described above, but was later found riddled with bullets. Piper Willie Scott, a shipyard worker, was one of the first to reach the German lines, and when his pals saw his body, he was still clutching his pipes. After James Phillips' pipes had been shattered, he took up a rifle and started fighting with bombs, yet perhaps the saddest tale belongs to eighteen-year-old Piper E.R. Grieves, who proudly led his Company over the top, wearing his kilt, and fell mortally wounded in No Man's Land. On 7 July his bagpipes were found close to La Boisselle, shot to pieces, and were returned to the Union Club which had sponsored them in 1914.

Pte John McGurk, of the 26th Northumberland Fusiliers, provides us with an opportunity to admire the exploits of the Tyneside Irish Brigade on 1 July. Listed in the SDGW as being born at 'Berkley, Glos', the CWGC corrects this error by revealing the twenty-one-year-old actually hailed from Birtley in County Durham. The son of John and Maria, he died of his wounds on 3 July at Rouen. The 1st, 2nd, 3rd and 4th Tyneside Irish battalions – 3,000 strong – set off from a position known as the Tara-Usna line, a full one mile of exposed ground *behind* the British forward trenches, and advanced in support of the Tyneside Scottish, who were tasked with securing La Boisselle and its defences before the Irish swept through to maintain the momentum towards Pozieres. The 2nd and 3rd TI, on the left flank, did not even reach No Man's Land before the majority had been mown down, yet on the right, the 1st and 4th were still on their way, not quite as decimated as their comrades, heading towards the targets of the 101st Brigade (15 and 16th Royal Scots, and so on). Moving into Sausage Valley, they still had 500 yards to go before the German firepower which was causing such carnage was reached, but a few made it, fought their way in, and kept going. The CO of the 4th TI was still with them, although he was recalled, as the Brigade Commander had been wounded, and the fifty or so men who were left pondered their next move. Cut off behind enemy lines, a consolidation of the position was perhaps the most likely, if ultimately unachievable, option. Their objective, Contalmaison, could be seen in the distance, fortified by defensive systems in its own right as it contained the HQ of a German Division. These fifty soldiers – all that were left of 3,000 – possessed a remarkable devotion to duty, and continued their advance towards almost certain death. Such gallantry brings tears to the eyes.

The Machine Gun Company attached to the Tyneside Irish '…went into action with the [103rd] brigade in the neighbourhood of La Boisselle'.[16] Casualties were not assessed until the 103rd Co., MGC, proceeded to billets on 7 July, when it established:

> Capt. Millar (Co. Comm.) & 2/i/c Lt Morse, killed, & 2nd Lt Harrison. 6 officers wounded. Co. Sgt Major wounded. 8 Sergeants missing (7 wounded.) 2 Corporals wounded and 2 missing. 15 Privates wounded, 43 missing, of whom 24 wounded.[17]

Eighteen-year-old Pte Jesse Charles Surman (26186), formerly of the King's Royal Rifle Corps, had lost his life in the attack. Born in Gloucester and enlisting in his home city, he was the son of Harriet, a native of Westbury-on-Severn who later lived at Wellesley Street in Gloucester. The family resided in the St Paul's area of the city, and the soldier is remembered on a plaque in the Salvation Army Citadel, Eastgate Street, as well as at Thiepval (5C & 12C).

The 175th Brigade of the Royal Artillery provided support for the Tyneside Scottish, targeting enemy machine-guns (knocking out three emplacements) and firing upon uncaptured enemy trenches in La Boisselle. At 11.00 a.m., 2nd Lt William Christie Hickman, a Liaison Officer, was standing under a tree near HQ when a German bombardment began, and an eyewitness stated that the former was killed when a '…blast blew him apart'.[18] His body was originally buried '…close to a crater where [the] road crossed original German front line',[19] but the grave is now situated at the Ovillers Military Cemetery (II.A.I.). 2nd Lt Hickman, aged twenty-eight, was the cousin of Revd Noott, who lived at St Luke's Vicarage in Berkeley Street, Cheltenham, during the war. Two of the officer's brothers were taken prisoner between 1914 and 1918, whilst his wife, Elizabeth, worked at the War Office in London.

The words of Brig.-Gen. R.C. Gore that 'The Divisional Commander congratulates his Troops on their fine reputation they have earned for themselves. With them he mourns deeply for our absent comrades'[20] bear further scrutiny. They reinforce the statistic that the 34th Division had suffered over 6,000 casualties – the highest along the whole Somme Front – yet not even La Boisselle had been taken on the first day, let alone the final objective of Pozieres. By nightfall, most battalions were back where they had started, minus thousands of men from all ranks. Setting statistics aside, J. Percy Marshall, of the RFA, wrote to his former tutors at Wycliffe College in Stonehouse:

> The other day I surveyed the front through a telescope from some high ground, and both the English and German trenches could be plainly seen, but the only sign of 'life' was 'death'. At one particular spot between the trenches I could discern many dead bodies scattered about in the open ground where they had lain since some past attack.[21]

An unnamed officer told the *Gloucestershire Echo* of his impressions of the 1 July assault, 'Our men walked through the raging fire exactly as though on parade. And if they had been soldiers all their lives they could not possibly have shown cooler discipline.' The *Gloucester Citizen* added:

> A Captain of the Lincolns, whilst leading his company across a perfect inferno, was hit in the leg, and again in the thigh, and again in the arm, but continued to stagger on, crying to his brave boys, 'Get at 'em, get at 'em!'. A fourth bullet brought him to earth, and his soldiers swept on as he himself would have wished. When later the body of this valiant officer was recovered he was lying stretched in a posture of pointing eagerness towards the German position.

A soldier wounded at Contalmaison implored to the general public back home:

> It boils down to munitions of war – that's all, munitions of war. You can't send us too much. For God's sake, be sure you send us enough. You can measure the blood we've got to pay before it's over by the guns and shells and cartridges you send out. The more you send the less we'll have to pay…Drop every other mortal thing, but for God's sake send us plenty of munitions. You can trust us to do the rest.

10

8TH DIVISION

With the valiant attempts of the 34th Division to deliver the offensive's knockout strike at La Boisselle having failed, the rest of the line to the north was experiencing similar frustration and immobility. The War Diaries of all participating battalions took on a familiar tone, with the 2nd Middlesex – alongside the 1st Tyneside Scottish – proceeding up the murderous 'Mash'Valley:

> As soon as the leading wave left our trenches to assault it was caught by heavy machine-gun fire and suffered heavy losses. As soon as the succeeding waves came under this fire they doubled forward and before anyone reached the German front line the original wave formation had ceased to exist. About 200 of all ranks succeeded in reaching the German lines – passing over the front line they entered the 2nd line of trenches, but after a short fight, during which about half became casualties, they were forced to retire to the German front line. There, under the leadership of MAJOR H.B.W. SAVILE [and other officers] the survivors proceeded to consolidate. By 9:15 a.m. the handful of unwounded men, numbering perhaps a dozen, were forced to retire to shell holes outside the enemy front line, where the majority remained until darkness enabled them to regain own lines. Of the 23 Officers who took part in the assault only 2nd-Lt H.C. Hunt regained own lines unwounded. Of the 650 N.C.Os & men who took part in the assault a bare 50 answered their names in the early hours of July 2nd.[1]

Pte William Lethbridge (SR.7200) was born in Stroud but had moved with his family to Middlesex by 1901, when he was still only three years old. His mother, Rose, was also a native of Stroud, although his father, John, is listed in the Census as being a 'gamekeeper's packer', originally from Chelsea. The new recruit joined up in Ponder's End, Middlesex, and his body lies buried at the Ovillers Military Cemetery (XVI.I.6).

There was to be yet one more casualty from the 2nd Middlesex – its Commanding Officer, Lt-Col E.T.F. Sandys, DSO – who had voiced his concerns to his superiors over his opinion that the German wire at the head of 'Mash' Valley was untouched by the British bombardment. Wounded on 1 July, Sandys returned to London for recuperation, but he was haunted by the loss of so many of his men, and in early September he took a room at the Cavendish Hotel before shooting himself in the head. He had previously intimated he wished he had died on the battlefield with his beloved battalion, and at an Inquest held after his death, the Coroner concluded the officer had committed suicide whilst temporarily insane. It is interesting to read the citation for his DSO, which appeared in the *London Gazette* several days after his death:

> For conspicuous gallantry when leading his battalion and keeping its direction during an attack under very heavy fire. Although wounded in several places, he continued to lead it

until further wounds made it no longer possible to do so. The fine behaviour of the battalion was largely due to the Commanding Officer's personal qualities.[2]

The book *The V.C. & the D.S.O.* also indicates that Lt-Col Sandys 'died of wounds' – a point of fact as he lingered for a week before succumbing to the effects of the self-inflicted gun-shot – but it tends to suggest he was injured in battle. The story itself, however, was widely and accurately reported in the newspapers of the time.

The 2nd Devons, which advanced to the left of the 2nd Middlesex, also suffered heavily, and were equally unsuccessful in reaching their objective. One of the casualties was 2nd Lt Edward Jago, whose sister, Dorothy Balkwill, lived at Badgeworth, near Cheltenham. This surname was especially common in Devon and Cornwall around this time, but in the early 1900s, a Henry Balkwill is first listed in the Gloucestershire village (by *Kelly's Directory*) as a farmer, and was still residing there in 1916 when the Plymouth-born officer fell. The latter, who had passed an entrance exam into Cambridge University just a month prior to the outbreak of war, set aside his studies to take up arms, losing his life at the age of twenty-two. (Thiepval 1C.) Amongst the officers detailed to remain behind on 1 July in order to replace casualties in the 2nd Devons was 2nd Lt Henry H. Jago, the brother of Dorothy and 2nd Lt E. Jago. Seeing so many of his comrades – including his sibling – go forward into a maelstrom of bullets and explosives must have been a time of extreme emotions for the young subaltern, who would later rise to the rank of Acting Major in the battalion, receiving a Distinguished Service Order, a Military Cross and Bar, as well as a Mention in Despatches. Two years older than Edward, he would be killed in action on 24 April 1918, when the 2nd Devons were heavily attacked by the Germans using tanks, gas and masses of infantry at Villers Bretonneux, to the south of the river Somme. (One of the 2nd Devons' most senior officers to take part in the attack on 1 July 1916 was Lt-Col A.J.E. Sunderland, who survived the first day of the Somme Offensive, but fell at the beginning of 'Third Ypres' (Passchendaele) on 31 July 1917. His mother, Florence, was a native of Redland in Bristol.)

Immediately opposite the village of Ovillers La Boisselle, the 2nd Royal Berkshires endured a torturous day. With the wire outside their own trenches not sufficiently cut, parties were sent out before Zero Hour to rectify the problem, and the enemy took advantage by opening up a heavy fire from 7.15 a.m. Already knowing what awaited them, the three assaulting Companies went forward at 7.30 a.m., and all but a small group on the left flank failed to reach the German lines. The CO, Lt-Col A.M. Holdsworth, received fatal injuries at 7.45 a.m., and with his second-in-command, Major G.H. Sawyer, DSO, also injured, the battalion was passed into the hands of its Acting Adjutant, 2nd Lt C. Mollett. With the British front trenches now subjected to an intense barrage, further progress was impossible, and the attack was postponed indefinitely. 'Steel helmets proved invaluable and in numberless cases saved men's lives',[3] declared the War Diary. All ranks had suffered heavily in the attack, and 2nd Lt Mollett is one of the handful of officers who had not been killed, wounded or reported missing by the end of the day.

Sgt Jonah William Trimmer, DCM (9311), is to be found within the SDGW as being born in Gloucester, and there are certainly individuals with this name connected with the city. In 1881, Benjamin (forty-two) and Mary (forty-one) were living at College Green, close to the Cathedral, with their five children and two servants. Gloucester-born Benjamin was a 'brewer' who employed sixteen people. By 1901, members of the family had moved to Islington in London. A snag appears with the register of a birth in Chipping Norton, Oxfordshire, at the end of 1891, under the exact name of 'Jonah William Trimmer', but it is likely that the Sergeant was related to the above in some way. He received his Distinguished Conduct Medal – second only to a VC for men in the ranks – for '…conspicuous gallantry and cool judgement in handling his machine-gun. On one occasion, after a withdrawal from the enemy trenches, he succeeded in getting his gun out of action under circumstances of great difficulty'.[4] An experienced soldier, the newer recruits would have looked to him for

Lt-Col A.J.E. Sunderland (pictured in 1914), CO of the 2nd Devons on 1 July 1916. He was killed in action a year later at Passchendaele. His mother was a native of Bristol.

guidance in combat, and it is likely he fell early in the assault, as his grave can be found at the Aveluy Communal Cemetery Extension (F.29).

Pte Gilbert George Garlick (No.19732) has more verifiable links with Gloucester. Born and raised in the city, he was the twenty-year-old son of Mrs G. Garlick, from Thomas Street, and he enlisted in Reading. (Thiepval 11D.)

The 2nd Rifle Brigade was in reserve behind the 2nd Royal Berkshires, and proceeded along the communication trenches to the front line once the first attack had been launched. The forward trenches were heavily congested with wounded troops and those unable to advance due to the heavy bombardment, resulting in 'A', 'B' and 'C' Companies being withdrawn to ease the overcrowding. Casualties amongst the 2nd RB were nearly all caused by shell-fire, according to its War Diary, and these totalled five officers wounded (including 2nd Lt H. Daniels, VC★), and 128 ORs dead or injured.

Rifleman Harry Skinner (No.3485), a native of Cheltenham, was an old soldier, having served five years prior to re-enlisting in August 1914. His service record[5] indicates that he had a fresh complexion, grey eyes, light brown hair, and his occupation was that of a 'gardener'. He worked at Newlands Nurseries near Frimley, in Surrey, which was the soldier's stated place of residence in the SDGW. His father was called William, and there were a number of siblings. The soldier is commemorated at Thiepval (16B & 16C).

★2nd Lt Daniels had received his V.C. at Neuve Chapelle the previous year when, as a Company Sergeant Major, he and another man cut wire entanglements which were impeding their advance under very heavy fire, suffering injuries in the process. Daniels survived the war and later became a Lieutenant-Colonel.

The *Gloucestershire Echo* reported in July 1916 that former Gloucestershire resident Lt Maurice Wallich, of the 6th Queen's (Royal West Surrey) Regiment, had been listed as missing in action on the 1 July. His CO told the Lieutenant's family:

> Wallich led the first wave of the Queen's attack, and did magnificently. He was last seen firing his revolver into a German trench, standing on top of their parapet. One man near him said he was seen to fall, and nothing more has been heard…All his men are loud in their praise and he evidently, from all accounts, led his men forward like a real hero.

The 6th Queen's of the 12th Division was actually in reserve on 1 July, and relieved the 2nd Rifle Brigade the following day with orders to capture Ovillers on the third. Lt Wallich, whose family was farming at Cooper's Hill, Brockworth (near Gloucester) in 1901 (there were also Wallichs living at nearby Cheltenham), was taken prisoner following the assault on the village, and he was not repatriated until December 1918, over a month after the Armistice.

On 22 June 1916, Maj.-Gen. Hudson, DSO, addressed the assembled troops of the 8th King's Own Yorkshire Light Infantry, informing them of their role in the forthcoming attack: 'You may carry bombs, but bombs are for bombers; your weapon is the bayonet.'[6] With their backs to Authuille Wood, just to the north of Ovillers, the battalion lost 10 per cent of its strength to enemy artillery in the hours immediately before 7.30 a.m. on 1 July, and although the first two waves 'met little resistance' crossing No Man's Land, those following suffered an estimated 60 per cent casualty rate due to the intense machine-gun fire levelled upon them. However, in this particular part of the Front, the German wire had been sufficiently breached to allow the survivors to employ their rifles and bayonets at close quarters, pushing the defenders back beyond their second line and towards the third. At some stage during the heavy fighting which followed, an order to 'retire' was passed along the British forward positions, and it was believed to have originated from the Germans, as no such edict had been issued. Officers and NCOs rallied their men, but losses were now extensive, and reinforcements were pinned down at the British trenches. Of the twenty-five officers, one Medical Officer and 659 ORs who went into battle, only the MO and 110 men returned.[7]

The fate of Lt Edward Maurice Baldwin Cambie's family is typical of the confusion, frustration and overwhelming grief experienced by those back in the UK desperately waiting to hear news of their missing loved ones in France. Born at The Vicarage, Gorsley, near Newent during 1894, he was the son of Solomon – a 'Clerk in Holy Orders' – and Alice, and attended Dean Close School in Cheltenham before studying at Hertford College, Oxford. For nearly two months after 1 July, Revd Dr S. Cambie, who was living in Ipswich by 1916, had no details as to the whereabouts of his son other than that he was unaccounted for after going into action. As we know today, the War Office was inundated with requests for information during the Somme campaign, and with the details of tens of thousands of casualties to be collated, it is understandable that delays of weeks and sometimes months were commonplace. Lt Cambie's father, however, informed the authorities that his next door neighbour, whose son fell on 15 July, received notification of the death almost immediately, and demanded to know what was being done about his own situation. Finally, eyewitness accounts were brought together, but before these were processed, Dr Revd Cambie was told in relation to his son, 'I fear I cannot hold out any hope of his living.'[8]

The 8th KOYLI had been led by Capt. K.E. Poyser on 1 July, and its temporary CO was wounded during the advance. Pte R. Firth, of 'D' Company, stated that he had seen Lt Cambie between the German front line and 'their wire'[9] (presumably the German second line), and had witnessed the officer being 'hit' before he stumbled on for a few yards and then fell dead. This was at 8.00 a.m., and the same soldier saw the body again in the evening, certain that life was extinct. Lt R.S.P. MacKarness interviewed three men separately, who were all in agreement that Lt Cambie had been killed at 'Hautville [Authuille] Wood', and his corpse had not been recovered at once. Pte Joseph Day of 'C' Company, 10th Platoon, crawled into a

E.M.B. Cambie, 8th Battalion,
KOYLI. He was educated at Dean
Close School in Cheltenham, and
died valiantly on 1 July 1916.

shell-hole on 1 July after being injured, and shortly afterwards an officer rolled on top of him, wounded in the neck. The identification disc confirmed that the deceased was Lt Cambie, and Archibald Ceacin also concurred that the former had been struck in the head 'by bullets', killing him almost at once.

The *Gloucestershire Echo* obtained the words of Capt. Poyser, who spoke of Lt Cambie, 'He had shown himself to possess to a remarkable extent the qualities of leadership, and the men who saw him in battle tell me that the courage, skill and resource shown by him were extraordinary.' Having fallen on ground which was soon re-taken by the Germans, Lt Cambie is now remembered at Thiepval (11C & 12A). The CWGC lists him as being aged twenty-two, but he was actually a year younger.

To the left of the 8th KOYLI, the 8th York and Lancasters suffered a day of similar trauma. Before they had even left their trenches, the parapet was swept with machine-gun, artillery and rifle fire, which killed the battalion's CO – Lt-Col A.J.B. Maddison – and his Adjutant when the attack began. The wire opposite the 8th was intact, and further casualties were caused as the survivors tried to find a way in, although the War Diary does note that it was believed some of the leading platoons reached as far as the German third line, never to be seen again. Hand-to-hand fighting and bombing raids took place for much of the day, but with telephone communications cut, the dwindling band of men still holding out in the enemy positions could not repel a number of strong counter-attacks which eventually drove them out. The War Diary states, grimly, 'Out of a total of 680 NCOs & men, & 22 officers, the following returned unwounded: 1 Sergeant, 3 Corporals, 10 Lance Corporals, 54 men, no officers.' It added, somewhat bizarrely, 'It's reported that an enemy machine-gun was found in the German front line with two Germans chained to it. Both were dead.'[10] This revelation prompted a soldier to comment to the *Bristol Times & Mirror,* 'Being chained to a gun would certainly help a doubtful man to make up his mind whether he would go or stay.'

This apparently brutal example of total warfare has been hotly debated ever since. As revealed previously, German machine-gunners were highly trained, supremely disciplined and undoubtedly prevented an Allied breakthrough on 1 July, so to suggest they had to be forced to stay at their post unto death seems a little far-fetched. Escape routes and relocation sites were all part of their training, and the method employed to move a weapon at short notice involved the crew attaching it to harnesses on their uniforms, which may account for the predicament described above, as the defenders were in the process of withdrawing when they were gunned down or hit by a shell. The propaganda value for the Allies, however, is self-evident.

Lt George Graham Hicking, the brother of 2nd Lt Francis Hicking of the 10th West Yorkshires, fell on the same day as his sibling. Born in Nottingham during 1893, he also attended Uppingham School, and is included in this text due to the residency of his parents, Joseph and Kate, who had moved to Halsey House, Pittville, Cheltenham by the 1920s. As with his brother, it is unlikely G.G. Hicking had any link with Gloucestershire during his lifetime. Originally posted as 'missing' on 1 July 1916, the situation had not changed by the following March, when it was finally concluded that the officer must be dead. Although listed by the ODGW as serving with the 6th Battalion, Lt Hicking (who had contracted dysentery in Gallipoli the year prior to his death) was attached to the 8th. (Thiepval, Addenda Panel.)

The 8th York and Lancasters, along with the 8th KOYLI, recorded combined casualty figures of over 1,100. These types of losses prompted the newspapers to change their approach to reporting the Somme campaign. From the jingoistic belief that the Germans were on the verge of capitulating they now changed to the sober view that the attacks had failed and left deadlock on the Western Front. The *Gloucestershire Echo* summed up this state of affairs in late July 1916, and behind the justifiable plaudits for the infantry, there is the thinly veiled truth that the war was far from over:

> And never, perhaps, have men been put to severer test than to advance, as battalion after battalion has had to do, through shells bursting so thickly that they made almost a solid wall, so that to those watching from behind whole waves of men have disappeared simultaneously behind a bank of smoke and tossing earth, while beyond the ground was swept with machine-gun and rifle-fire from, it might be, only 50 yards away. Yet one after another, wave following wave, our men have gone into it without one faltering. It might be laughing or cheering, or, with set teeth, silently – but they have gone. And only those have failed to reach their ultimate objective who fell on the way. Not once but half a score of times troops have gone forward with orders to reach a certain point – a wood, perhaps, or ruined building, a bit of trench or mere spot upon the map. They have gone and been lost to sight until half an hour, an hour, or two hours later tidings have come that they were there. And so they were – the shattered remains of half a company, a lieutenant and seven men; 20 men under command of an NCO – all that were left had got there, though behind them the enemy might have closed up and the supports had been wiped out upon the way.

32ND DIVISION AND 36TH DIVISION

In between Authuille Wood and Thiepval stood the German-held 'Leipzig Salient', which jutted out into No Man's Land towards the British lines. At its narrowest point, the two opposing armies were barely one hundred yards apart, and when the barrage was underway, before 7.30 a.m. on 1 July, men of the 17th Highland Light Infantry crept across the intervening space and rushed the Redoubt, catching the defenders by surprise. At 8.30 a.m., the 11th Border Regiment left the cover of Authuille Wood and immediately came under heavy machine-gun fire, causing widespread casualties. With the communication trenches congested, the 11th Battalion – known as the 'Lonsdales' – had to advance across open country, and as soldiers were falling all around, the man who was responsible for raising, training and commanding the Lonsdales, fifty-four-year-old Lt-Col Percy Wilfrid Machell, CMG, DSO, was also killed as he urged his men forward. Joining the army in 1882, he took part in many of Queen Victoria's campaigns in North Africa, and was already a vastly experienced soldier when the Lonsdale Regiment was formed in the north-west of England during the autumn of 1914. As with many Commanding Officers, Lt-Col Machell took a keen interest in the welfare of his troops, and the sight of so many of them succumbing to the bullets and bombs fired from a position known as the 'Nord Werk' (which the 8th Battalions of the KOYLI and York and Lancasters of the 8th Division were attacking at the time) must have been devastating. The official records of the Lonsdales notes: 'Men could do no more'.

The *Bristol Times & Mirror* reported the CO's death in its columns, and further investigation revealed that he had attended Clifton College between 1878 and 1879 before training at Sandhurst. The Lieutenant-Colonel lies buried at the Warloy-Baillon Communal Cemetery (A.17), although it is perhaps surprising that his grave is not situated in the Lonsdale Cemetery, which, as the name suggests, contains many of his men. (Lt-Col Machell married Lady Valda Gleichen – who was related to Queen Victoria – in 1905, and his wife's sister, Princess Helena, died at Ashmead House in Cam, near Dursley, at the beginning of 1947.)

One of the Lonsdales' officers injured in the assault was 2nd Lt Frederick Martin Ransom, the son of the late Mr G.F. Ransom, who was the former proprietor of the Belle Vue Hotel in Cheltenham's High Street. Born in 1883, FM Ransom served with the South African Constabulary during the Boer War, and the Natal Carabineers immediately after the conflict. Back in the UK he joined the 5th Glosters (Territorials), and had risen to the rank of Colour Sergeant by 1915, based at The Barracks in Sharpness, when he received an officer's commission in the Border Regiment. His 'good moral character' was certified by Sir J.T. Agg-Gardner, Cheltenham's MP (who would later unveil a memorial to the fallen Old Boys of Dean Close School), and the Second Lieutenant's wife is listed as Florence Mary Ransom, of 'Bell View Hotel'.[1] Originally serving with the 10th (Reserve) Battalion of the Borders, he transferred to the Lonsdales shortly afterwards and received a gun-shot wound to his head on

1 July 1916, necessitating an operation at Rouen before he was repatriated to a Bristol War Hospital. By 1919 he was living at Matlock House on Gloucester's Barnwood Road.

At 7.10 on the morning of 1 July, the 1st Dorset Regiment moved south towards Authuille Wood and came under immediate fire, wounding Captain Kestell-Cornish as well as ten other ranks. The officer was a native of Bisley, near Stroud, the son of Mr and Mrs Vaughan Kestell-Cornish, and grandson of the Revd Canon Thomas Keble, a former Vicar of the ancient Cotswold parish. Robert Vaughan Kestell-Cornish received a Military Cross at Ypres on 1 May 1915, when, despite being asphyxiated, he rallied his men during a gas attack and held on to the position until reinforcements arrived. The injury he received on 1 July 1916 was caused by a bullet above his left clavicle, and this was removed two days later. He had Gloucestershire links with Chalford, Lechlade and Fairford – Keble House in the latter town was his one-time residence – and he was awarded a Bar to his MC in November 1916, when he was in charge of a working party under heavy fire. Appointed Adjutant to the 1st Dorsets, Capt. Kestell-Cornish – who was mentioned three times in Despatches – was attached to the Staff at Divisional HQ when he was severely wounded in action on 8 March 1918. He died of his injuries over three months later, at the age of twenty-two.

Most of the 1st Dorsets reached Authuille Wood on 1 July, and the leading platoons advanced in a similar direction to that of the 11th Borders later in the day, attracting the same fire from the Nord Werk which had decimated the Lonsdales. 'It was apparent that matters were not progressing quite as favourably as had been anticipated',[2] noted the War Diary, as many casualties were being caused, '…during the dash across country from AUTHUILLE WOOD to our own front line'.[3] This exposed ground was about one hundred yards in length, and it was soon '…covered with our killed and wounded, yet the men continued to jump up and advance over their fallen comrades as the word to go was given.'[4] Upon reaching the forward-most British positions, they were found to be heavily congested with dead and injured, plus those unable to push forward due to the intensity of the barrage. 'Lateral movement was practically impossible',[5] reported the War Diary, and only six officers

Lt-Col P.W. Machell, CMG, DSO, CO 11th Borders ('Lonsdales'). Educated at Clifton College in Bristol, he was a casualty of the first day of the Somme Offensive.

Capt. R.V. Kestell-Cornish, MC & BAR, 1st Battalion, Dorsets. A native of Bisley, he was wounded on 1 July 1916, then mortally so in March 1918.

along with approximately sixty men actually reached the Leipzig Redoubt, where they began bombing the enemy at close quarters. The rest of the battalion remained pinned down in their own lines, and the Germans sent over an increasingly heavy bombardment during the afternoon, so with the situation becoming 'almost untenable', the 1st Dorset Regiment was withdrawn in the evening. Sixty-seven men in the ranks were dead (SDGW), whilst twenty-one officers and 368 ORs had been wounded (War Diary).

Lance Corporal Walter Edgar May (No.11684) was one of the fatalities. Born at Shirehampton, on the north bank of the river Avon to the east of Bristol, his service record[6] reveals that he enlisted at Bristol Recruiting Office No.2 on 2 September 1914, at the age of nineteen years and seven months. He had a fresh complexion, brown eyes and fair hair, and was working as a 'labourer' prior to joining up. Originally in the 3rd Dorsets, he joined the 1st Battalion 'in the field' during August 1915, and he was appointed an unpaid Lance Corporal the following January. Reported 'missing' on 1 July, it was later confirmed to the soldier's parents – Albert and Lydia – that Walter was dead. Letters, cards and a writing pad belonging to the deceased were returned to the family at Crown Terrace, West-town, Shirehampton, and his medals were forwarded later in 1921. As the whereabouts of L/Cpl May was not known initially, it is fair to assume that he had reached at least as far as No Man's Land before being struck down, although his body was eventually recovered to be buried in the Lonsdale Cemetery (I.A.24).

When the 1st Dorsets set off towards Authuille Wood, the 2nd King's Own Yorkshire Light Infantry advanced almost due west to support the assault on the northern part of the Leipzig Salient. The left flank of the 2nd KOYLI came under heavy fire from the direction of Thiepval, stalling the attack which had also immobilised the 16th Highland Light Infantry in No Man's Land. 'The hostile machine gun and shell fire was so intense that all efforts to cross the fire swept zone between the opposing lines failed and the survivors were forced to remain in our own front line,' recorded the War Diary, 'Capt. E.J. Millin was killed attempting to advance in this part of the field.'[7]

Capt. E.J. Millin, 2nd Battalion, KOYLI. Born and bred in the Cirencester area, he was awarded the *Medaille Militaire* in 1914, but was mortally wounded on 1 July 1916.

Captain Edward Job Millin is listed in the CWGC as being with 'C' Co. when he fell, but the War Diary indicates he was actually in command of 'D' Co., which had been detailed as a carrying party. Born in Cirencester, he enlisted into the KOYLI during 1899, leaving his job as a waiter when he was one month short of his twentieth birthday. Seeing active service during the Boer War, he was stationed at St Helena towards the end of the conflict – possibly guarding POWs – and then went to Malta for three years. He married Alice in Sheffield on 15 October 1906, and there are three known children of the marriage – John, Christopher and Muriel. A Company Sergeant Major by 1912, the military experience of E.J. Millin was put to the severest test when he was sent to France with the 2nd KOYLI in mid-August 1914, and he had received a *Medaille Militaire* for 'distinguished service at Mons' by the end of the month. Also Mentioned in Despatches, CSM Millin was wounded in the head by shrapnel and returned to the UK, obtaining a commission from the ranks during his recuperation. He did not see combat again on the Western Front until November 1915, when he rejoined his old battalion, and his wife, by this time, was living at Ampney St Peter near Cirencester, close to her father-in-law. She was told of her thirty-eight-year-old husband's death several days after it had occurred, and the *Wilts & Glos Standard* revealed that Mrs Millin had been sent a message of sympathy from the King and Queen. The newspaper concluded: '[Capt. Millin's] old friends and neighbours deeply deplore his loss while exulting in his fine career.' The officer's body was not recovered to be identified, and he is now remembered at Thiepval (11C & 12A).

At the village of Thiepval, the 15th Lancashire Fusiliers attacked with the 16th Northumberland Fusiliers, but only a handful managed to breach the German front lines before being cut off. The 16th LF went up in support of its sister battalion just after 9.00 a.m., yet with the enemy defences still standing firm its machine-gun emplacements were able to pour their murderous fire upon any reinforcements, and the 16th LF was soon back where it had started, minus sixteen men from the ranks. Pte William Dennis Cronin (No.11274) was one of them, born in Gloucester before moving to Salford in Lancashire by the time he was six years old. His Irish-born father, Denis, was a shoemaker, whilst his mother, Gentilla, hailed from Gloucestershire. Pte Cronin is commemorated at Thiepval (3C & 3D).

Of this particular sector, the *Western Daily Press* would report:

> The fighting around Thiepval seems to have been of the most terrible description…High explosive and lyddite simply poured into the little town, while the air above was thick with exploding shrapnel, and the trench mortars played incessantly, the projectiles of the last-named being clearly visible in the air, travelling, as they do, at a low velocity. In the sunshine each mortar shell in its slow fall gleamed amid the smoke like a great fiery spark – much as a large brass plate might look if tossed up into the sunshine. The place was a veritable devil's cauldron, a mere bowl of seething fumes, black and green and white.

36TH (ULSTER) DIVISION

No individuals from Gloucestershire or North Bristol were found to have clear-cut links with this Division, which, by its definition, comprised regiments which were entirely raised in Ireland. Advancing to the north of Thiepval, straddling the river Ancre, many of the Brigades made stunning initial progress, surrounding the strong-point known as 'Schwaben Redoubt' and pressing on towards 'Stuff Redoubt', covering nearly a mile by mid-morning. Strong German counter-attacks gradually pushed the Irishmen back, and despite dogged determination and some fierce resistance, dwindling supplies of reinforcements, supplies and ammunition forced a withdrawal, although a few small parties were still holding out in the German front lines when darkness fell. Several weeks later, the *Gloucester Citizen* reported how a five-minute period of commemoration was set aside for the citizens of Belfast, '…as a tribute of respect to the memory of the officers and men of the Ulster Division who fell during the recent British advance.' At 12 noon on the appointed Wednesday, '…traffic was suspended for the same period, and blinds in the business establishments and private houses were drawn, while flags on public buildings were flown at half-mast. A special memorial service was held in the Cathedral.'

This brief summary does not do justice to the heroism of the Ulster Division, but their story is told in much more detail within other texts, and we must now move on to the 29th Division at Beaumont Hamel.

12

29TH DIVISION

The line which stretched northwards from Beaumont Hamel to the village of Serre, covering three Divisions, produced some of the most enduring and tragic tales of the Somme Offensive. On the southern flank of the 29th Division, a bulge protruding towards the German positions provided the starting-point for an attack led by the 1st Royal Inniskilling Fusiliers, with the 1st King's Own Scottish Borderers and 1st Essex following on behind. The leading platoons were soon held up, and when the 1st KOSB advanced it met a similar hail of bullets:

> 8:10. Our attack not progressing due to intense enemy machine-gun fire.
> 8:31. Advance still going on but being constantly checked.
> 8:45. The attack ceased.[1]

Another battalion which recorded over 500 casualties, the 1st KOSB War Diary indicates that eleven officers were killed and nine wounded. As the assault only lasted for just over an hour, the carnage in that time was particularly gruesome, and one Second Lieutenant to fall had already witnessed death and destruction on a large scale in another Theatre of War. Second Lieutenant John Altham Stobart Graham-Clarke was born in Sheffield during 1894, the son of Captain Lionel Graham-Clarke (Royal Artillery), and Frances, although the family moved to Frocester Manor, near Stonehouse, a few years later. Capt. Graham-Clarke received a DSO in recognition of his services in the Boer War, and ended his military career as an Honorary Major in the Royal Gloucestershire Hussars. He died in July 1914 and lies buried in St Peter's graveyard, Frocester, along with several other relatives, some of whom are remembered on the lych-gate which leads to the now abandoned church.

J.A.S. Graham-Clarke joined the 5th Royal East Kents (the 'Buffs') as a Private soon after his father's death, and later received a commission with the 9th KOSB, giving his mother's address – Frocester Lodge – as his permanent residence. A character reference for the young man was provided by Revd Gerard Unwin, the local vicar, who stated that he had known the new recruit since 1911. Attached to the 6th Border Regiment, he sailed from Liverpool bound for Gallipoli on 1 July 1915, and took part in the Suvla Bay landings on 7 August. Wounded six weeks later, he recuperated at the Red Cross Hospital in Giza, close to the Egyptian pyramids, and the next mention of him is in the *Stroud News*, which revealed that he had arrived on the Western Front during May 1916. (This could not have been with the 6th Borders, which left Egypt on 30 June, and did not disembark at Marseilles until 6 July.) The *Stroud News* again provides the necessary data on 14 July: 'Lt J.A. Graham-Clarke, 1st King's Own Scottish Borderers, only son of the late Capt. J.A. Graham-Clarke, DSO, of Frocester Manor, was reported killed in action on 1 July.'

A telegram was sent to Sir Lionel Darell of nearby Fretherne Court, informing him that 2nd Lt Graham-Clarke was 'missing', and it was soon confirmed that the officer had indeed fallen in battle. Upon hearing the news, Frances Graham-Clarke went to stay with the Darells, as the two families were related by marriage, and a muffled peal was rung on the bells at Frocester Parish Church in memory of the nineteen year old. The *Wilts & Glos Standard* was told that the young soldier had '…died gallantly leading his platoon'. Originally buried close to where he fell, 2nd Lt Graham-Clarke's body was reinterred at the Ancre British Cemetery, Beaumont Hamel (II. A.26) in 1920, and a letter was sent to his mother by the War Office to this effect.

At 7.20 a.m. – a full ten minutes before the general attack – a mine placed beneath the German-held Hawthorn Redoubt was detonated. Although this occurred immediately opposite Beaumont Hamel, its 40,000 pounds of high-explosives could be heard and seen in the wider vicinity, thus warning the defenders of an imminent advance. As the debris fell to earth, men of the 2nd South Wales Borderers '…immediately commenced getting out of the trenches and through our wire',[2] yet they had not even breached their own entanglements when machine-guns and shrapnel shells were opened upon them. The two leading Companies were cut down and the battalion's objective – the enemy front line – was not even reached. The fate of Captain Alexander Arbuthnot Hughes is indicative of the ferocious attempts to repel the assault, as Capt. (Temp. Major) G.T. Raikes, DSO, witnessed:

> On the 1st July 1916, I saw Capt. Hughes leading his Company, he was walking forward about 50 yards from the [German] wire leading 6 or 7 men forward, all these men were knocked out a few yards further on…Practically all those reported missing were probably killed…[3]

In a separate report relating to another officer, a soldier of the 2nd SWB noted that only a handful of his comrades got anywhere near the enemy trenches before being picked off. He also saw Captain Hughes at a similar distance to the objective as Captain Raikes had reported, and that the casualty was lying '…crumpled up just about where he fell, he was dead…'.[4] Pte Shoreland, of 'B' Co., saw Captain Hughes being shot through the shoulder and falling, whilst both Sgt B. Jones and Pte Higgins confirmed that they had seen the Captain die. Even so, Captain Hughes was officially 'missing believed killed' for over a year until his body was found in No Man's Land by the 5th Salvage Corps on 3 August 1917. A cigarette case was discovered and returned to the officer's parents, who were also informed that their son had been interred at 'Y' Ravine Cemetery (the modern grave reference is C9).

Born at Woolwich in 1887, A.A. Hughes was the son of Col A.J. Hughes, RFA, and Caroline, and attended Clifton College between 1901 and 1904. Aged twenty-nine when he died, his home address was at Tunbridge Wells.

With its close proximity to the river Severn, the South Wales Borderers had a number of Gloucestershire men in its ranks. Pte William Buckland (No.10329) was a native of Eastville in Bristol, and in 1901 he was aged nine, living with his family at Cloud Hill Road, St George. His father, William, was a 'horse keeper' from Kingswood, whilst his mother, Elizabeth, hailed from Essex, and there were three younger siblings. (Thiepval 4A). Pte Alfred William Stephen Jones (No.18504) was born at Coleford in the Forest of Dean, and enlisted in Newport. His mother, Mary, was residing at Usk in Monmouthshire by the 1920s, and her twenty-eight-year-old son is also remembered at Thiepval (4A.) Pte Albert Woffenden (No.9821) is possibly the Gilbert Woffenden who is to be found in the 1901 Census, aged nineteen and working as a 'bread maker'. The SDGW lists him as being born in Kingswood, Bristol, and with such an unusual surname, this is the only family to be found in the same eastern district of the city at the beginning of the twentieth century. Edwin Woffenden, a 'coal haulier', hailed from Pucklechurch, and his wife, Emma, was a Somerset woman. They had five children, with Gilbert being the eldest. Pte Woffenden, who enlisted in Pontypool, is another whose name is at Thiepval (4A).

The War Diary of the 1st Border Regiment notes how the 2nd SWB was, 'wiped out by machine-gun fire in our own wire'.[5] On the previous day, German gunners had found the range of the British forward trenches, and when the 1st Borders advanced into No Man's Land 'at a slow walk', the inevitable barrage confronted them, thinning the ranks with every step until small groups of men were all that was left of an original strength of twenty-three officers and 809 men. Twenty of the former became casualties (the CO, Lt-Col Ellis, was injured and brought in by Pte Newcombe), whilst 559 other ranks were killed, wounded or reported missing within less than thirty minutes. Pte John Henry Gray (No.10025), who was born at Tredegar, enlisted in 'Bristol, Glos.' according to the SDGW, but there are no residential or family details to be found in either Casualty Roll. He lies buried at the Hawthorn Ridge Cemetery No.2 (B.34).

With the first two battalions brought to a standstill, the CO of the 1st Newfoundland Regiment – Englishman Lt-Col Hadow – now received orders to advance from his position 300 yards behind the British front trenches, in conjunction with the 1st Essex. The latter moved forward along the congested communication trenches, whereas the Newfoundlanders went into battle across open ground, in broad daylight, with no artillery support. Having already decimated the 2nd SWB and 1st Borders, the German machine-gunners had a new target, and set to work with ruthless efficiency. Bunching through the narrow gaps in the British wire, few of the attackers even made it out into No Man's Land, and those who did were soon shot down. In forty minutes, 91 per cent of the battalion had become casualties, yet such was the pride in their cause and background, even some of the officers who were meant to stay behind had joined their comrades in the disastrous advance. Raised in North America with much patriotism at the start of the war, it had ceased to exist as a fighting force in less than an hour. The Ayre family suffered more than most, with two brothers and two cousins falling in the advance. All four were officers whose grandfather was a prominent merchant back in St Johns. The Newfoundland Memorial Park now commemorates this most appalling of human tragedies by preserving the trenches, battle-field and bomb craters, watched over by a bronze caribou. 'Y' Ravine – the first day objective – was so heavily defended by the Germans that it was not attacked again until November 1916.

Beaumont Hamel itself was also garrisoned and fortified in great strength, and the unenviable task of storming the town on 1 July was allotted to the 1st Lancashire Fusiliers and 2nd Royal Fusiliers, with the 16th Middlesex in close support. When the Hawthorn Mine was blown, men of the 1st LF were out of sight, but the War Diary notes that, 'all felt the ground shake'.[6] This was the prompt to move into position, and at 7.30 a.m. the attack was met by a 'storm of bullets', pinning it down in No Man's Land. An hour later, it was clear the advance had not reached the German lines, and Beaumont Hamel was still in enemy hands. Dead and wounded men were all around, and following a sudden retirement on one flank, it was feared a German counter-attack was commencing, although the situation was retrieved by the swift building of barricades. The rest of the day was spent assisting the wounded or dodging artillery shells, and the bitterness expressed at the end of the Lancashire's War Diary for the opening attack is barely concealed:

> The day had cost the battalion many valuable lives. Casualties were 7 officers killed, 14 wounded & 500 O.R.s. The battalion fought well, but the enemy was ready for us & [our soldiers] had plenty of M.G.s against them. No troops of only 1.5 men per yard can hope for success.[7]

One of the fallen officers was Captain Edward Granville Matthey, who attended Cheltenham College between 1907 and 1911. Born in 1893, he left the Royal Military College at Sandhurst and received a commission with the Lancashire Fusiliers prior to the outbreak of the war. The 1st LF was one of the most famous regiments of the Gallipoli campaign, when; on 25 April 1915 six of its officers and men were awarded Victoria Crosses for getting ashore under the most withering fire from the Turkish defenders high up on the cliffs at Cape Helles. One of them – Captain (later Major) Richard Willis – would spend his final years in Cheltenham. Capt. Matthey is mentioned by name only once in the War Diary for 1 July 1916:

'A' Company had also suffered in their advance to the Sunken Road, the three subalterns all being hit [as well as] many men. Capt. Matthey reached the road and dashed on with the men who entered near Northern End.[8]

This was not long after 7.30 a.m., and it is probable he was killed a short while later. His body was recovered and interred at the Redan Ridge Cemetery No.2 (C.44). His father, Captain G.E. Matthey, of the Inniskilling Fusiliers, had passed away by the 1920s, whereas his mother, Cara, was living in Kensington.

In the ranks, Sgt Bertie Dight (No.288) was also amongst the dead. Born at 'Bristol, Glos', according to the SDGW, he is almost certainly the same person as eleven-year-old Albert J. Dight, living in Lincoln Street close to Temple Meads, in 1901. His parents, George and Eliza, came from Somerset, whilst his older siblings – all natives of 'Bristol, Glos' – held down varying occupations such as 'leather merchants', 'porter', 'tailoress' and 'cigar maker'. Enlisting in Birmingham, Sgt Dight is now commemorated at Thiepval (3C & 3D).

At the end of June 1916, the 1st LF and 2nd Royal Fusiliers were sent the best wishes of Gen. H.B. de Lisle, the General Officer commanding 29th Division, who described the forthcoming attack as 'the most important battle in which British troops have ever fought.'[9] Immediately opposite the left flank of the 2nd RF was the Hawthorn Redoubt, and when it was blown to pieces 'Z' Company rushed forward to occupy the crater, only to be met by instant machine-gun fire. The War Diary reports the cause of this as being the fact that the British artillery bombardment – which had been 'fierce' until 7.20 a.m. – was lifted to the German second and third lines, thus enabling the enemy's front trenches to fill with survivors and deal with the attack which had been signalled by the mine exploding. Fruitless attempts to storm the objectives continued until mid-day, when the few stragglers still out in No Man's Land were forced to retire. Lt-Col Johnson, the CO, had been severely shaken by the effects of a high explosive shell landing close by, whilst Major Cripps, who had taken over as Brigade Major, was dangerously injured within two hours. Casualties included twenty-one officers and over 350 men, with the War Diary revealing rather coldly on July 2nd: 'Salvage of dead and wounded still remaining in our own trenches actively carried on.'[10] Captain Swift then assumed command of the battalion.

Pte Henry Frank Lovell (No.G/16655), who was born, enlisted and lived in Bristol, had been killed in action. This surname is common in the city during the nineteenth and early twentieth centuries, and the only added information is from the CWGC, which reveals he was married to Mrs F. Pratt (formerly Lovell), of Tankard's Close in St Michael's Hill. Previously in the 9th Reserve Cavalry, Pte Lovell is remembered at Thiepval (8C, 9A & 16A).

The War Diary of the 16th Middlesex (Public Schools) Battalion for 1 July gives little information as to the nature of the fighting it encountered, other than that it was 'in action' from 7.30 a.m. German eyewitnesses later recalled how the soldiers advanced slowly towards them with their bayonets glistening in the morning sun, so it is little wonder the 2nd Royal Fusiliers and 16th Middlesex both lost over 500 men in such a short space of time. Pte Herbert Nelmes (PS/2612) was born at Ruardean, in the Forest of Dean during 1891, the son of Dan – a carpenter – and Alice. He was baptised in his local church, but by the time of the 1901 Census the family had moved to Gloucester, and the soldier's parents were living in the city's Goodyere Street by the 1920s. Pte Nelmes, who enlisted in Cardiff, is commemorated at Thiepval (12D & 13B).

The Battalion War Diary established that thirty-seven men in the ranks were 'missing believed killed', whilst a further 138[11] were simply unaccounted for by the end of the day. Pte Murray Percy Howard Blumer (PS/133) was one who did not answer the next roll call. Born in Sunderland, he attended Dean Close School in Cheltenham, and when the 1901 Census was taken he was an eleven-year-old student living on the campus. His service record[12] reveals that he enlisted into the Public Schools Battalion in London on 7 September 1914, aged twenty-five years and three months, from his employment as a 'stockbroker's clerk'. An unmarried man, his home address was that of his parents, William and Jessie, along with his sisters Gertrude, Gladys and Muriel, in Muswell Hill.

In January 1917, news was finally received from a Pte D. Chuter, incarcerated in Germany, that he had seen Pte Blumer in an enemy dug-out on 2 July 1916, wounded, several hours after being taken prisoner. As no trace of the latter could be found in the POW lists, it was 'accepted for official purposes' that Pte Blumer must have succumbed to his injuries on or after the date he was last seen. The historical records note that no soldier from the 86th Brigade – of which the 16th Middlesex formed a part – reached the German wire on 1 July, and it is documented that a number of injured men from the Public Schools Battalion were removed from the crater by the Germans following the advance. The Adjutant, Capt. Francis Cockram – riddled with bullets – was one of them, spending the rest of the war as a POW. (The bodies of around 180 of his fallen comrades in the vicinity were not recovered until the following November.) Pte Blumer is commemorated at Thiepval (12D & 13B).

Ten officers and 139 ORs of the 86th Brigade's Machine Gun Company joined the attack on 1 July, moving out across the open ground when the debris from the Hawthorn Mine had cleared. Positioning several guns around the lip of the crater, the men were immediately subjected to the same hostile fire which devastated the infantry battalions around them. Even though the German trenches had been '…badly knocked in' by the British artillery, Germans were spotted 'from the waist upwards'[13] resisting the assault, and a vicious exchange of bullets ensued when the enemy brought up their own heavy duty weapons on the opposite side of the depression. It was noted in the War Diary that the barrage tailed off towards 12 noon, by which time the British attack had failed.

Pte Norman Fulton (No.11643) was amongst the MGC casualties. Born in Fife, Scotland, he was formerly in the Gordon Highlanders, and his place of residence in the SDGW is given as 'Northbeach, Glos.' Bearing in mind that he enlisted in Cirencester, it is highly likely this is Northleach, on the Fosse Way. (Thiepval 5C & 12C.)

The Pioneer Battalion for the 29th Division was the 2nd Monmouthshire Regiment, which had arrived on the Western Front during November 1914, and had taken on its new role precisely two months prior to the opening day of the Somme Offensive. Various Companies were attached to different regiments in the Division, and during the hours of darkness, as 30 June gave way to 1 July, the Pioneers were busy digging saps to conceal bombers, or communication trenches to enable the assault troops to move up to their positions whilst the enemy barrage was ongoing. Between 1 and 4 July, four officers were wounded, eleven ORs died and a further eighty-one received injuries, according to its War Diary.[14]

In the 21 July 1916 edition of the *Dean Forest Guardian*, the Obituaries column revealed: 'Yarworth. Killed in action. Pte★ Ralph Yarworth, of the Post Office, Clearwell.' The newspaper would later report that Ralph Yarworth (No.1543) had been born, baptised and confirmed in the small Forest of Dean village near Coleford. At a memorial service in St Peter's Church held shortly afterwards, relatives and friends were told that the soldier had 'laid down his life for King and Empire'. One of four members of his family serving in the Forces, he was a single man who formerly worked as a miner at the local Flour Mill Colliery. (In 1881 a number of Yarworths were living at Dean Pool Farm and Clearwell Road, Newland, although the name 'Ralph Yarworth' does not appear in the Baptism Register for St Peter's between 1876 and 1906, or on the 1901 Census. The occupations of the men-folk mentioned in the former are mainly those of a 'collier', 'quarryman' or 'stone-cutter'. There was also a butcher named Yarworth in the hamlet during the early 1900s.) Cpl R. Yarworth, who may have been known by a different Christian name, is commemorated at Thiepval (16B.)

Clearwell is said to have sent more soldiers to the Front in proportion to the population than any other village in England. One of its most famous sons was Pte Francis George Miles of the 1/5th Glosters, who, on 23 October 1918, was awarded the Victoria Cross in France, when, under his own initiative, he went forward alone through heavy machine-gun fire, located the enemy weapon and put it out of action. He then captured the crew of another

★Both the SDGW and CWGC give his rank as Corporal. His date of death in the Casualty Rolls is 1 July.

Pte M.P.H. Blumer, 16th Battalion, Middlesex Regiment. A former pupil of Dean Close School in Cheltenham, he died of his wounds on 2 July 1916.

gun before signalling to his comrades the best route to advance, thus enabling them to secure a further sixteen enemy machine-guns and their operators. Pte Miles survived the war and died in his native hamlet during 1961. In such a close-knit community he would almost certainly have known Cpl Yarworth when they were both growing up.

Pte Arthur John Bullock (No.3238) had also lost his life. Born at Arlingham, to the south of Gloucester on the banks of the river Severn, he too had strong Forest of Dean connections, and by the time of the 1901 Census, when he was aged twelve, his family was living at Plump Hill, East Dean. His father William – a 'road labourer' – and mother Alice, were both Foresters, whilst his three older brothers all worked in a coal pit. He also had three younger siblings. Enlisting in Pontypool, Pte Bullock was living in Mitcheldean at the time, and he is now remembered at Thiepval (16B).

The *Gloucester Citizen* noted within its section 'Incidents in the Assault' in mid-July:

Some of the men talk about the mine which went up at Beaumont Hamel with great glee. A hearty sergeant, with an unusual power of description, said it reminded him of the pictures you sometimes see in cinemas of petroleum stores blowing up – always in America. 'I'd been in that part of the line for some time,' he said, 'and, Lord, how we used to curse that mine. Fatigue parties always were wanted to carry the stuff out, and then later on to take in the explosive. The exploding chamber was as big as a picture palace…and the long gallery was an awful length. Of course we used to be working under some of the crack Lancashire miners. Every time a fresh fatigue party came up they'd say to the miners:"Ain't your damned grotto ever going up?" But, my Lord, it went up alright on 1 July. It was the sight of your life. Half the village got a rise. The air was full of stuff, wagons, wheels, horses, tins, boxes, and Germans. It was seven months well spent getting the mine ready. I believe some of the pieces are coming down now.'

The decision to blow the mine ten minutes early was, however, a horrendous error, and settled the fate of the 29th Division before it had even begun its assault. Under the headline, 'There Have Been A Dozen Balaclavas!', one correspondent in the *Gloucestershire Echo* likened the recent fighting in France to the ill-fated Charge of the Light Brigade in the Crimea during October 1854 – an historic military blunder which doomed a band of gallant men:

> What I hope I have made plain, however, is that there is no measure of pride which the people at home may take in the performance of their Armies which is not justified. You who are mourning need have no misgivings. In so far as pride can console grief, you have consolation to the full.

13

4TH DIVISION

The Front allotted to the 4th Division, between Beaumont Hamel and Serre, was relatively narrow compared to other sectors, but its casualty rate was to be the fifth highest overall by the end of 1 July. Advancing to the left of the 29th Division's 1st Lancashire Fusiliers, the 1st East Lancashires were followed soon afterwards by the 1st Hampshires, with the latter receiving machine-gun fire 'from all directions'[1] before the attack was aborted. Survivors took refuge in shell-holes until darkness fell, when they returned to their original lines. The War Diary states that every officer became a casualty (on 10 July only six battalion officers – excluding those at HQ – were still in the line), and one of the fatalities was India-born Lt Hugh Irving Adams. His father, George, worked for the Indian Civil Service, and the youngster was sent to Cheltenham College as a boarder between January 1896 and July 1900, from where he went to the Royal Military College at Sandhurst. After tours of duty with the Light Infantry of the Indian Army, H.I. Adams took up farming in Canada with his wife and young son, but returned to England when war was declared. By 1916 his sister, Muriel Parsons, and parents were living at two addresses along Sydenham Villas in Cheltenham, and the Lieutenant was posted to No.4 Entrenching Battalion 'in the field' during the January prior to his death.

On 6 July 1916, a telegram was sent to the officer's mother in Cheltenham informing her of her son's death in action on the *second*, but it undoubtedly occurred on the previous day. Mrs Adams then told the War Office of her daughter-in-law's address in Canada. Shortly afterwards, Pte Chas Ford, 1st Hampshires, explained to an official who was investigating the fate of fallen officers:

> …on 1 July, quite early in the day…he [Ford] saw Lieutenant Adams killed, and actually had to step over his body in the advance. Lt Adams was his platoon commander, he thinks he came from America, or somewhere far away, for when he [Ford] went on leave he remembered that he [Adams] said his home was too far away to get to it.[2]

Cpl Webb added that at 8.15 a.m., '…Lt. Adams fell and then rose, saying "come along eleventh!" (his platoon) and then fell back and did not move again. It was beyond the first line of trenches approaching the second to the left of Albert, in front of Matie…'[3]

Aged thirty-four, Lt Adams' body was buried at the Sucrerie Military Cemetery, Colincamps (I.H.12). His effects – which included a photo case and two locks of hair – were sent 'care of' Lloyds Bank in Cheltenham.

L/Cpl Richard Eeles, of the Hampshires, was awarded a Military Medal for gallantry on 1 July, and received the distinction in person from Gen. Plumer just over a month later. It is highly likely that he served with the 1st Battalion, as the only other unit of the regiment on the Somme – the 2nd Battalion, in the same Brigade as the ill-fated 1st Essex and 1st

Newfoundlanders of the 29th Division – did not take part in the opening day of combat. The soldier lived at Wells Road in Stow-on-the-Wold with his wife and three children, whilst his parents resided at nearby Temple Guiting. A Boer War veteran, he was recalled in August 1914 and had two brothers, four brothers-in-law plus a nephew serving in the Forces.

At 9.10 a.m. the 1st Royal Warwickshire Regiment, which had already experienced the front-line horrors of gas attacks in the last week of June, received orders to move up from its reserve position and towards the battle-zone. Just after 1.00 p.m., reports were received that British troops had been spotted in the German forward trenches, and a patrol belonging to the 1st RWR set off into No Man's Land under Lt R.R. Waters of 'A' Company. Pinned down by machine-gun fire from Beaumont Hamel, the sortie was forced to withdraw having suffered a number of casualties, including the death of Lt T.F. Breene. In the ranks, Gloucester-born A/Cpl Albert Henry Boucher (No.8609) had also fallen. By 1901 he was an eighteen-year-old working as a 'railway shunter' in Birmingham, boarding with a family in the All Saints district of the city, and he later enlisted at Warwick. Married to Nellie, he was thirty-two when he fell, and his name can be found at Thiepval (9A, 9B & 10B).

The centre of the 4th Division was held by the 1st Battalions of the Rifle Brigade and Somerset Light Infantry. In mid-July, one survivor from the latter told the *Dursley Gazette* of the 'encouraging words' spoken by Brig.-Gen. Powse DSO before they went over:

> Remember, the old Somersets have always had a good name. Keep it, and no lagging behind…If anything wants shifting, the Somersets will do it.

The soldier in the ranks added, 'Our boys were only too anxious to get over the parapet, and there were several mouth organs going.'

Advancing upon the 'Quadrilateral Redoubt', an officer of the 1st RB recalled in the *Bristol Times & Mirror*:

> They [the Germans] opened their machine gun fire exactly ten minutes before we started. I heard the clack, clack plainly through the big stuff…There's no doubt in my mind that if Master Boche had no machine guns he would have stood no chance at all.

The machine-gun guarding the 'Quadrilateral' jammed at precisely the time the British assault started, although the defenders had buried a mine beneath the position in the event of it being over-run, and this blew a short while later, killing the engineers who had placed it. A significant number of attackers reached the 'Quadrilateral', as the distance which had to be crossed was much shorter than in other parts of the line, yet the resistance faced was as strong as ever. Sgt Holley from Bath, of the SLI, told the *Bristol Times & Mirror* of his experiences, reprinted under the rousing headline: 'UP AND AT 'EM! How The Somersets Charged The Foe!'

> I shall never forget the morning of [July] 1st, the longest day I have lived. It was hell upon earth. We went into the trenches about midnight the night before, and we all went over the top the next morning. All our watches were fixed at zero; that was for us to go over at 7:30 a.m

Following the British bombardment, Sgt Holley continued:

> At 7:30 the fire was lifted and the order was sent down the line, 'up and at 'em', and we met such a storm of machine gun and shell-fire that you could think it impossible to ever live in. But I will say for our boys they never flinched. Our boys and the Rifle Brigade took the lead, but I don't think many of us reached the [enemy] trench before being cut down. I did not last very long. We got up [to] within 20 yards of their front line when my officer collected the platoon together to make a charge. He asked us if we were all ready and I said 'yes'. We got up to charge, but if you ever saw the vanishing trick put on about sixty men it was when he

said 'charge'. They were waiting, and we went down like sheep. They gave me [my wound] in my left thigh, right in the bone, and there it stopped. It was not being hit that I worried about, it was having to stay out there all day, but I suppose I must think myself lucky that I am in the land of the living.

With the Divisions on either flank faltering, the gains made by the 4th were under severe threat. The War Diary for the SLI states:

> It is impossible to get a detailed account of the fighting that ensued, but the situation after the first hour or two was that men of various battns were holding part of the Quadrilateral and were engaged in a fierce grenade fight. Our men were for some time severely handicapped by [the] shortage of grenades, but these were afterwards sent up.[4]

Small parties of British soldiers had reached as far as the German third line – a rare accomplishment in this part of the Front – yet they were now in danger of being cut off. Only two officers of the Somersets had achieved this position, and both were wounded, so the decision was made for the latter to return as best they could, leaving Company Sergeant Maj. P. Chappell in charge of the outpost. Realising he could not hold out where he was, the NCO from Bath gathered his troops and made a concerted dash for a trench already held by a separate party of men in khaki uniforms, who turned out to be from the Seaforth Highlanders. Close by was another group of Germans who were causing considerable disruption, and just as a deliberate British charge was being planned to alleviate the peril, a Corporal in the Scots regiment picked up a handful of grenades and began walking towards the enemy, hurling bombs as he went. His brave actions enabled the line to successfully rout their unwanted neighbours, yet the Seaforth Highlander fell dead in a most gallant sacrifice. His name is not known.

With the noise of battle raging in the near-distance, the immediate vicinity of the 'Quadrilateral' now took on an uneasy air of calm. In the afternoon, grim news was brought across No Man's Land of the deaths of Brig.-Gen. Prowse – a long-standing officer of the Somersets, recently appointed to command the 11th Infantry Brigade – and Lt-Col Thicknesse, the 1st SLI's CO. CSM Chappell knew Brig.-Gen. Prowse well from their days in the Somersets, and the blow must have been doubly severe for the men still holding out in enemy territory. As the afternoon wore on into the evening, the Germans began to gather in strength close to the 'Quadrilateral', and in the early hours of 2 July the small garrison was ordered to withdraw. CSM Chappell – who was awarded the Distinguished Conduct Medal for his supreme endeavours on 1 July – brought the remnants of his battalion back. The War Diary concluded:

> The Battn. lost very heavily. With the exception of 2nd-Lt Marler, Bde. Dump officer, no officers, with the exception of Capt. Acland, R.A.M.C., who formed up in the Assembly trenches, returned unscathed at the end of the day. Lt Col. Thicknesse & Capt. Ford (Adjutant) were both killed before our trenches were passed…Brig.-Gen. Prowse died of wounds.[5]

The most senior officer to die on 1 July 1916, Brig.-Gen. C.B. Prowse, DSO, was a native of Somerset, but his family had links with Clifton, as two of his brothers – Cecil★ and Llewelyn – were born here. Commissioned into the SLI during 1892, Charles Prowse fought with them during the Boer War, being Mentioned in Despatches three times. Proceeding to Flanders in August 1914, he was soon involved in the early skirmishes of the First World War, and was the subject of an entire paragraph in Viscount French's first despatch of the conflict when he saved the line at La Gheer, for which he was promoted to Brevet Lieutenant-Colonel – the first such appointment of the war. The site of a stand by the Hampshires and Somersets in October 1914 became known as 'Prowse Point', and Prowse Point Cemetery was later constructed here. It remains the only Commonwealth burial ground to be named after an individual.

★At Royal York Crescent, 1866.

Brig.-Gen. C.B. Prowse, DSO, CO 11th Infantry Brigade. The most senior officer to die on 1 July. His parents once lived at Frampton Cotterell, to the north of Bristol, whilst two of his brothers were born at Clifton.

At the Second Battle of Ypres in April and May 1915, Lt-Col C.B. Prowse was given command of the 11th Infantry Brigade – which included his old regiment, the Somersets – and at one stage he was in overall charge of fifteen battalions, three of which were French. Of these operations, Maj.-Gen. Sir Henry Wilson, commanding the 4th Division, noted: 'He maintained a thorough and complete grip of the situation throughout, and dealt with every emergency in a most masterly manner.' Several months later, Lt-Col Prowse oversaw the successful capture of a considerable length of German trenches at Pilckem, near Ypres, and had accomplished an astonishing rise through the ranks from a junior Major to Brigadier-General in less than a year. Mentioned in Despatches a further three times – once by Sir Douglas Haig – he was created a Companion of the DSO for 'distinguished service in the field' just a month before his death.

The *Wilts & Glos Standard* reported that C.B. Prowse was the former commander of a detachment of the Bath Volunteer Cyclists, and had once spoken at a smoking concert held in The King's Head in Cirencester. An eyewitness watched his demise on 1 July, telling the same newspaper:

> Between the newly captured German lines, the Brigadier was cheering us on when a big shell dropped about 20 to 30 yards away. A piece must have hit him, for he was seen to fall. Several men rushed to his assistance. Before he died he cheered the men and told them to keep up the name of the Stonewall Brigade.

(The latter title was given to the 80th Brigade after its defence of the Ypres Salient during May 1915.)

Other accounts of the Brigadier-General's death in action indicate that he had moved the Brigade HQ up to its new position in the enemy lines when he became frustrated at the lack of progress and left his position to organise the attack, subsequently falling to machine-gun fire. (See Chapter 21 for more details of the death and funeral.) His loss was widely reported in West Country newspapers, and it came only weeks after his brother, Capt. Cecil Prowse,

The original grave of Brig.-Gen. C.B. Prowse, DSO.

RN, died when HMS *Queen Mary* exploded during the Battle of Jutland in the North Sea. Aged forty-seven, Brig.-Gen. Charles Bertie Prowse, DSO, lies buried at the Louvencourt Military Cemetery (Plot 1, Row E, Grave 9). He left a widow, Violet, back in England. (His parents, George and Emmeline, once lived at The Grange in Frampton Cotterell, to the north of Bristol.)

The Bristol newspapers also informed their readers that the Somersets' CO, forty-six-year-old Lt-Col John Thicknesse, was amongst the dead. Another long-serving soldier of the SLI, he hailed from the Midlands, was married to Phyllis, and his remains were later interred at the Sucrerie Military Cemetery (I.H.15), Colincamps.

Lt Edward Crozier MacBryan, 3rd (attached 1st) SLI, has closer links to Gloucestershire, as he attended Cheltenham College between 1902 and 1903 before continuing his education at Oundle School, followed by Jesus College, Cambridge. Born in 1893, he was the son of Dr Henry MacBryan, of Kingdown House, Box, in Wiltshire. His brother, Reginald, spent four years at Cheltenham College, becoming captain of the Rugby XV during 1913/14, and he was wounded whilst serving as a Lieutenant with the King's Own Scottish Borderers at around the same time his elder brother was reported 'missing, believed killed'. (The oldest sibling, John, was captured at Mons in the first weeks of the war whilst holding the rank of Captain in the Somersets. He was another Old Cheltonian.)

Wounded in the left thigh by bullets on 2 May 1915, Lt E.C. MacBryan attended a Medical Board at Bristol's Beaufort War Hospital the following August, and was still unfit for duty. On 1 July 1916, Pte C. Strickland recalled that Lt MacBryan led his platoon past the first German line and on towards the second when the officer received gun-shots to the head, causing him to fall. 'I think he was killed at once',[6] the Private stated from his hospital bed. However, in a separate testimony, Sgt Harry Hunt, of the 1st Rifle Brigade, informed the authorities that he had tended to a dying officer of the Somersets in the German *third* line, bathing his head with silk handkerchiefs before placing him in a dugout when it was clear he would not live for much longer. 2nd Lt Codner, who took over the role of the 1st SLI's Acting Adjutant following the death of Captain Ford, was given Lt MacBryan's revolver and belt by Sgt Hunt,

2nd Lt A.V.C. Leche, attd SLI. He perished with many of his comrades on 1 July 1916. His father once lived in Clifton.

who informed him that the stricken man had been, 'hit through the abdomen and was sinking fast'.[7] The NCO later informed Dr Henry MacBryan, 'Your son faced the music like a man.'[8] The dates cited as the Lieutenant's official date of death vary between 1 and 2 July, but his body was never recovered to be identified, so he is now commemorated at Thiepval (2A).

Another officer whose fate was not immediately known was Second Lieutenant William Herbert Treasure, born in London during 1897. His father, Herbert, took up the post of a Bristol Bank Manager a few years later, bringing his wife, Grace, and family with him to live at 196 Redland Road. From his Lloyds Bank employment address at 'Brisbank', Bristol, Mr H.G. Treasure wrote a letter to the War Office on 24 July 1916, demanding: 'Can you inform me how long my family and I are to be kept in suspense?, and when may we expect to hear officially what has happened?'[9]

The following month Major Majendie, the new CO of the 1st SLI, told the grieving father that his son's body had been found by another battalion patrol just outside the enemy wire on or about 18 July, and added:

> As it was so close to the German lines, the only thing they could do was bring back his i.d. disc. Though your son was with us only a short time, we saw enough to know that he was an excellent officer, and he is a great loss to us.[10]

Cpl Thomas Robertson, who took part in the advance, was apparently told by a comrade that 2nd Lt Treasure had been killed, but due to his (Robertson's) 'dazed state', he could not recall the officer's name. However, the Corporal did later record, 'He was my platoon officer but did not go with us in the attack.'[11]

It would appear that 2nd Lt Treasure was originally detailed to remain behind as the bulk of his battalion went forward on 1 July, but evidently the officer did not wish to do so and requested an attachment to a trench mortar battery. 2nd Lt A.H. Collins, himself wounded, testified that:

He [Treasure] was in charge of a Stoke's Gun Party and from what I could gather his was one of the few teams to get their gun across to the German lines and successfully into action. They fired 150 rounds with it and I believe your boy was one of the last with the gun.[12]

Pte A.E. Miller added from Etaples Hospital, 'Lt. Treasure was in charge of a Stokes Trench Mortar belonging to the battalion…The Lance Corporal who was in charge of us was by the side of him. As I was coming back wounded he said to me "Poor Mr Treasure is killed."'[13] There is also a reference to the officer's servant, a man named Boult, who lost his life at the same time. (This was forty-four-year-old Pte Louis Boult, from Bedminster.) An obituary for 2nd Lt Treasure appeared in a mid-August edition of the *Bristol Times & Mirror*, announcing that he was '…previously reported missing, now reported killed in action on 1 July…' His parents later lived at Hyde Lodge in Bristol. (Thiepval 2A.)

Another officer with Bristol connections was 2nd Lt Arthur V.C. Leche – attached to the Somersets from the Devons – whose medical practitioner father, Arthur, lived in Clifton's Cornwallis Crescent as a teenager. Also reported missing on 1 July, the death was not officially recorded until the following year, when a Trooper Herbert, of the Yorkshire Dragoons, claimed that he had buried the remains of 2nd Lt Leche and placed a cross above his grave. Pte Nicholls – presumably of the 1st SLI – later recalled that he had seen the same officer fall, and the corpse was blown to pieces by a shell. Tpr Herbert's actions may well have ensured that the final resting place is still marked today – in the Serre Road Cemetery No.2. Arthur Leche senior was living in Axbridge by the 1920s.

The *Bristol Times & Mirror* contained many accounts of the SLI's attack, including:

One of the bravest actions I saw was that of a captain in the Somersets who was badly wounded in the left arm. Although the arm was useless he refused to leave his post, and was still firing his revolver when I last saw him, while the Germans were sniping him in all directions.

(According to the War Diary, Captains Ford, Leacroft and Neville were killed, whilst Captains Llewellyn and Harington were injured.)

The West Country newspaper also revealed the tale of Lt Harold Colville, who apparently predicted he would receive four wounds during the war, with the final one proving fatal. On 1 July he suffered a fracture to the base of his skull – his fourth combat injury – and died five days later.

The following list of fatalities in the ranks is a lengthy one, with most of the individuals having strong Bristol connections. Halfway through, the impressions of a *German* officer who witnessed the British attack at first-hand are reprinted as a reminder of the impact of war upon both sides.

CSM Frank Edward Day, MM (No.4399), was born at Bedminster, to the south of the river Avon, enlisted in Taunton, and his residence is given as 'Bristol'. In the absence of an exact address, he is included here. (Serre Road Cemetery No.2 – II.A.32.) Cpl Henry Guest (No.5949) was born at Westbury-on-Trym and joined up in his home city. In 1901 he was a Private in the SLI, aged nineteen, and living in barracks. (Serre Road Cemetery No.2 – III. E.13.) Cpl Frederick Langdon (No.6383) hailed from St Michael's in Bristol, the thirty-one-year-old son of George and Kate. His wife, Mabel, was living at Meyrick Street in Barton Hill by the 1920s. (Thiepval 2A.) L/Cpl Albert Victor Govier (No.11236) died of his wounds in the UK on 8 July, having been evacuated from the Front, and he was almost certainly injured either in the final week of June or during the attack itself. Born in St George, Bristol, he was living in Woodbine Road with his family by 1901. His father Reuben – who appears to have had the occupation 'labourer at furnace' – his mother Martha, and his four siblings, all came from the same part of the city. Aged nine in 1901, A.V. Govier was later employed by Messrs Lysaght's Works, the steel factory in the centre of Bristol, and had moved to Albion Street,

Cirencester and its immediate vicinity was the home of Pte R.C. Freebury, 8th Battalion, SLI. He was killed on 1 July 1916.

Redfield, by the outbreak of war. His body lies buried at the nearby Avon View Cemetery (DB5 48) – the only known casualty of the beginning of the Somme Offensive (in this text) to be laid to rest in Gloucestershire or North Bristol.

Pte William Ashford (No.10814) was the twenty-year-old son of Sarah, who later lived in Eyers Lane, St Judes in Bristol. Born in the city, Pte Ashford is commemorated at Thiepval (2A). Pte Eli George Bartlett (No.7001) came from St Phillip's in Bristol (born at the end of 1883), and by 1901 he had moved to Wembdon in Somerset, working as a 'groom'. Joining the army in Taunton, he gave his place of residence as Bradford in Yorkshire. (Thiepval 2A.) Pte Francis George Fear (No.10786) was twenty years old when he died, a native of Bristol's St Clements; his next of kin is given as 'A.J. Fear' of Vicarage Road, Whitehall. (Serre Road Cemetery No.2 – I.C.30.) Pte Reginald Charles Freebury (No.17240) has the rather peculiar birthplace in the SDGW of 'Big Lambhill, Glos.', but the 1901 Census reveals him to be a native of 'Lechlade, Glos', whereas the *Cheltenham Chronicle & Glos. Graphic* indicates that he originally came from Ampney St Peter, near Cirencester. The family was living at Ready Token at the beginning of the twentieth century, with George – a 'carter on farm' – his wife Mary and their five children all to be found in the household. Reginald, who was aged eight at this time, enlisted in Cirencester during January 1915, and went abroad on active service the following May. Formerly employed by the Great Western Railway at Llanelli, he was gassed at Ypres shortly after his arrival in Belgium, and later informed his family at the end of June 1916, 'I shan't be able to write again for six weeks, as we are going into the big push, but don't fret, dear mother.' His comrade, W.J. Knight, later told Mrs Freebury, 'He was much loved by us all, as he was one of the best...We all join in sending you our deepest sympathy.' The *Wilts & Glos Standard*, which published all of the above correspondence, also revealed a memorial service was held at Ampney St Peter Parish Church when news of the soldier's death came through. (Thiepval 2A.)

Pte Francis Henry Hart (No.11261) came into the world at St Mathias in Bristol towards the end of 1878. Three years later the 1881 Census reveals him to be residing at York Buildings in St Paul's with his mother, Sarah, and three older sisters. Aged thirty-nine when he fell, he is commemorated at Thiepval (2A), as is nineteen-year-old Pte Alfred Archie Haskins (No.20452) from Kingswood, Bristol, the son of Alfred and Fanny. Pte Sidney William Holbrook (No.6881) came from the St Andrew's district of Bristol. The surname was common in the city and beyond around the time of the First World War, but his lower service number suggests he was an old soldier. (Serre Road Cemetery No.2 – III.E.10.) Pte Frederick E. Horsford (No.10736), aged thirty-eight, has the middle name 'Edward' in the SDGW, but the 1881 Census reveals it to be 'Edwin'. Both sources agree that he came from St Paul's in Bristol. He was the son of Edwin – a 'chair frame maker' – and Sarah Louisa, who were residents of Earl Street, in the heart of the city, when Frederick was two years old. When the CWGC compiled its data forty years down the line, the couple were to be found in Picton Street, off the Ashley Road. (Thiepval 2A.) Pte William Samuel Jenkins (No.5724), thirty-four years old when he died, is confirmed by the CWGC as being a Boer War veteran. Born at Hotwells in Bristol, he was married to Elizabeth, who later lived at Easton Road. (Thiepval 2A.) Pte William Thomas Jennings (No.3/7292) was a native of St Phillip's in Bristol, and was aged twenty-nine when he fell. He is almost certainly the same person as the fourteen-year-old William Jennings who was working as a 'dairyman' when the 1901 Census was taken in St Silas Street, near Temple Meads. His parents, Elias and Mary, along with his four younger siblings, were all Bristolians. The soldier's widow, Sarah Jane, later lived at Barton Hill. (Serre Road Cemetery No.2 – I.A.23.)

The *Western Daily Press* managed to obtain the following description of events on 1 July by Lt Dambitsch, a German officer who was in his own front line when the British attack began. Although his location is not given, his account is indicative of how strong the resistance was to such a large-scale assault:

> What we have just met on The Somme makes our experiences of last September [at Loos, 1915] mere child's play. No previous war affords any comparison to it. It was [our] dug-outs that had to be battered down, so that at the moment of assault, all the defenders except a few survivors, and all the machine guns should be buried.

(He then makes reference to the solid construction of the German communication trenches, which allowed reserves, food and ammunition to be brought up whilst a barrage was ongoing.)

> This fire lasted seven days, and finally there came a gas attack…Although the offensive was made by great masses of infantry, and had been prepared with all the latest improvement of the science of war, the attempt to break our line utterly failed. Even today, when war is so largely a matter for mechanical contrivances, the old truth still holds good that in the long run it is always the men who are the deciding factor.

Continuing with the 1st SLI's fatalities, eighteen-year-old Pte Leslie Ernest Knight (No.17307) came from St Michael's in Bristol, and was living at Thornhill Place at the start of the twentieth century. His Somerset-born mother, Annie, is mentioned in the 1901 Census, but there is no trace of his father, Thomas, who may have been serving abroad in the Forces at the time. The family had moved to Twerton in Bath by 1916, and Pte Knight's parents later relocated to Burnham-on-Sea. (Euston Road Cemetery, Colincamps – IV.E.3.) Pte Charles William Lock (No.9223) died of his wounds on 2 July. A native of 'St Peter's, Glos' (SDGW), he was the twenty-two-year-old son of William – a 'dock labourer' in 1901 – and Minnie, and was living with them in Brislington, to the south of the river, in the early years of the twentieth century. His parents would subsequently move to Anchor Road, on the north bank of the Avon. (Gezaincourt Communal Cemetery Extension – I.G.3.) Originally reported 'missing' on 1 July, Pte Arthur Martin (No.10572) was actually a prisoner of war, and his father, Mr G.T. Martin, of Derby Street in Bristol's Redfield district, must have had a mixture of emotions when the fate of so many of his son's comrades became known. However, the Bristol-born soldier died on 9 October 1918 – most probably due to an illness or disease – whilst still a captive in Germany. His body now lies at the Niederzwheren Cemetery at Kassel (II.N.7), and this burial ground constituted the amalgamation of a number of Commonwealth POW graves after the war. (The *Western Daily Press* indicated that Arthur Martin was a Lance Corporal, but this is not corroborated in the Casualty Rolls.)

Pte Ernest Luke Moss (No.19306) is probably the same person as the ten-year-old Ernest Moss who was living at Blacksworth Road in Bristol during 1901. Both the Census and the SDGW give his place of birth as 'St George, Bristol', and his parents in the former are named as Alfred and Emily. (Thiepval 2A.) Pte Henry O'Brien (No.15287) was born at Redcliffe, Bristol, but a match does not appear in the 1901 Census. Enlisting in Yeovil, his residence is given as 'Bristol' in the SDGW. (Thiepval 2A.) Pte William Pearce (No.10715) hailed from Easton in Bristol, and was aged twenty-one when he fell. His father, Samuel, had moved to Wates Road in Kingswood by the 1920s. (Thiepval 2A.) Barton Hill-born Pte Charles Petheram (No.11081) is also remembered at Thiepval, and his parents were living at Lincoln Street after the war. Pte Ernest Charles Radford (No.9792) was another Easton boy, and is most likely to be the Ernest C. Radford, aged ten in 1901, residing at Air Balloon Hill with his father, Willie – a 'black smith' – his mother, Sarah, and two siblings. (Thiepval 2A.) Pte Thomas Charles Sheppard (No.3/7843) came from Redcliffe, and there is a family with this surname living at Slee's Court in the same district during 1901, although the eleven-year-old son is listed as 'Thomas A. Sheppard'. Somerset-born Kate – a 'bacon packer' – was the mother to five children, all aged twelve or under. In St Mary Redcliffe Parish Church there is a War Memorial dedicated to the men connected with the surrounding area who fought and died in two world wars:

> Those of this parish who are inscribed below left all that was dear to them, endured hardness, faced danger and finally passed out of the sight of men, by the path of duty and self-sacrifice; giving up their own lives that others might live in freedom. Let those that come after see to it that their name be not forgotten.

'T. Sheppard' is one of the many listed for the 1914–18 conflict. (Serre Road Cemetery No.2 – I.H.34.)

Pte Charles Richard Tozer (No.11056, SDGW; No.11058, CWGC) was born at St Paul's in Bristol. The surname is another which was common in the city at the time, and in the absence of further data, his subsequent background is unclear. (Thiepval 2A.) Pte Fred Upton (No.5657) was a native of St Michael's, Bristol, and in 1881 he was living at Oxford Court in Westbury-on-Trym with his parents, Frederick and Alice, plus his four siblings, including a one-month-old sister who had yet to be named. Another who was almost certainly an experienced soldier, he joined up in Taunton from his Bristol home, and was aged thirty-seven when he fell. Pte Upton's mother and father would later move to Alfred Hill in Kingsdown. (Thiepval 2A.) The birthplace of Pte Thomas Frank Wakeman (No.6743) is given as 'Easton, Bristol' in the SDGW, and there is an individual with this name whose arrival into the world was registered in the Barton Regis area of Gloucestershire (central Bristol) at the end of 1896. He is almost certainly the same individual as the four-year-old Frank Wakeman to be found in the 1901 Census living within the St Gabriel Fenchurch Parish of St Phillip and St Jacob, in the heart of the city. His father, also listed as 'Frank', was a 'baker's carter', whilst his mother was named Lily, and he had two younger brothers. (Thiepval 2A.) Pte Frederick William Wood (No.11054), who must have joined up at the same time as Pte C.R. Tozer, was born in Bristol's St Phillip's district (registered in Barton Regis during the spring/summer of 1897), the son of Edwin and Elizabeth. The 1901 Census reveals the family to be in the St Gabriel Fenchurch Parish, close to the Wakemans, with Bristolian Edwin – a 'shoe maker' – the Head of the household, married to 'Bessie' (from Dorset), and looking after their three children, with three-year-old Frederick being the middle in age. The CWGC indicates that Pte Wood was in 'B' Company on 1 July 1916, and the War Diary states that four platoons of 'B' Co. occupied the left flank of the first and second lines in the attack: 'The advance was

Lt H. Jones, 1/6th Battalion, North
Staffordshire Regiment, was a former scholar
of Wycliffe College, Stonehouse. He was one
of the many who perished on the first day of
the Somme Offensive.

carried out excellently to start with, and a severe barrage was not encountered.'[14] However, once the enemy had rallied, the inevitable resistance opened up, 'The battn. had to ease off to the left, owing to the ridge which it should have crossed being swept by machine guns…and (then) found itself in the German trenches in the neighbourhood of the Quadrilateral.'[15] Aged nineteen, Pte Wood was possibly one of the latter, as his body was not recovered. His parents had moved to Eagle Street in Easton by the 1920s. (Thiepval 2A.) Both Irishman Pte Alfred Cole (No. 19897) and Dartmouth-born Pte Arthur Harold Dyer (No. 11676) enlisted in Bristol and are remembered at Thiepval, but their residential details are not to hand.

CSM Percy Chappell, DCM, received a commission soon after the Somme Offensive began. He was the highest ranking soldier of the 1st SLI to return to the British lines unhurt on 1 July. But, as with so many battalions along the front line, the next roll call would reveal devastating gaps where familiar faces once stood. The man from Bath finished the conflict as a Major, second-in-command of his beloved Somersets, yet virtually all of his pre-war comrades were dead, wounded, or in captivity. The above list – all in the main linked to North Bristol – is but a proportion of the 151 soldiers in the ranks who had lost their lives by the end of the day. Inevitably, a great deal more were from rural Somerset, and although the 1st SLI was never even classed as a 'Pals' battalion, the sense of loss in *every* part of the United Kingdom and Ireland which added their names to regimental badges soon becomes grimly apparent. The *Western Daily Press*, along with other newspapers, were informed that the first German lines had been occupied on a twenty-mile front, whilst on a ten-mile sector, the second enemy positions were also in British hands. Although some units of the 4th Division *had* advanced this far, the reports of their gallant but ultimately doomed stand were not forthcoming to the general public back home.

However, the carnage in this Division was not yet over. Two battalions of the Royal Warwickshire Regiment – the 1/6th and 1/8th, with a heavy Birmingham bias – had been drafted into the line from the 48th Division, further to the north. With the 1/8th to the fore, followed by the

1/6th, the Warwickshires advanced at 7.30 a.m. on 1 July, passing the enemy front trenches with little opposition, but were held up beyond the second and third lines. On a number of occasions, parties of men were bombed out of their positions when their own supply of grenades was exhausted, and with no ammunition being brought across No Man's Land, this proved to be a critical handicap in the progress of the attack. The inevitable fire from enemy machine-gunners and snipers also harassed the British, and the War Diary of the 1/8th estimated 90 per cent of its strength of 800 men became casualties. The CO, Lt-Col Innes, was amongst the twenty-nine of thirty-two officers who were killed, wounded or taken prisoner, and the demise of the former was described to the *Wilts & Glos Standard* by an eyewitness, who told the newspaper:

> [His death] occurred on the morning of 1 July, at 8 o'clock, when he fell gallantly taking his regiment into action – the regiment he loved so well and had done so much for. He was a thorough soldier and a patriot.

Second Lieutenant Francis Basil Freeman was reported to be wounded and missing by the War Diary, and 'missing believed killed' in an article published by the *Dursley Gazette*, which revealed the officer was last seen after being shot through the stomach whilst leading his men towards the German third line. A former pupil of Berkeley School and Evesham Grammar, the twenty-six-year-old Second Lieutenant was a pupil then a teacher at Bengeworth School in Evesham, and had joined the local Territorials before transferring to the 14th Warwickshires, reaching the rank of Sergeant. Six of these original volunteers received their commissions with the same regiment, and all perished on the Somme battlefield during the first day of fighting. Born in Staffordshire, 2nd Lt Freeman – the son of Albert and Ellen – was buried at the Cerisy-Gailly French National Cemetery (II.G.16), to the south-west of Albert. This originally seemed to be an error, as the location of the grave is some ten miles from the spot where he fell, but it transpired that bodies found after the Armistice were taken in turn to burial grounds which were 'available' for new interments at the time. Having fallen deep within German territory which was soon retaken, it is perhaps surprising that the officer's identity could later be established in such a positive manner.

The remains of Gloucester-born Pte Archibald Morgan (No.1843) are to found at the Serre Road Cemetery No.2 (II.A.35), and therefore he almost certainly fell close to his own lines.

Right: Sapper T.R. Lane died on 1 July 1916. He was born in Gloucester.

Opposite left: Pte A. Morgan, 1/8th Battalion, Royal Warwickshire Regiment, was mortally wounded on 1 July 1916. Pte Morgan was born in Gloucester.

Opposite right: Capt. K. Herne, 1/6th Battalion Royal Warwickshire Regiment. He attended Wycliffe College in Stonehouse. Severely wounded on 1 July 1916, he died in 1919.

Enlisting in his home city, he was formerly with his county regiment, and came from a large family of ten children. He was aged six in 1901, living with his parents, Thomas and Mary, in Gloucester's Alfred Street, and his father worked as a 'plumber's foreman'.

The combined 1 July losses of the two Warwickshire battalions exceeded 1,000 men. Wounded in the abdomen during the advance, Captain Keith Herne, of the 1/6th, was helped back to the British lines by his servant, who had to drag his officer across the bloody mess of No Man's Land a few inches at a time before both men caught their breath. Within sight of a Casualty Clearing Station, the Captain's rescuer was decapitated by a shell, but, due to his endeavours, his comrade did manage to reach safety. Repatriated to England, Captain Herne partially recovered from his devastating ordeal and was sent back to the Front the following December, where he was subsequently incapacitated once more by an exploding bomb. His injuries were assessed as 'severe but not permanent', and it was noted that the individual, 'complains of headaches and inability to concentrate. He is depressed and nervous,' whilst the effects of shell-shock prompted a military doctor to add: 'his nervousness is increased by any loud sound.'[16] The bullet which had struck him down on 1 July passed straight through his body, close to his spine, and he did not see active service again. Living in North America when war was declared, the former Wycliffe College pupil had returned to the UK to join up, and received his commission in March 1915. One of four brothers who were all injured during the conflict, Captain Herne's constitution was severely weakened by his experiences in battle, and he succumbed to the effects of the Spanish Influenza epidemic on 3 March 1919, having never fully shaken off the horrors of war, which affected him for the remainder of his life. His cremated remains were later taken to his native Wales.

The 2nd Lancashire Fusiliers left their assembly trenches at 8.00 a.m. on 1 July, and moved out into No Man's Land shortly after 9.00 a.m. Just over half an hour later, the first Companies reached the German trenches, but with no support on either flanks, and mounting resistance from the enemy, the advance began to 'telescope' as the positions around the 'Quadrilateral' were occupied. The remainder of the battalion then came across carrying supplies, and the area was held until 11.00 a.m. the following day, when the survivors were ordered back to their own lines. Parties were sent out to bury the dead, although the threat of a counter-attack was ever-present. Sixteen officers and 352 ORs had become casualties, including Pte Frank Gooch (No.4426), the twenty-year-old son of Mrs F. Gooch, who lived at Chapman's Place, Kilcot, near Newent. Born

A. Hurley survived the 1 July attack with the Warwickshires and later lived near Cheltenham.

in Manchester, where he subsequently joined up, Pte Gooch is remembered at Thiepval (3C & 3D). His father Frank, a native of Kilcot, was a Manchester greengrocer in 1901.

Sapper Thomas Robert Lane (No.101853) was from Gloucester, the son of Thomas and Charlotte. In 1901 he was aged five, living at Columbia Street in Kingsholm, and later joined the 9th Field Company of the Royal Engineers, which was attached to the 4th Division on 1 July. Between this date and 7 July different sections were serving along the entire sector, deployed in rewiring and restoring damaged defences and trenches. The War Diary indicates that two men in the ranks were killed and nine wounded on the first day of the Somme Offensive. The *Cheltenham Chronicle & Gloucestershire Graphic* revealed that the soldier's widowed mother was living in Gloucester's Tredworth Road by 1916, as well as adding her three other sons and one grandson were all serving in the Forces. The grave of Sapper Lane is to be found at the Sucrerie Military Cemetery (I.D.9), Colincamps. He was most probably shot by a sniper or hit by a shell.

One of the youngest casualties in the Division was Pte John James Perkins, of the 1/6th Royal Warwickshires, who lies buried close to Sapper Lane. Pte Perkins, a Birmingham lad, was aged just sixteen when he fell on 1 July 1916. Exactly seventy years later one of his comrades in the RWR – Albert Hurley – was living near Cheltenham, and at 8.30 a.m. (taking into account British Summer Time) Mr Hurley's son laid a wreath at Cheltenham's War Memorial to coincide with the precise moment the attack was launched. Mr Hurley junior told the *Gloucestershire Echo* in 1986 that he 'wanted to honour my father and all those brave and glorious young men who went so fearlessly into the bloody, horrific battle.' Enlisting into the City of Birmingham Battalion at the outbreak of war, Albert took part in many of the major offensives of the conflict, receiving three Mentions in Despatches, being buried alive twice when trenches collapsed on top of him, and suffering from the effects of mustard gas. He joined up again during the Second World War, and spent another six years in uniform.

The ex-serviceman's son continued, 'I felt I had to do something to make sure the first of July was not forgotten. It will be a sad day if this country ever forgets what people like my father and those men who died did for us – they all gave so much. That terrible war has haunted my father all his life.'

31st DIVISION

The battleground around Serre is often focused upon as representing a microcosm of the wider fighting along the Somme on 1 July 1916. The 93rd Brigade was comprised of three West Yorkshire battalions – 15th, 16th and 18th – along with the 18th Durham Light Infantry. It was the 15th (also known as the Leeds Pals) which led the way, on the left flank of the 8th and 6th Royal Warwickshires of the 4th Division. The Pals' War Diary reveals an all too familiar summary of events:

> 7.30 a.m. The Battle of the Somme commenced. The attack was launched in successive waves. Every wave was held up by a very severe sweeping machine gun fire. There had been an hour's intense artillery bombardment of the enemy's front line trench and a 10 minute intense 'hurricane' trench mortar bombardment, but when the advance was made, the enemy front line was thick with men…Large numbers of our men were casualties long before reaching the German wire. Some were reported to be over the front enemy trenches and in their final objective. [This was an error]. Our casualties were 24 officers and 504 O.R.s. By the end of the day we were holding our front line. Dead and wounded were being brought in from No Man's Land for several days.[1]

One of the bodies to be recovered was that of Cirencester-born Pte Harold Allen (No.15/1570), who had joined up in Leeds from his residence in the city. Aged five in 1901, he was living at Somerford Road in Chesterton, near his native town, with his father William – who worked on the railways – his mother Ellen, and three older brothers. The eldest, William, had been born in Stonehouse, near Stroud, whereas the other two hailed from Swindon. Pte Allen, who was married to Helene, lies buried at the Serre Road Cemetery No.2 (VII.C.11).

With the leading battalions suffering heavily, the 18th West Yorks' received orders at 8.20 to move forward, and were immediately hit by shrapnel, high explosives and machine-gun fire. Its CO, Lt-Col Maurice Nicholl Kennard, MC, was killed by German artillery at around 8.30 a.m., and most of his men were struck down before they reached No Man's Land. With the situation hopeless the attack was called off, and the 18th DLI was spared further bloodshed. Formerly in the 6th Dragoons, Lt-Col Kennard was the second son of Robert and Rose (who later lived in Wiltshire), and grandson of Mr R. Nicholl Byass, JP, who resided for many years at 'Wyck Hill' near Stow-on-the-Wold. (In 1901, the latter was in residence with his wife, Mary, and fourteen servants. The same year saw the next generation of Kennards living in Monmouthshire – the birthplace of seventeen-year-old Maurice, whose father was described as a 'gentleman', JP and Deputy Lieutenant of the county.) At the end of July 1916, a memorial service was held at Wyck Rissington Church in the Cotswolds in memory of the fallen officer. The official history of the 18th Battalion – the Bradford Pals – notes that the men received heavy cross-fire from the 'Quadrilateral' as soon as they began their march towards the guns, and everyone dropped to their stomachs except for the CO, who, carrying just a walking stick, stood upright and called upon his men to follow. Soon afterwards, the thirty-two-year-old was the victim of an exploding shell. Mentioned in Despatches during October 1914, he was wounded a month later, and was at one time the second-in-command of the 13th York and Lancasters. (Thiepval 2A, 2C & 2D.)

The West Yorkshires as a whole endured a torrid time during the summer of 1916. One of its officers, Old Wycliffian Alfred Martin, recalled:

> I was in the Somme battle for the first two months of the offensive, July–August, and after our regiment had been cut up we were sent to a quiet part of the line, where I managed to get 'pipped' by an aerial torpedo.[2]

In the centre of the 31st Division stood the men of the 11th East Lancashire Regiment. Early in September 1914, the Mayor of Accrington offered to raise an entire battalion, and within ten days thirty-six officers and 1,076 soldiers had enlisted. The following February the Accrington Pals left their home town bound for training in North Wales, and 16,000 citizens cheered them on their way following an inspection by Old Cheltonian Maj.-Gen. E.T. Dickson. Eventually sent to Egypt, the Pals guarded the Suez Canal before being transferred to France in March 1916, in preparation for the Somme Offensive. The fate of the Accrington Pals on 1 July has come to symbolise the futility and heroism not just of the first day, but of the entire war.

One man who was not part of the genesis of the Pals, yet nonetheless shared in its immortality, was Second Lieutenant Arthur Beacall, born at the School House, Quedgeley (to the south of Gloucester) in August 1895. His father, Thomas, was the headmaster of the village school, as well as being the Clerk to the Parish Council and an assistant overseer. (The educational establishment, which used to stand just along from the church on the junction with the modern A38 road, has since been demolished and replaced by a row of shops.) Baptised less than two months after his birth, Arthur was one of nine children, four of whom were natives of Quedgeley, the family having moved to Gloucestershire around the year 1890. There is a link with Lancashire, as nineteen-year-old Thomas was born there, although whether this played a part in Arthur's future choice of regiment is unclear.

Following the completion of his education, Arthur found employment at Lloyds Bank in Stroud and also played for the town's Rugby Football Club at Fromehall Park, where the *Stroud News* noted him to be a 'robust forward who always "played the game"'. On the outbreak of war, he joined the 6th Somerset Light Infantry as a Private, giving his permanent address as 'The School House, Quedgeley', and he was examined at The Armoury in Stroud before being passed fit for military service. The new recruit was 5'6" in height, had brown hair and grey eyes, and his 'good moral character'[3] was confirmed by Lt-Col Heyworth, of Quedgeley House, who stated that he had known the young man for four years. Pte Beacall made rapid progress through the ranks, and was appointed a Lance Sergeant several months before the 6th SLI arrived in France during May 1915, serving with them until mid-November. Upon his return to England, he received an officer's commission with the 10th East Lancashires – a UK-based unit – and on 7 June 1916 he married Edith Brewer, of Lansdown in Stroud, at the town's parish church. Just weeks later, he joined up with his new battalion on the Western Front – the Accrington Pals. In position by 4.00 a.m. on the morning of 1 July, the following Appendix to the War Diary – written in chronological order by the CO, Lt-Col A.W. Rickman, as the day's dreadful events unfolded – gives an insight into the confusion, desperation and slow realisation of what was happening to the 11th East Lancashires. The vast majority of casualties occurred during the tragic first twenty minutes, but this was not known until later:

> The assembly trenches for the attack on Serre extended from MARK COPSE to MATTHEW COPSE inclusive, with the 12th Batt. York & Lancaster Regt on the left, and the 93rd Brigade on the right. The 13th and 14th [Battalions] York and Lancaster Regt were

2nd Lt A. Beacall (above) was born at Quedgeley, near Gloucester, and fell in with the famous Accrington Pals. He died on 1 July 1916.

in support of the 11th East Lancs Regt The battalion was ordered to go forward in 4 waves accompanied by details of the 94th Machine Gun Company and the 12th Batt [King's Own Yorkshire Light Infantry] Pioneers; the hour of the attack being 7.30 a.m.

(The first platoons went out into No Man's Land at approximately 7.20 a.m. in readiness for the Gen. advance.)

7:22 a.m. The 2nd wave proceeded to follow the 1st wave.

7:23 a.m. Two platoons 13th [York & Lancasters] followed second wave.

7:29 a.m. I saw [our] 3rd & 4th waves advancing. By this time there was intense rifle [and] m.g. fire and a very heavy barrage of artillery fire. They crossed out into No Man's Land crossing the front line about 7:32 a.m.

7:39 a.m. Reported by runner via Mark Copse – 1st two waves advancing according to timetable. Heavy M.G. & rifle fire still coming from German front line. Intense fire of all descriptions.

7:50 a.m. Reported by runner – all four waves have gone forward – M.G. fire still coming from the North. [This was from the direction of the defences opposite the neighbouring 48th Division, which were not under attack]. Report from Lt Gay – led platoon through 1st [German] line. Lt Gay wounded, M.G. fire much less intense.

(This is significant – by this time most of the Pals were dead or wounded.)

I sent Lt Macalpine to establish telephone communication [between] Mark Copse & H.Q. Lt Macalpine returned & informed me all communication was cut and it was not re-established all day.

8:10 a.m. Reported M.G. fire still coming from the North.

Capt. [name illegible], 13th Y & L, arrived with only nine men in his two platoons.

I further reported I could see odd groups in my front [trenches] believed to be wounded; also that I could not see any of [the] waves.

No further report from waves. Heavy artillery barrage on [British] front line.

Looking towards Hebuterne from Serre in 1920. This photograph covers the area occupied by the 31st, 48th and 56th Divisions on 1 July 1916. Many thousands fell on this bleak landscape during the Somme Offensive.

This last statement is another indication of the slaughter which had just taken place. Because the Germans had no more infantry advancing towards them, they were able to shell the trenches which the Pals had just left. Similar disjointed scraps of data were received over the next fifty minutes. 'No information from any waves' is repeated twice.

9 a.m. Report from Corporal Riply, wounded, belonging to 1st wave. States that only seven of his platoon got into enemy 1st lines. They held it for about twenty minutes, bombing Germans back till bombs were exhausted. Corpl. Riply saw remains of 2nd wave in front of [German] barbed wire. Germans still holding out. Saw no sign of 3rd or 4th wave. Heavy barrage on [British] front line.

10:10 a.m. No report from any waves. Message from [Officer Commanding] 13 Y & L that C Company Y & L was going forward to occupy German 1st line trenches. Heavy barrage. M.G. fire from right [possibly originating from the 'Quadrilateral' in front of the 4th Division]. 10 wounded men 11th E.L. [Accrington Pals] have returned and they state front line is still in enemy hands.

11:25 a.m. No information from any waves. Pte Glover (1st wave) states 1st wave encountered heavy M.G. fire, bombs & artillery fire crossing No Man's Land. Capt. Livesay, 1st wave, with remnants of 2nd wave, together with 3rd wave, charged German trenches. Capt. Livesay sent back a message for reinforcements – this never reached me. A number of wounded in Sap C. Field dressings urgently required.

11:50 a.m. No reports from any waves except statements of wounded men.

12 noon. I proceeded to put [the British] front line in state of defence as far as possible against counter attack.

(This represents a stark realisation by the officer in charge that instead of breaching the German lines as expected, an unthinkable reversal was very much feared.)

3:10 p.m. I have left [only] 1 officer and 25 [other ranks] of my own unit available

3:50 p.m. Very intense bombardment of [British] front line. All posts driven in by artillery fire. Urgently require more men: I have 55 men in all, some of whom are wounded. 2 Lewis guns only – two men to work them, one of whom wounded.

9:20 p.m. I beg to report I saw 2 Germans removing our wounded back to their lines from No Man's Land. There are no Lewis or [machine-guns] in [our] line. I am getting the wounded evacuated as soon as possible but there are a good number yet to be attended to.[4]

(Lt-Col Rickman was knocked unconscious by a shell shortly after this entry, and later received a Distinguished Service Order for his actions on this day. Surviving the war with further wounds, a Bar to his DSO and a number of Mentions in Despatches, he died in Wiltshire during 1925.)

What had begun as a confident advance in the bright sunshine of 1 July had ended in carnage. 700 of the Accrington Pals lined up at 7.30 a.m. and walked slowly across 300 yards of No Man's Land towards the German positions. Instead of encountering little or no opposition, they headed straight into a murderous hail of rifle and machine-gun fire, leaving 235 dead and 350 wounded within twenty minutes. 2nd Lt Beacall, leading his men into action, was probably one of the first to fall. It was noted that, 'Not one man wavered or went back.' Perhaps one of the saddest yet noblest entries in the War Diary reported that, 'Small parties penetrated as far as the German fourth line, but were not heard of again.' Like their comrades of the Tyneside Irish at La Boisselle, a handful of Pals were determined to carry out their orders and reach Serre. Their dedication to duty is extraordinary.

Original front-line trenches. The 1st King's Own Scottish Borderers of the 29th Division left these positions on 1 July 1916, suffering heavy casualties before the attack was called off. Their objective was 'Y' Ravine later to become a Commonwealth Cemetery.

On 6 July a telegram reached the Beacall household in Quedgeley. It read:

> Regret to inform you that 2nd Lt Beacall reported missing 1st July. This does not necessarily mean that he is killed or wounded. Further news upon receipt.

Two days later, the family's worst fears were realised:

> Deeply regret to inform you that 2nd Lt A Beacall, Lancashire Regt, previously reported missing 1st July, now reported killed in action. The Army Council expresses their sympathy.[5]

The *Stroud News* soon heard of the Quedgeley officer's death in action, and added: 'only seven of [his battalion] returned to answer the call.' (This figure turned out to be erroneous, but nonetheless is indicative of just how many men were known to have been lost.) Recalling his sporting exploits, the newspaper continued, '…we can fully realise how Lt Beacall went into the fight, because we had learned to appreciate his dash on the football field.' The *Gloucester Journal* noted:

> His many friends will hear with deep regret that [2nd Lt Beacall] has now been officially reported 'killed'. He was a son of Mr Thomas Beacall, of Quedgeley. Lt Beacall was very popular at Stroud, where for some time he was on the staff of Lloyds Bank. He was a keen sportsman, and for two or three seasons played forward for Stroud Rugby Club.

The officer's body now lies at rest in the Euston Road Cemetery, Colincamps (I.D.6), another reason for suggesting he fell early in the assault. With No Man's Land swept by enemy fire, retrieval of the dead and wounded – as confirmed in the War Diary – was no easy task.

But the conflict was not yet done with the Beacalls. Alan, a Private in a Canadian Regiment, lost his life on the Western Front during September 1918. Both he and his brother are commemorated on the Quedgeley War Memorial, whilst their parents' graves can be found close by, in the churchyard. The village today is virtually unrecognisable from the rural landscape which became their home.

The devastation and grief felt in Lancashire following the decimation of the Accrington Pals ran deep. The towns which had so patriotically cheered their men to war were plunged into mourning, and, in time, a Memorial Chapel was dedicated to the 11th East Lancashire Regiment in the local St John the Evangelist Church. In 1991 a new monument to the Pals was constructed on the lip of one of the trenches from which the attack was launched back in 1916. Built of Accrington brick, it is a permanent reminder of their sacrifice, and there are similar inscriptions dedicated to other units close by. The Sheffield Memorial Park, for example, was adopted by the Yorkshire city after the First World War, and is the only part of the Somme battlefields preserved by the British. (The Newfoundland Memorial Park to the south is, of course, Canadian.) A raid by the 12th (Sheffield) Battalion of the York and Lancaster Regiment on 26 June 1916 reported the German wire to have been 'badly damaged' in places, and during the early hours of 1 July white tapes were laid out in No Man's Land to guide the men into the attack the following morning. However, these had been removed by the enemy before dawn, and with the communication trenches in, 'exceedingly bad condition owing to heavy rain' (the water was 'above knees'[6] in some places), the advance appeared doomed before it even began.

The intense bombardment of the German forward positions in the lead-up to 7.30 a.m. prompted the compiler of the 12th York and Lancaster's War Diary to declare: 'Our intention to attack must have been quite obvious to the enemy.' Finding the barbed wire undamaged, the narrative continues: 'A great many casualties were caused by the enemy's machine-guns,' whilst, '…whole sections were wiped out. The failure of the attack was undoubtedly due to the wire not being cut.' The officer believed that the machine-gun emplacements should have

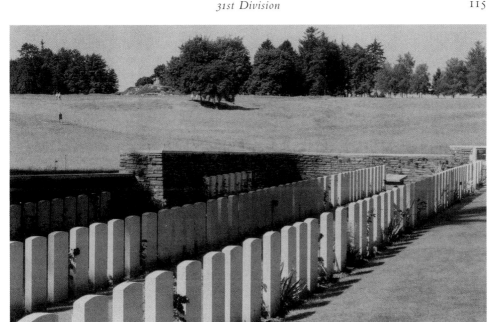

'Y' Ravine pictured in 2006. The 29th advanced from their trenches in front of the line of trees on the horizon (these were planted after the war) and across the exposed ground of No Mans Land, which is still pitted with shell craters. The 2nd South Wales Borderers, 1st Borders and 1st Newfoundlanders also lost thousands of men on the opening day alone. This area now forms part of the Newfoundland Memorial Park.

been dealt with by bombers, but as a consequence of this not being so, there were, '...no means of stopping their fire. Consequently, succeeding waves were wiped out and did not arrive at the German wire in any strength.'[7]

Corporal Francis Edwin Watkins, MM (12/548), is listed in the SDGW as being born at 'Boughton-on-the-Water, Cheltenham, Gloucs'. He enlisted in Sheffield from his home in Chesterfield. The 1901 Census provides a more accurate place of birth for the sixteen-year-old 'ordinary agricultural labourer' (then living at The Borders in Defford, Worcestershire), revealing him to be a native of 'Bledington, Glos'. (This is a village on the Oxfordshire border, approximately five miles to the east of Bourton.) His father, John, was a 'stockman on cattle farm' at the turn of the twentieth century, whilst his mother, Olive, came from the county in which they then resided. The soldier's service record[8] is amongst those stored at the National Archives, and states that F.E. Watkins married Mabel in 1907, with the couple becoming parents to Mabel and Mary in due course. Aged thirty in 1914, the new recruit was 5ft 9in and gained promotion to Lance Corporal in October 1915; he was made a full Corporal the following May and was appointed Acting Lance Sergeant★ less than two weeks before the Somme Offensive. The documents also reveal that he was awarded his Military Medal on 16 May 1916. The battalion had taken over the front line from a West Yorkshire unit the previous day. Just after midnight the Germans began shelling the British positions – a regular occurrence designed to unnerve and disrupt the newcomers before they had the chance to settle in. Fifteen soldiers were killed and many more wounded, including a number who had been buried by collapsed trench debris. The War Diary noted, 'Our men were very steady during the bombardment',[9] and rescue operations were carried out by groups from different

★This rank is not corroborated by the Casualty Rolls.

regiments. Citations for Military Medals were not published in the *London Gazette*, so it is fair to assume that Cpl Watkins received his gallantry award for his part in the extrication of stricken comrades. .

Aged thirty-two, Cpl Watkins, MM, has no known grave, and is remembered at Thiepval (14A & 14B). On 13 November 1916 soldiers of the 3rd Division briefly entered Serre and discovered a small number of bodies belonging to the Sheffield Battalion, suggesting that – along with their outnumbered comrades from the Accrington Pals – the heavily-fortified village *had* been reached against overwhelming odds, although this has never been verified. These men could have been taken prisoner and withdrawn to Serre by their captors, yet some British observers were convinced that the position had been achieved as signals or flares were seen within the hamlet itself, indicating a partial success which was the possible prompt for *German* artillery to then open up on the new targets. Brigadier Loe, who was a Forward Observation Officer on 1 July, was not convinced, however, and stated afterwards that he did not see any survivors of the 12th York and Lancasters get beyond the enemy front line.

On the same November date as this grim find, 2nd Lt Richard G. Morgan, of the 12th East Yorkshires (a native of Chalford near Stroud, and an Old Wycliffian), was reported to be 'wounded and missing'. At 5.30 a.m. he led his men across No Man's Land towards Serre and was hit by a shell, but shouted: 'Don't mind me, lads! Get on! Get on!'[10] Bandaged by medics, the stricken officer was unable to stand, and stretcher bearers sent to rescue him were shot by the Germans. Later on the same day, Pte John Cunningham, of the 12th East Yorkshires, accompanied a section of men up a communication trench and met with heavy resistance, leaving him as the only unscathed member of the party. Collecting all the ammunition he could from the dead and wounded, he went on alone and bombed the enemy until his supply was exhausted, whereupon he went back for more supplies and repeated his heroics, clearing the trench. Cunningham was awarded a Victoria Cross for his actions. A German counter-attack soon afterwards meant that 2nd Lt Morgan's body was not found until the following March when the enemy had already evacuated the hamlet. Held in reserve on the morning of 1 July, the 12th East Yorkshire Regiment had little idea of the day's progress, but their subsequent involvement in the Somme battles were as bloody as most in the line. 2nd Lt Morgan fell during one of the last major engagements of the offensive, crossing ground which was still covered by the bodies of soldiers who had made the first attempt back on the first day of July. Over four months later the British front line had barely moved.

The 92nd and 94th Companies of the Machine Gun Corps were attached to various regiments of the corresponding Brigades in the 31st Division on 1 July. At 7.50 a.m. the 92nd MGC received orders to move eight of its machine-guns forward into a position where a German counter-strike was feared. This time coincides exactly with that quoted by the Accrington Pals' War Diary as to when the enemy fire lessened in its intensity, indicating that most of the infantry had already fallen. The MGC account continues, '2nd Lt E.B. White, who was in charge of four of these guns, was killed by a rifle bullet.' At 4.00 p.m., another weapon and its crew were urgently requested '…to stop enemy who were observed to be bayoneting and robbing our wounded. The result was successful.'[11]

Second Lieutenant Edward Beadon White was born at St Paul's in Bristol during December 1879, the son of John, and the family later lived at the Ship Inn on the city's Deanery Road. Serving with the North Somerset Yeomanry for many years, E.B. White married Jeannie in 1912, and the couple's daughter, Nina, was born in February 1916. Living in Glasgow at the outbreak of war, he was working as a surveyor for HM Customs and Excise when he received his mobilisation papers on 5 August 1914, returning to Bath as a Regimental Quarter Master Sergeant to serve with his old unit. Crossing to France in November, he was discharged to a commission in September 1915, having connections with the 11th Yorkshire Regiment before becoming a Machine Gun Officer early in 1916.

2nd Lt A.M. Herapath, Yorks & Lancasters attached MGC. He was educated at Dean Close School in Cheltenham and fell on 1 July 1916.

The Officer Commanding the 92nd MGC confirmed that 2nd Lt White – whose loss was reported in the *Western Daily Press* – had 'died of wounds' on 1 July, and the latter's widow was sent a telegram to this effect one week later. Originally buried in an isolated graveyard to the south of Hebuterne, his remains were reinterred at Euston Road Cemetery, Colincamps (V.G.7), during 1919 (close by is the headstone of 2nd Lt Beacall of the Accrington Pals). His father was living in Coronation Road, Southville, by 1916, whilst his uncle, Mr Wood, was the one-time owner of the Full Moon Hotel in Bristol's North Street.

Four officers and nine gun teams of the 94th MGC were assigned to the various assault battalions during the last days of June, and although details of their endeavours are not given, the War Diary reveals that from the total of sixty-seven men who went into action on 1 July, only one officer and twenty-two ORs returned uninjured. One of the former was suffering from shock, another did not answer the roll call and two were wounded, whereas five soldiers in the ranks had lost their lives, nineteen were incapacitated, and a further seventeen were unaccounted for.

The officer whose whereabouts was unknown is almost certainly Second Lieutenant Alfred Maltravers Herapath, who for many months was declared to be 'missing believed killed.' Born in Dublin during 1887, he was the son of Edwin – a Captain in the 19th Regiment (the Yorkshire Regiment, or 'Green Howards') – and Caroline, and a nephew of the future Major Herapath, who was commanding the Severn Bridge Guard in 1916. Educated at Dean Close School in Cheltenham, A.M. Herapath enlisted into the ranks of the Royal Fusiliers when war was declared and later obtained a commission with the York and Lancaster Regiment.

Last seen going into battle on 1 July, his details were circulated amongst German POW camps, but no positive clues as to his fate were forthcoming. The CO of the 94th MGC later confirmed that he had seen 2nd Lt Herapath fall injured, adding: '…just afterwards, a shell exploded close to this officer and when the fumes, etc., had cleared, nothing could be seen of him.'[12] In January 1917 it was concluded that the twenty-eight-year-old must be dead, as '…no further information regarding him has been received.'[13] His father conceded, 'There seems no room to doubt that my son was instantaneously killed by a shell as reported.'[14] The body was buried at John Copse – one of the front line trenches held by the left flank of the 12th York and Lancasters on 1 July – but it was another to be relocated to the Euston Road Cemetery (IV.5.10) after the conflict. The officer's brother, Norman, fell at Arras in April 1917 whilst serving with the 1st Somerset Light Infantry.

The savage cost of the loss of so many 'Pals' is starkly illustrated in the fate of some family members in the 31st Division. Frank and William Gunstone were brothers who served in the 12th York and Lancaster Regiment alongside Cpl Watkins, MM. Both fell on 1 July, as did three Barnsley siblings – Charles, Fred and Ernest Walker – fighting with two different battalions of the York and Lancasters. The camaraderie, pride in their background and sense of togetherness engendered by the 'Pals' came at a huge price. Yet there were also tales of an unyielding sense of duty, personified by the gallantry of Reginald Battersby, who, still weeks short of his fifteenth birthday, added five years to his real age and joined the ranks of the Manchesters. With the help of references supplied by his former headmaster, as well as the local Lord Mayor, the teenager received an officer's commission and was eventually posted to the Accrington Pals. On 1 July 1916 the boy who was only as old as the century itself led a platoon 'over the top' at Serre, sustaining gun-shot wounds in the attack. Following his recuperation, he returned to the Front and lost a leg as the result of an explosion, yet he remained in uniform until beyond the Armistice. In later life he became a clergyman in Wiltshire and was a key figure in his village's Home Guard during the Second World War.

15

48TH (SOUTH MIDLAND) DIVISION

The 48th Division held the northern most sector of the Fourth Army Front, with the 31st Division on their right flank, and the Third Army's 56th (London) Division to the left. Two battalions – the 6th and 8th Royal Warwickshires – had been sent south to join the 4th Division's ultimately disastrous attack, but for the units which remained behind, including several of the Glosters, no orders had been issued to advance along with the rest of the offensive at 7.30 a.m. Once this was realised by the German defenders immediately opposite they were able to assist in repelling the 31st and 56th Divisions on either side, so it is little wonder that the Accrington Pals and the Sheffield Battalion of the former suffered so heavily. The 1st Gloucestershire Battery (3/1st South Midland Brigade), which recorded the first casualty mentioned in this text back on 24 June (see Chapter Two), revealed in its War Diary on 1 July:

> …until 12 noon, covered left flank of 31st Division. 18 pounders fired 2,000 [rounds] per battery. 4.5" howitzers – 1,500 rounds per battery…During the days of bombardment and day of assault the Brigade's casualties were 7 O.R. killed and 9 O.R. wounded.[1]

On 1 July Gunner F.A. Bosworth, of the 1/2nd South Midland Brigade, was awarded a Military Medal 'for good work in maintaining telephone cables during operations'.[2] This is almost certainly the same Cpl F.A. Bosworth who lost his life in Russia during June 1919 whilst serving with the 420th Brigade of the Royal Field Artillery. He had added a Bar to his MM in the intervening years, but his details are not included in the SDGW. The various Batteries of the South Midland Brigade lost a number of officers during the Somme campaign, including Major Geoffrey Browne from Clifton, Captain Arthur Stone – who worked for Bristol Tramways prior to the conflict – and Lt Edward Gedye, who also had links with Clifton. All three men are buried at Aveluy.

As an example of the progress of the Glosters on 1 July 1916, the 5th Battalion's War Diary indicates '…artillery continuous on front'.[3] The following day it received orders to attack three lines of German trenches, although this operation was cancelled in the early hours of 3 July. (The 5th had strong links with Gloucester, continuing up until its disbandment during the 1960s.) The 1/6th Glosters – stationed at Bristol's St Michael Hill in August 1914 – were to be involved in the same attack, only to be withdrawn '…just as we were forming up'.[4] (On the 6th, 'B' Company *did* carry out a raid, with the password 'Old Market' issued for their return, which occurred after being driven back by bombs.) The 1/4th Glosters – a City of Bristol Territorial Battalion based in Clifton when war broke out – had been on the Western Front since March of 1915. They were also in reserve to the south of Sailly on the first day of the Somme campaign when an 8in shell came over in the morning, landing amongst the 'transport'. One man was killed, two wounded, and six horses were '…put out of action'.[5]

In the SDGW, the dead soldier is listed as Pte William James Holcoop (No.2136), a native of St Mark's in Bristol who enlisted in his home city. This individual appears in the CWGC as Pte 'Hulcoop', the husband of H. Hulcoop, who was living at Penfield Street (now Penfield Road), off Mina Road in North Bristol by the 1920s. W.J. Hulcoop was a sixteen-year-old 'Porter (Cotton Works)' in 1901, residing at Church Street in the St Mark's Parish of Easton with his parents – William (forty-six), a 'Stone Mason's Labourer', and Mary Ann (forty-seven) – plus three younger siblings, all of whom were natives of 'Bristol, Gloucestershire'. The body of Pte Hulcoop was interred at the Couin British Cemetery (I.B.13), a burial ground which had been created by Field Ambulances of the 48th Division the previous May. There are five Glosters buried here amongst the 401 graves. (Close by, at Couin Chateau, was the Divisional HQ.)

On the very same day the latest edition of the popular *Fifth Gloucester Gazette* was distributed amongst its readers, and within its eagerly awaited pages was a mixture of humour, progress reports on the war, as well as – inevitably – obituaries detailing the losses of familiar faces in the ranks. By the end of July, the 48th Division had been sent into action at Pozieres, with the Glosters distinguishing themselves admirably. The poet F.W. Harvey, who received a DCM whilst serving with the 5th Glosters in the First World War, was a regular contributor to the *Gazette*, and some of his most famous works were read first in the Somme trenches. On a more light-hearted note, the following anonymously penned text appeared in the next publication:

CORPS SHIPPING INTELLIGENCE FROM LLOYDS, JULY 1916:

S.S. BACK BADGE – due August, 1914
S.S. LEAVE – service practically suspended
S.S. REST – all hope abandoned

EXCHANGE AND MART:

German Dug-outs at BAPAUME. Vacant shortly. Rent Free'

Returning to their most pressing duties, reference was made to men from Gloucestershire who were with different units. Of the 1 July assault the endeavours of the 6th and 8th Royal Warwickshires received a salutary mention, as did the grim news of the death of Brig.-Gen. Prowse, DSO, who was said to have died whilst attempting to capture an enemy machine-gun. This is not corroborated in other reports, even though several sources indicate he *was* felled by M.G. bullets. Soldiers of the 5th Glosters were reminded of 'Prowse Point' (now a Commonwealth Cemetery), which was well known to them following their stint at Ypres the previous year, and expressions of sorrow at the senior officer's demise were put forward.

At its height 1,500 copies of the *Gazette* were printed, and it remained an integral part of the battalion's morale until 1919, when the survivors of the 5th came home.

16

56TH (LONDON) DIVISION

The line at Gommecourt, to the north of Serre, 'bulged' towards the British trenches, and was a heavily fortified section as a result of its exposed position. Now part of the Third Army's sector, the 56th Division occupied the right flank, whilst the 46th (North Midland) Division was to their left, the latter was the furthest away from the river Somme amongst the 1 July assaulting infantry. There was a mile-long gap between the 56th and 48th Divisions where no advance was sanctioned, and the consequences of this have already been explained in the previous chapter. Likewise, beyond the 46th Division the limit of the offensive had been drawn, so these two Divisions were effectively isolated, fighting their own battle within a battle which was originally designed as a 'diversion' to the main attack centred around Albert. The salient itself had been a constant nuisance to the British since they arrived in the area, so the plan had two distinct aims: over-run the defences whilst at the same time prevent the Germans from sending reserves to the south, where the strategic breakthrough was intended.

The target of the 56th Division, therefore, was the 'underbelly' of Gommecourt, moving forward from Hebuterne in roughly a south-west/north-east direction to storm the enemy trenches and link up with the 46th Division. They were supposed to join them from a north-westward direction around Foncquevillers to catch the defenders in a 'pincer' movement *behind* the fortress. Gen. Sir Edmund Allenby was the commander of the Third Army, and he had his reservations about the policies at Gommecourt. He was concerned about the concentration of fire his troops would have to overcome from the relatively unhindered flanks, as well as the previously issued order that every preparation must be of the highest profile, leaving the defenders in no doubt that their man-power was most definitely needed here and nowhere else. In addition, the width of the stretch of No Man's Land which opposed the 56th Division was close to 800 yards, and the problems of crossing it under heavy fire were addressed prior to 1 July when it was decided to dig a new trench, halfway across from where the attack would be launched. This delicate operation, in full view of the Germans, was carried out with great skill over three nights, and had the crucial benefit of a communication sap leading back to the original forward positions – although it was proof to the watching enemy that action was imminent.

The southern end of the Third Army was held by the 14th Battalion of the London Regiment, better known as the London Scottish, which had been on the Western Front since September 1914. Marched into the trenches by pipers, the Territorial unit wore 'Hodden Grey' kilts, which were the same colour as the hunting coat of their founder, Lord Elcho, but it was not a tartan as the 14th was raised by Scots 'in exile'. Although they provided good camouflage, the kilts themselves tended to snag on barbed wire, became waterlogged in wet weather, the hems froze and cut the legs of the wearer, mustard gas stuck to bare flesh and the pleats harboured numerous lice. However, the distinctive uniform was worn with pride, and the Germans referred to Scottish soldiers as 'ladies from hell'.

At 7.28 a.m. on 1 July, Companies of the London Scottish moved onto the tapes which marked their path through the wire, and advanced promptly to time, sweeping across No Man's Land in spite of a British smoke barrage which actually hindered the progress of the infantry. All of the enemy lines were taken within a short space of time, but as early as 10 a.m. grenades were urgently required, and by mid-afternoon the War Diary notes that the intensity of high explosive fire from the German artillery had increased. At 4.00 p.m., Captain Sparks sent a message back telling his superiors that all bombs had been expended, forcing a withdrawal of the survivors. Of the twenty-three officers and 811 men in the ranks who were on active service, only nine officers and 236 other ranks answered the next roll call. Some had been held back, yet it was an all too familiar statistic and even the Medical Staff suffered casualties as they tended to the wounded.

Scottish-born Pte Herbert Muir Murdoch (No. 5612) had fallen at the age of thirty. Enlisting in the capital, his residence in the SDGW is given as 'Bristol', and the CWGC reveals that he was the son of George J., whilst his widow's name was Florence. She later lived at Richmond Terrace in Clifton and her husband lies buried at the Gommecourt British Cemetery No. 2 (II.D.17), Hebuterne, a post-war amalgamation of smaller burial grounds now situated in the old No Man's Land across which the Division attacked. (The soldier is also remembered on the St Paul's Church War Memorial in Clifton.)

Following behind, the Queen Victoria's Rifles (1/9th London Regiment) and the Queen's Westminster Rifles (1/16th Battalion) also made good initial progress, even though the War Diary concedes that the German defences were far more strongly held than had been expected. The Diary noted that the deep dug-outs which were captured appeared to have been practically undamaged by the British artillery bombardment. The wire was also virtually uncut, causing the Londoners to '…file in close order through the gaps',[1] and losses began to mount. The official account continues:

> …as no officer who got as far as this has returned, and only one Sergeant, it is extremely difficult to know in detail what happened, and still more difficult because no communication across No Man's Land was [ever] able to be established.[2]

With all Company Commanders dead, the momentum was kept up by junior officers who led the remainder of their platoons on bombing raids along the trenches until supplies dried up. 2nd Lt J.A. Horne was singled out for his superb courage, organising and directing operations before he was incapacitated, whilst Second Lieutenants Bouill and Upton were, at one stage, 'the only officers left fighting'. Holding on into the evening, Bouill was later reported to be 'wounded and missing', whereas Upton was the last to leave the German lines, losing his life on the parapet of the British trench just as he reached apparent safety. 2nd Lt Engall had earlier manned a machine-gun single-handedly until he was shot dead. 2nd Lt Horne was later commended:

> I desire to bring to notice the most gallant conduct of 2nd Lt J.A. HORNE, who by his example and leading inspired and helped all who came within his reach. I have every reason to believe that his gallantry and leading merit a recommendation for the Victoria Cross. I deeply regret to fear that there is practically no chance of [him] having survived as he was seen to be wounded very severely.[3]

2nd Lt Horne, from Kensington, did not receive a posthumous medal of any description, and his comrades only numbered 198 the following day when the battalion marched to Bayencourt. Under the headline 'AMONG THE MISSING', the *Gloucester Citizen* newspaper revealed shortly afterwards:

> Mrs A.W. Williams, late of Hawksley, Dean's Way, Gloucester, has received official intimation that her son, Arthur Victor, of the Queen's Westminster Rifles, is missing after the action on 1 July. He joined on August 3rd, 1914, and went to France on 14 February 1915.

Rifleman Williams (No.2179) was a nineteen-year-old native of Gloucester (attending the local King's School), and enlisted in Westminster from his residence in nearby Gower Street. His parents, Arthur – who served in the Army Service Corps during the war – and Georgina, were living in Wiltshire by the 1920s. (Thiepval 13C.)

The same scenario awaited the 5th (City of London) Battalion – the London Rifle Brigade – as they began to consolidate their swiftly made gains in the enemy trenches. 2nd Lt R.E. Petley and his small group of men at first believed they were part of a larger British contingent, but when German bombers and snipers began harassing their position it soon became clear that the situation was untenable. At 4.00 p.m., having erected desperate barricades, Petley sent a message back to HQ: '…I [want] more bombs. Quite out of touch to right and left…It is quite absurd to lay here at night as we are.'[4] Given permission to withdraw, the wounded were reluctantly left behind, and a mere handful managed to regain their own lines.

Sgt Frost, of 'A' Company, recalled that around 8.00 p.m. the Germans finally took the upper hand and drove the British out of their bolt-holes:

> There was no hope of holding on any longer and our party of 'A' Co. joined in the rush for the open…What a pity we could not get up some supports. We could easily have cleared the PARK [the 'point' of the salient which jutted out into No Man's Land] I am sure…I was hit in right side of face when leaving the German trench and lost much blood. My body is much bruised from concussion earlier in the day.[5]

An obituary in the *Wilts & Glos Standard* informed its readers that Rifleman Horace Edgar Bishop (No.2472), aged thirty, the youngest son of Francis William and Jane Bishop, had been killed in action on 1 July. The SDGW does not give a place of birth for the soldier, but it does indicate that he enlisted in London from his home in Wimbledon.

In his future narrative, 2nd Lt Petley would note:

> It was really magnificent the way every man, cool and collected, strolled out through quite a stiff barrage…The smoke lifted for a few seconds when we were out….. I shouted an order and they shook out as if they were on Wimbledon Common.[6]

Further research in the 1901 Census revealed that fifteen-year-old Horace Edgar Bishop, who had been born in Cirencester, was living with his parents at Horton House in the town's Sheep Street in this year. His father was a grocer, and there was also a commercial enterprise known as Bishop Brothers along these lines in Cricklade Street around the time of the First World War. Rifleman Bishop is another remembered at Thiepval (9D), and casualty figures for the London Rifle Brigade on 1 July topped 570.

The role of the Pioneer Battalion for the 56th Division was filled by the 1/5th Cheshire Regiment, which went over in support of the Queen Victoria's Rifles (QVR) and the Westminsters (QWR). Some of its men became pinned down in the forward positions alongside the two aforementioned units, assisting them in blocking the ends of the newly-occupied trenches in order to resist enemy counter-attacks. In several eyewitness accounts the name of 2nd Lt Arthur is mentioned, and here was an example of another unrecognised act of outstanding self-sacrifice. An officer of the 1/5th Cheshires, he nonetheless took command of a group of QWR bombers and proceeded to engage himself in the more pressing task of resisting the German threat all-round. When all of the grenades were expended, 2nd Lt Arthur ordered his men to withdraw, whereupon he remained behind to allow his comrades to escape. After a short fight, the gallant Yorkshireman was killed.

Pte Norman Randolph Perry (No.2430) also fell. Born in Bristol, he enlisted in Chester under an alias, and his real name was 'Broadribb'. The CWGC indicates that he was the son of William and Eliza (of Chester), and although the seven-year-old future soldier was living in Somerset by 1901, his birthplace is given as 'Bristol, Gloucester'. He is commemorated at Thiepval (3C & 4A).

Gunner William James (No. 19964), of the 56th Divisional Ammunition Column, is the final fatality in this chapter. Born in Cheltenham, he joined up in Newport, Monmouthshire, and lies buried in the Hebuterne Military Cemetery (IV.M. 55). His position was most likely hit by an enemy shell. There are seven 'possibles' in the 1901 Census, and in the absence of an age or family references in the CWGC, it is once again unwise to speculate as to the exact identity of the casualty.

A small group of soldiers from the 56th Division *did* reach the rear of Gommecourt village, but they had no hope of linking up with the 46th Division even if they were able to consolidate their position. 2nd Lt Arthur, therefore, was one of the few men in either Division to reach this far at all. 2nd Lt Petley, of the London Rifle Brigade, finally realised in the late afternoon that the situation was hopeless:

> Sgt ROBINSON brings me verbal <u>orders</u> to withdraw which of course we reluctantly must obey. Sgt Robinson is bringing all the men down to you [Capt. De Cologan] and Sgt AUSTIN and I are trying to get Sgt Olorenshaw. Should like some hot dinner when we get back.[7]

46TH (NORTH MIDLAND) AND 37TH DIVISIONS

The 37th Division – not involved in the advance on 1 July – has already featured in this text, when the 13th King's Royal Rifle Corps took part in a significant raid on enemy lines during the early hours of 29 June, leading to the death of T/Major Charles Simonds. (See Chapter Two.) Brevet Colonel C.S. Collison, DSO, of the 11th Royal Warwicks, later recorded his own observations of the infantry assault on the first day:

> At 6.30 a.m. our artillery opened an intense bombardment of the German positions about Gommecourt. At 7.23 a.m. smoke was discharged along the fronts of the 37th, 46th and 56th Divisions, and at 7.30 a.m. (zero hour) the two latter Divisions attacked from the N. and S. Up to midnight no really accurate record of the results of these actions is obtainable; but the advance of a Brigade of the 46th Division was stopped, and renewed at 3.30 p.m. I watched this phase from the Divisional line, but was unable to see any progress, though there was some apparently. The attack of the 56th Division (hidden from us by the bend of Gommecourt Wood) is reported to have been satisfactory – also unsatisfactory. Very heavy fighting was going on here [until] about 10 p.m. At 1 a.m. (2 July) information was received that the 46th Division was to be withdrawn to its original line, after attempting to extricate two battalions which had not been located since the commencement of the attack.[1]

The above account was written in the senior officer's own personal diary. He went on:

> …I only record it as an example of the confused and scanty nature of the information that reaches those whose knowledge of battles is usually confined to what takes place in their immediate neighbourhood. In this case the event was the advance of the left brigade of the 46th Division [the 139th Brigade, containing four battalions of the Sherwood Foresters], but the clouds of smoke from our trenches and from those of the attacking troops, combined with the vapour and dust from the bursting shells, made even this movement very hard to follow. It was, however, apparent to us that the smoke cloud put up at 3.30 p.m. to cover a renewal of the attack on the left was ineffective. Probably it was found impossible to arrange it effectively in the stress of battle; moreover what wind there was, was not then in the right direction. It had been a day of intense heat and of strenuous fighting against a resolute resistance, and in this part of the field, at any rate, the action seemed to die out during the afternoon.[2]

The smoke barrage mentioned by Bt.-Col Collison proved to be a severe handicap to the assaulting troops, and a number even lost their way in the initial stages. Moreover, the wet weather of the previous week had rendered this particular sector a quagmire of water-filled shell holes and slippery mud, making progress extremely difficult, and this was on top of a heavy enemy bombardment which had continued all through the night of 30 June/1 July, causing many casualties.

Almost immediately opposite the village of Fonquevillers, the 6th North Staffordshires – part of the 137th Brigade – attacked Gommecourt Wood, leaving their trenches which were between two and three feet deep in water. Under extreme fire and suffering heavy losses, few reached the German wire, which was found to be largely uncut, and the confusion was further exacerbated by the smoke which obscured the minimal gaps in the entanglements, rendering the attack hopeless. According to the War Diary eight officers were dead, four were missing and six were wounded, whilst thirty-four men in the ranks had been killed, 122 unaccounted for and 170 incapacitated (The SDGW puts the final figure of OR fatalities at 162). Lt Horace Birchall Jones, who had written to his family on the eve of battle, 'I go in with every confidence, but realising that I may fall, I cannot do so without expressing my gratitude to you all', did not return. A Major of the battalion informed the Lieutenant's parents:

> It is with feelings of great sorrow that I have to write to you with news about your son. From statements of men who saw him I fear there can be little doubt he died fighting hard on 1 July. He is missing, so there is a chance he is wounded and a prisoner, but I can hold out little hope. Please accept the deepest sympathy of us all with you in your loss. Your son was a wonderfully good soldier who did not know what fear was, and his loss is a heavy blow to the regiment. He was so popular with everybody, always cheery and in good spirits. Many of his comrades have, alas, gone with him.[3]

A keen boxer, swimmer and motorcyclist, H.B. Jones attended Wycliffe College in Stonehouse between 1905 and 1907, joining the 1st Birmingham City Battalion (14th Royal Warwickshires) before receiving his commission with the North Staffordshires. A native of Solihull, he is commemorated at Thiepval (14B & 14C).

The fate of the 1/7th Sherwood Foresters (Notts and Derby Regiment) had been partially witnessed by Bt.-Col Collison, DSO, from his position on the left flank of the attack. Through the acrid smoke, the War Diary estimated that only around twelve men reached as far as the German second line before being driven back to a precarious position held by a slightly larger group, although *they* in turn were unable to put up much of a fight due to their rifles '…in some cases being muddy, and having no supply of bombs'.[4] The lack of a man-made screen to cover the supporting waves now had an adverse effect, as the German machine-gunners soon picked them off, and their artillery opened up with devastating accuracy. A party was assembled at 3.30 p.m. in order to transport boxes of bombs across No Man's Land, but in the event this did not occur. Isolated and fired upon by more and more reinforcements who had emerged from their dug-outs, the beleaguered garrison stranded in enemy territory endured a torturous day, with only a handful returning to safety by nightfall. Nineteen officers and 424 men were classed as casualties, including the CO, Lt-Col L.A. Hind – 'missing believed killed', and his Adjutant, Capt. R.M. Gotch – 'missing believed wounded.' (Both men were in fact dead, as was the Commanding Officer of the 1/5th Sherwood Foresters. Their counterparts from the 1/5th and 1/6th North Staffordshires both lost their lives on 1 July.)

Listed by name in the 1/7th Sherwood Foresters' War Diary is:

> Lieut. J. MACPHERSON, O.C. B. Co., Killed.[5]

'B' Company was one of the first to go over the top, led by Lt John MacPherson, another Old Boy of Cheltenham College (1905–09), whose Register gives his rank as 'Captain'. The son of Alexander and Mary, he was a Private in the 6th Royal Fusiliers before becoming an officer in the Notts and Derbys. Born in January 1891, he was twenty-five when he died, and is remembered at Thiepval (10C, 10D & 11A).

Ruins in Foncquevillers. The village was the base for the 46th (North Midland) Division prior to its 1 July 1916 attack on Gommecourt.

In the ranks, Pte John Smith (No.266785) was also amongst the dead. Born at 'Eastville, Glos.' (Bristol), he enlisted in Nottingham from his Hartlepool home. His grave is located at the Gommecourt Wood New Cemetery (II.E.24), Foncquevillers, suggesting that he fell close to the British lines. Another burial ground situated in the old No Man's Land, 465 of the 749 interments are unidentified. Most of the men to be found here fell on 1 July.

The War Diary for the 46th Company of the Machine Gun Corps indicates on this date that:

> A large number of rounds fired behind enemy lines caused retaliation, in the course of which an emplacement and dug-out [were] blown in. One O.R. was killed and one wounded.[6]

The dead soldier was Pte Alfred William Ernest Willey (No.26885), born in Westbury-on-Trym and joining up in Bristol. His service record[7] reveals that his home address was at the Prince of Wales Cottages, Stoke Lane, Westbury when he enlisted in November 1915 at the age of twenty-two years and eleven months. His former occupation was that of a 'gardener', and he originally served in the ranks of the 16th Glosters before transferring to the MGC in March 1916, whereupon he was attached to the 46th Company 'in the field' on 22 June that year. He was one of ten siblings, and his father, James, had passed away by the time of the First World War, whereas his mother, Annie, was living on the Southmead Road. Aged twenty-three when he died, Pte Willey is buried at the Foncquevillers Military Cemetery (I.L.22).

By coincidence, the 46th Divisional Ammunition Column – like its counterpart in the 56th Division – also recorded a casualty with links to Gloucestershire and North Bristol. Twenty-three-year-old Lt Trevor Arthur Manning Davies, who attended Clifton College between 1909 and 1912, was originally reported 'missing' on 1 July before it was later confirmed that he had died in action. The son of Arthur and Ada, his body now rests at the Gommecourt British Cemetery No.2. (II.H.26), Hebuterne.

Returning to the 37th Division, the 154th Field Company of the Royal Engineers had been stationed around Bienvillers during the build-up to the Somme Offensive, and the decision was made to transfer its HQ into chalk caves dug beneath the village church. However, when soldiers of the RE were joined by 250 infantrymen below ground, '…the air became so foul that all had to be taken out.'[8] Slit trenches were then hollowed out to shelter the men from enemy barrages and the 154th also accompanied patrols with the intention of blowing up German machine-gun emplacements, but none of these sorties was successful. The strength in June 1916 comprised seven officers, 202 in the ranks, one French interpreter, twenty horses and fifty-seven large mules, plus a small number of servicemen attached from other battalions.

On 1 July the War Diary of the 13th King's Royal Rifle Corps noted, 'Guns were heard in the distance from the very early hours, and news is expected at any moment of the progress made by our troops.'[9] Meanwhile, the 154th Field Company was standing by in Bienvillers at 6.30 a.m., minus its Mounted Section which was bivouacked at Pommiers, when two 5.9in shells landed amongst Numbers 3 and 4 Sections, killing fifteen and wounding a further seventeen. One of the dead was Sapper William Paxton (No.69902), who was born in Preston-on-Stour at a time when the Cotswold parish lay in Gloucestershire, whereas today it is situated just within the Warwickshire county boundary. In 1901 W. Paxton was aged nineteen and working as a 'wheelwright and carpenter', almost certainly for his sixty-six-year-old father William, who was in the same occupation. His mother was called Ellen, and both parents were local to Preston. The young man later moved to Stratford-upon-Avon, where he married Lily in November 1913, and the family grew with the arrival of William Henry in May 1914, plus Ethel May the following year. By the time of his daughter's birth in September of 1915, William Paxton had joined the army and his employers – G. Whately, Builders and Contractors of Rother Street – gave the following testimony: 'W. Paxton worked for us some months as a Joiner and Carpenter, and we always found him a good, efficient and industrious work-man.' The new recruit's service record[10] also noted that he was aged thirty-three years and 350 days (in March 1915), was 5ft 10in in height, and his home address was at Arthur Road, Stratford. Originally with the 82nd Field Company, RE (part of the 19th Western Division, which included the 8th Glosters), he transferred to the 154th Field Co. prior to the Somme campaign.

The *Stratford Herald* revealed on 7 July that:

> News has been received of the death of Sapper W. Paxton, RE, who was killed in action by a shell on the 1st of this month when he was in France. In a letter to his widow the officer in charge of his section describes him as a willing, hard-working man, always ready to do his bit. Paxton, who hailed from Preston-on-Stour, leaves a widow and two young children to mourn his loss.

Following her husband's death, Lily Paxton forwarded the couple's birth and marriage certificates to the Royal Engineers' Record Office, but she later became anxious that they had been 'mislaid'. She also enquired whether any letters or articles were found in the pockets of his uniform, as she desired them back, and although the official documents were eventually returned to her, there was no mention of any personal items relating to Sapper Paxton.

Apparently the only brother to five older sisters, William Paxton (thirty-five) lies interred at the Bienvillers Military Cemetery (VIII.B.6). By the 1920s his widow (who received her husband's posthumous medals in 1921) was living in Percy Street, Stratford – close to their marital home – and the soldier is also commemorated on the town's War Memorial. His elderly parents remained in Preston-on-Stour, which became part of Warwickshire in 1931.

By the end of the day on 1 July, the Gommecourt salient was still very much in German hands. The attack was immediately closed down, and Bt.-Col Collison, DSO, noted:

> Unusual quiet marked the 2nd July in this Sector, and only the thunderous rumblings and mutterings to the South indicated that the struggle was still in progress in the region of Albert, and on the French front. The 46th and 56th Divisions had now withdrawn to positions they occupied before their advance, and an uncanny silence succeeded to the noise and turmoil of the last week.[11]

18

19TH (WESTERN) DIVISION

This Division was in reserve at Albert on 1 July, but it was soon to be involved in the attack on La Boisselle during the night of 2/3 July. The 57th Brigade comprised the 10th Royal Warwickshires, 10th Worcesters, 8th Glosters and 8th North Staffordshires. The CO of the 8th Glosters – Lt-Col A Carton de Wiart – was awarded a Victoria Cross for his part in assuming command at a critical stage of the eventually successful assault on the village through a devastating hail of fire. Afterwards, he dedicated the medal to his men, claiming '…each has done as much as I.'[1] However, he would later express his dismay at the omission of the 8th Glosters' part in the advance by the Official History of the Somme battles, written by the War Office beyond the Armistice. (Nearly all of the officers were either killed or wounded, with 84 ORs dead.) Inevitably, the 8th Battalion contained a high proportion of men from Gloucestershire and North Bristol, with the 10th Worcesters also registering a percentage of soldiers from its neighbouring county to the south. (La Boisselle, and the nearby hamlet of Ovillers, were both 'adopted' by the City of Gloucester during the 1920s, symbolising the strong link between that particular sector of the Somme and the number of men from the Glosters who fell in its liberation and subsequent defence.)

On 1 July, the War Diary for the 9th Welch Regiment – part of the 58th Brigade – reveals that its position was on the Albert-Bapaume Road, but that '…no casualties reported.'[2] However, the SDGW lists that eight men in the ranks of the 9th Welch lost their lives on the first day of the Somme campaign, two of whom had connections relevant to this book. Pte Herbert Worsley Conway (No.1655) was born in Wiltshire, but by 1901 he and his family had moved to Bristol. He was aged four by this time, and would have been either nineteen or twenty when he fell in 1916. Enlisting in Pontypridd, he is commemorated at Thiepval (7A & 10A), and his parents – Robert and Eliza – were living at Warwick Avenue, Eastville, by the 1920s. Pte David Rosenbloom (No.19263) was also aged four in 1901, a native of Stepney in the East End of London, and resided with his family at Mile End Old Town. He joined up in Cardiff, although the SDGW does not reveal his place of residence, whereas the CWGC indicates his mother, Leah, gave her address as 'St James' Churchyard, Bristol' when the Debt of Honour Register was compiled. (Thiepval 7A & 10A.)

The dates of death of these eight men may be an error, unless they were attached to another battalion on the front line at the time. The most likely explanation for the loss of eight soldiers in reserve would be the explosion of a shell, but this is not mentioned in the War Diary. One of the octet is buried at the Cerisy-Gailly French National Cemetery, to the south-west of Albert, and the Commonwealth section here was created when bodies of Somme casualties were brought in after the conflict. Another lies buried in the A.I.F. Burial Ground at Flers – a village on the Somme battlefield which was not captured until September 1916. (Flers is famous for seeing the first use of tanks during the First World War.) The 9th Welch itself lost three men when La Boisselle was taken, and the total number of deaths in their ranks during July 1916 was sixty-seven, which, in comparison with other regiments, was fairly low. In the absence of any definitive evidence as to the fate of the eight soldiers listed as dying on 1 July, it is pure speculation whether the date is accurate or not, but the duo with Bristol links (the fact they are both remembered at Thiepval also suggests they may have been assault troops) are included because of the official records.

So ended the most costly day in the long history of the British Army. Yet this was only the beginning of an offensive which would last until November, and a month before a halt was called to the fighting, the *Stroud News* reported:

> The Somme Pictures proved to be the greatest cinema attraction ever presented to the public of the Stroud district, and we congratulate the management of the Empire Theatre on securing the wonderful film for its patrons. The pictures gave us some little conception of the tremendous amount of energy expended in this one theatre of war. They gave us, too, some faint inkling of the immense and tragic waste of war; the blasted land, the material wreckage, the broken men, and the irrecoverable lives. Their effect was saddening and at the same time inspiring. The half-demented German prisoners aroused sentiments not of derision but of pity. But the dominant impression was that of the buoyancy of our own incomparable men. Surely in all the tragic history of war a more light-hearted, high-spirited and fearless army has never marched into the zone of death and pain? The incalculable debt we owe to these heroes can never be liquidated: for all time the race will be their debtor. No words could record so convincingly…the splendid spirit of Britain's fighting men.

The *Gloucestershire Echo* had commented in mid-July:

> In a general way our success these past few days amounts to a magnificent artillery victory. Infantry say the shells burst in front of them, and they had nothing to do but march into some of the trenches we occupied with rifles slung. The proportion of German dead in some trenches was 80 per cent of the defenders. A German lieutenant who was taken prisoner with his company said that he had not used his machine gun. He wanted to save his men for Germany so that she might be able to begin another war in 50 years time.

The officer's prediction came true in less than half that time.

Above: Lochnagar Crater was visited by a party from Gloucestershire in 1936. The mine was blown at 7.28 a.m. on 1 July 1916, and the chalk sides of the crater were still prominent twenty years later. The village of La Boiselle – the target of the 34th Division on 1 July – is in the distance. Note the lack of trees. Both Ovillers and La Boiselle were 'adopted' by the City of Gloucester due to the area's strong links with the Glosters' Somme battalions.

Right: The large cross marks the original grave of Capt. L. W. Crouch (Oxford and Buckinghamshire. LI) at Ovillers La Boisselle. In reserve near Serre with the 48th (South Midland) Division on 1 July 1916, the Oxford and Buckinghamshire moved a few miles to the south three weeks later (along with the Glosters), where the officer lost his life in action.

Opposite: After the war, many ex-servicemen returned to the battlefields to re-discover where they had fought and lost comrades. The scene is labelled 'The Road Through Ovillers' and was taken in 1920. Ovillers was attacked by the 8th Division on 1 July 1916.

19

THE LOSSES

The initial casualty returns, taken as the combat battalions were withdrawn after the opening day's fighting, totalled nearly 62,000 men, with 36,000 wounded and a further 17,700 'missing'. The individuals of the latter category proved the most difficult to track down, and the task of doing so was gargantuan in the extreme. To be posted 'missing' could mean a soldier had been taken prisoner, fallen dead in action, survived the attack before returning with a different battalion than his own, or received injuries and was still out on the battlefield. With the assistance of countless eyewitness statements – some of which are included in this text – it took an official historian six months to collate, dissect and assimilate the records of each infantry unit which took part in the attack before coming up with a final figure for the dead, wounded and unaccounted for on 1 July 1916. The total reached was 57,470 servicemen. The total of those killed, or who died of their wounds as a result of the first day, rose to beyond 19,000, with the figure for the missing being reduced to just over 2,000, leaving those injured at roughly the same number as before. Bearing in mind that approximately 120,000 troops were sent into action on 1 July, it was therefore almost a straight 50/50 chance of being hit for those involved.

The fate of the 2,000 does not take too much imagination. These were the men who were blown to pieces by artillery fire, or last seen deep in enemy territory, pressing on towards certain death or capture. Casualty rates amongst the officers was inevitably high. Distinctively dressed, often carrying a revolver, and sometimes even a sword or just a walking stick, they advanced at the head of their men to become prime targets, with almost 2,500 lying dead or injured by nightfall. Only 585 of all ranks became prisoners of war – an extraordinarily small number considering the huge scale of the attack – yet it is indicative of just how ferocious the fighting became, both for those who were tasked with its success, as well as for the men who were so determined to repel it. The Germans had more men taken into captivity than their enemy, but overall, their losses were significantly smaller than the British, due in no small part to the devastating power of its machine-gun teams which wreaked such death and destruction upon the soldiers in khaki.

Only in the south of the line were there any territorial gains – at Montauban, Mametz and Fricourt – all of which had advanced the Allied line one mile further on. Yet elsewhere, the British were back where they started from, counting the cost of Divisional losses ranging from 2,000 to over 6,000. Some ill-fated battalions – such as the 10th West Yorkshires, the Tyneside Scottish and Irish, plus the Newfoundlanders – had been all but wiped out in a matter of minutes. The regions of the United Kingdom and Ireland were hit hard by the opening day. Yorkshire, Lancashire and the North-East of England suffered the most, along with Ulster, Scotland and London. Newspapers of the large industrial cities were crammed full of photographs depicting the dead and missing, but each and every county up and down the land lost a proportion of its men on 1 July 1916.

The scale of these figures was quite unprecedented. Even with the benefit of hindsight they astonish so it is hard to overestimate the impact at the time. British casualty rates in the two years of the Crimean War (1854–56) were nowhere near as high as for those of twenty-four hours of this one day during the First World War. Even later campaigns of the same conflict did not produce these staggering numbers over such a short space of time, although the Passchendaele Offensive of the following year, and the grim final battles of 1918, produced some horrendous overall losses in their own right.

To imagine 60,000 individuals out 'in the field' is difficult to comprehend, unless one equates the volume to a high-profile modern-day football or rugby match. The sixteen-mile front line, from Montauban in the south to Gommecourt in the north, produced the equivalent of two casualties every single yard. Statistics and analogies are all very well, but the slaughter is almost incomprehensible in mere black and white. So to return to the human aspect of this book, the strength of the camaraderie engendered by combat stress and pride in the regiment is personified in the fate of 2nd Lt Arthur James Maybrey, a Cheltenham-born officer of the 10th Glosters who had links with nearby Prinknash. Three weeks after the offensive began, 2nd Lt Maybrey led his men across No Man's Land on a night raid near Pozieres and was the only soldier to squeeze through the barbed wire into the German trenches. Forced back by hostile fire, his comrades lost sight of him, and he was not heard of again. Sgt Goulden, who was wounded in the operation, told the authorities, 'He was one of the finest officers England ever put into France. The men cried when we lost him.'[1]

20

THE VCs OF 1 JULY, AND THE PLIGHT OF THE WOUNDED

At the end of July 1916 one of the headlines in the *Bristol Times & Mirror* read, 'Unknown Heroes. Thousands of VCs Earned In A Month'. There were nine Victoria Crosses awarded for supreme courage on 1 and 2 July, and the exploits of these men – briefly detailed in relation to the wider text of this book – provides a snap-shot of recognition for those who were decorated for gallantry and for those whose extraordinary deeds never came to light.

At Fricourt, T/Major S.W. Loudon-Shand, of the 10th Green Howards, in the 21st Division, encouraged his men under heavy fire by climbing onto the parapet of the trench, in full view of the enemy, and was mortally wounded almost at once, yet he insisted on being propped up nearby in order to cheer his soldiers onwards. This was in the same sector as, amongst others, the 8th Somerset Light Infantry.

Sgt J.Y. Turnbull, 17th Highland Light Infantry, was one of a small group which captured an important enemy position near Authuille, in the 32nd Division part of the line. He then had to withstand sustained bombing attacks from the Germans, wiping out most of his comrades – along with those sent to replace them – several times. Virtually single-handed he maintained the post, and was shot dead by a sniper several hours later. His grave can be found at the Lonsdale Cemetery, close to the final resting place of Shirehampton-born L/Cpl Edgar May.

The 36th (Ulster) Division received four Victoria Crosses at Thiepval on the opening day. T/Capt. E.N.F. Bell, 9th Royal Inniskilling Fusiliers, took the initiative when an advance was faltering by moving forward and shooting the gunner of an enfilading machine-gun. On three further occasions, when the assault was held up, he went on alone and threw bombs amongst the enemy before he was killed in action rallying sections of men who had lost their officers. T/Lt. G. St G. S. Cather, 9th Royal Irish Rifles, spent five hours out in No Man's Land searching for, and tending to, the wounded, all while under heavy fire. The following day he repeated his mission of mercy, and lost his life in the process. Rifleman (later Sergeant) R. Quigg, 12th Royal Irish Rifles, went into combat with his platoon three times and was then told an officer was lying injured, exposed to enemy snipers. Quigg risked his life by bringing back no fewer than seven casualties, only stopping through sheer exhaustion. He survived the war and died in 1955. Pte W.F. McFadzean, 14th Royal Irish Rifles, was in a crowded trench prior to going over the top when a box of bombs which was being distributed amongst the men fell to the floor, dislodging two of the detonating pins. McFadzean immediately threw himself onto the grenades, smothering the blast but killing him instantly. His actions saved many lives.

Also near Thiepval, Cpl (later Captain) G. Sanders, 1/7th West Yorkshire Regiment, became isolated with a party of thirty men within enemy lines and impressed upon them that they had to hold out at all costs. Organising the defences, Cpl Sanders ensured that three counter-attacks were repelled, and the group was not relieved for thirty-six hours. Without food for the duration, their water had been given to the wounded on the first night. (Sanders passed away in 1950.) Two Companies of the 1/7th West Yorkshires – part of the 49th Division in reserve – were sent up in support of the Ulsters at Schwaben Redoubt.

Drummer (later Drum-Major) W.P. Ritchie, 2nd Seaforth Highlanders, stood on the parapet of his trench near 'Y' Ravine, south of Beaumont Hamel, under heavy machine-gun fire and bomb attacks to repeatedly sound the 'charge'. His display of courage, on his own initiative, stemmed the drift back of many British troops who had lost their officers. He died in 1965. Part of the 4th Division, the Seaforth Highlanders fought alongside the 1st Somerset Light Infantry.

At Foncquevillers, attached to the 1/5th Sherwood Foresters from the RAMC, Captain J.L. Green – despite being injured – rescued an officer caught on the German wire, dragged him into a shell-hole and dressed his wounds whilst bombs were being thrown at the duo. The Captain continued assisting the casualty back towards the British lines, but was killed before he reached safety. His remains were later interred at the Foncquevillers Military Cemetery, where Machine Gun Corps fatality Pte Alfred Willey, from Westbury-on-Trym, is also buried.

The retrieval of the wounded was a monumental task, and fraught with danger, as experienced by Capt. Green, Lt Cather, and many others. These accounts of the injured being bayoneted or robbed, and the men sent out to rescue them facing snipers' bullets, were not examples of British propaganda destined for the newspapers back home, for they were written down in highly confidential War Diaries which were never shown to journalists due to their obviously sensitive military content. The WD of the 4th Tyneside Scottish, which suffered dreadful carnage on 1 July, recorded:

> Our stretcher bearers were conspicuous by their daring in bringing in wounded men in daylight under fire. The dressing station and the trenches near were soon congested with casualties and only by continual and very exhausting work by Capt. J.W. Muirhead [our Medical Officer] and his staff were they able to gradually relieve this pressure which was not [lessened] until the following day.[1]

The 10th Lincolnshire Regiment (Grimsby Chums) told a similar story:

> Owing to continuous machine gun & rifle fire great difficulty was experienced in recovering the wounded many of whom lay out in No Man's Land for over 30 hours but through the constant exertions of all ranks during the nights of 1st & 2nd and 2nd & 3rd July as far as could be ascertained all wounded belonging to the battalion had been brought in before leaving the fighting area. Any attempts to do this during daylight was immediately met by heavy machine gun & rifle fire from the enemy's trenches and all our wounded when seen to move were at once fired on by German snipers.[2]

Even in the south of the line, where the injured lay on newly captured ground, the risks had not diminished. Lt-Col E.H. Trotter, DSO, the CO of the 18th King's Liverpool Regiment which had assisted in the taking of Montauban, ventured:

> The stretcher bearers whose ranks were thinned by casualties worked incessantly on the wounded of every battalion they came across. Many of our men and the wounded of the 90th Brigade remained on the field for 40 hours. The Medical Officer and every available officer went out to deal with them and marked their positions, and the 2nd Wiltshires, over-worked as they were, gave valuable help in clearing the race-course into our front trenches. I cannot help mentioning that I never heard a man of my battalion make a single complaint or request that he should be moved and they seemed to look upon it as a kindness that officers and M.O.s should come out and do their best for them when they were helpless.[3]

The frustrations in the aftermath of the assault also manifested themselves in the War Diaries. At Gommecourt, the 16th Queen's Westminster Rifles of the 56th (London) Division commented in its official summary of 1 July:

> R.A.M.C. ARRANGEMENTS. If arrangement had been made to send up 100 fresh bearers with stretchers on the evening of the battle to begin immediately it was dark to look for and collect wounded in 'No Man's Land' the whole of the wounded in our Sector could have been collected and evacuated the same night. The Regimental Stretcher Bearers and Volunteers from the survivors worked gallantly and indefatigably as they always do, but there is a limit to what men can do especially after a day of battle and the individual fresh men could have done much more; also there was a considerable shortage of stretchers.[4]

The CO of the 9th York and Lancasters, Lt-Col J. Addison, remained in No Man's Land for a number of days before he succumbed to his wounds, and this was proved by a brief diary he had written *in situ*, which was found on his body several months later. (The Casualty Rolls give his date of death as 1 July.) Some of the corpses from the same Division – the 8th – were later found to have been mutilated before or after death, probably by German night patrols. Reports of general barbarity from the Kaiser's men were published back in the UK, prompting one soldier to comment bitterly in the *Bristol Times & Mirror*: 'They've got no decency, like, they Germans.'

Yet there *were* instances of mercy shown by fellow human beings whose nationalities just happened to be at war. One former Wycliffe College student noted, 'I have conceived a profound admiration for the RAMC since this battle of the Ancre, when their coolness in working all day long under fire, doing their work individually, and without an officer to lead them, was beyond praise.' Commenting on the attitude of captured German doctors, he added, 'Many were the little acts of courtesy that I saw pass between men of grey and men of khaki. What an awful waste to be killing one another, when such noble qualities undoubtedly exist on both sides.'[5]

An officer of the London Rifle Brigade opposite Gommecourt recalled:

> There is an incident I should like to mention which shows that we have a decent lot of Huns opposite and which could prove a source of consolation to the relatives of the missing. About 9.45 p.m. (early twilight) a German came out to us, and as I saw his red cross I prevented our men from firing. He came up, saw I had been roughly dressed, and went on nearer to our own lines to attend to one of his own men. Some of our men got up to go and he shouted out and stopped one of their machine guns. I think this shewed [sic] pluck and decency and augurs well for our wounded which we had to leave behind.[6]

For those soldiers struck down early in the assault, medical assistance was more readily accessible if they could get to a dressing station under their own steam, or with the help of comrades. The 25th Field Ambulance at Millencourt revealed that, following the launch of the assault at 7.30 a.m., the first walking cases arrived half an hour later, whereas the more serious casualties were brought in fifteen minutes after that. By 10.00 a.m. there was a steady flow of individuals, and an hour further on a state of congestion was experienced. Those 'sitting' or 'lying' (i.e., the more seriously wounded patients) were sent to the Casualty Clearing Stations at Heilly, and, as the day wore on, all of the medical facilities set up to deal with the injured were hopelessly overwhelmed, leading to the closure of the CCSs at Heilly by 8.30 p.m. (These reopened the following afternoon.) The transport system put in place to ferry the stricken soldiers away from the Front proved to be 'insufficient', and the 24th Field Ambulance – dealing with the ongoing effects of the fighting around Ovillers La Boisselle – documented the fact that many of those who had been brought in were forced to lie on straw outside. At the same time the men who had been incapacitated in the 'chest and abdomen' were sent

Wounded soldiers at Cheltenham's VAD Hospital in either July or August 1916. Most of those in the care of nursing staff had been wounded on the Somme.

on to the 92nd Field Ambulance at Warloy, but even this prevented any more referrals in the afternoon. A journey of up to twelve miles then awaited those deemed fit enough to travel to Puchevillers, and the piles of blood-soaked stretchers grew with every passing hour. 'Some patients slept in the open', disclosed the 24th FA[7]

A great many troops had received 'Blighty' wounds, and they were now part of the colossal Casualty Clearing Chain which would eventually bring them back home in the dozens of Hospital Ships which had been specially requisitioned for this task. Four or five such vessels docked in Southampton each day, and one wounded Major told the *Bristol Times & Mirror*, 'Nobody can tell how much the Boche knew. It doesn't do to place too much reliance on what prisoners say. He undoubtedly knew we were going to make our advance.'

In 1908 the Territorial Forces Act instituted the forming of procedures to look after the wounded in the event of war, and the 2nd Southern General Hospital at Southmead in North Bristol was one of several regional bases set up to cope with the expected demand. With 520 beds at its disposal, the scheme appeared adequately prepared, and a new Surgical Wing at the Infirmary was opened by King George V four years later, adding more scope. When the conflict with Germany began, the medical authorities placed their facilities at the disposal of the War Office, which gradually increased the quota of temporary wards and even tents in the grounds to meet the regular influx of casualties from the Western Front. Smaller sites in the area were also requisitioned, including the Asylum at Fishponds which became the Beaufort War Hospital in 1915. There is a plaque within Bristol Cathedral which states that 89,000 sick and injured patients passed through the entire 2nd Southern General Hospital network between 1914 and 1919.

'Wounded in the Great Offensive' declared the *Gloucester Citizen* on 3 July, '546 Men Arrived Yesterday.' Two days later, the *Gloucestershire Echo* reported, '318 Wounded Arrive In Cheltenham. All were sitting cases, suffering from wounds in head and arms.' As if to reassure the general public it also revealed: 'SOLDIERS SLEEP THROUGH OPERATIONS'. Sixty injured troops disembarked at Lydney on 6 July and eighty-two were admitted to Gloucester's Great Western Hospital the following week.

The *Dean Forest Mercury* also commented:

> The Hon. Mrs Bathurst, Vice President and Hon. Treasurer of the Gloucester Branch of the British Red Cross Society, is raising a special fund to provide bedding, equipment and medical appliances rendered necessary by the large increase in wounded soldiers.

Captain Charles Bathurst, MP, then let the grounds of Redhill House near Lydney for the purposes of the Red Cross. As with the crowded Dressing Stations and Field Ambulances at the Front, these smaller sites were essential to the overall logistics of caring for so many incapacitated servicemen. In August, the *Stroud News* reported that: 'Over 130 wounded soldiers from Standish and Stroud Red Cross Hospitals were entertained at a special matinee given by the Directors of the Empire Theatre, Stroud.' Other recreational activities included special lunches, trips to see a stage play, and even a visit to Bristol Zoo.

After the war Mrs J. Middleton Martin, the Commandant of the Stroud Red Cross Hospital, informed a gathering assembled to congratulate the organisation on its work over the previous four years, that 1,040 patients had been cared for during this time. It was later decided to carry out extensive alterations and additions to Stroud General Hospital as a 'Peace Memorial'. At nearby Standish, its Commandant, Miss King, OBE, gave the 'colours' of the VAD Hospital – the Union and Red Cross Flags which had flown above the complex throughout the conflict – to the Parish Church during a '…solemn service of reception' on 25 February 1919.

Soon after the opening of the Somme campaign, the *Western Daily Press* published the following article from a 'reliable source' under the headline: 'Are We Downhearted? How Fresh Troops And Wounded Met.'

> In Southampton Docks today the writer [of the article] saw a strange dramatic sight…A long Red Cross train, just filled from end to end from one of the hospital ships, casualties from the present offensive in France, was pulling slowly out for its run to London. Almost every window in all its great length served to frame an outward-gazing soldier, officer or man, in ragged blood-stained muddy khaki. These were sitting up cases, nearly all with heads bandaged or arms in slings. It is not difficult to imagine or easy to tell how England looked to a wounded Englishman who has come direct from an intense bombardment and an advance from the trenches in France. Just near the dock gates the hospital train met another equally long train coming in and packed from end to end with fresh troops bound for France from some English depot camp, each one of its windows framed with not one but two or three men in khaki, red, lusty faces well sun-browned, looking out over the close cropped heads of their mates, full of eager curiosity and expectation, and full of the fresh, clean robustness which camp life in the English countryside brings to us all.
>
> For fifty yards or so, and at a foot pace, the two contrasting trains of King George's soldiers glided side by side in an uncanny silence. The writer watched them from an office window overhead and could plainly see in the faces of the untried troops their eager interest and profound respect for their comrades who had been tried. A strange dumb kind of promise shone out from many of the eyes in those fresh faces. Assured pride, the easy fearlessness of the man who has proved himself in the very teeth of death, this was marked in the faces of the wounded. But not a man spoke a word…Suddenly, in a rather quavering voice most singularly vibrant with emotion, a very young lance-corporal of the Dorsets…whose right arm was in a white sling and whose head was swathed in bandages, cried out in all the sunny silence: 'Are we downhearted?' Then the tension snapped. It seemed that hundreds of these brave fellows, coming home and going out, heaved long sighs. All had wanted to give expression to the powerful emotions inspired by the chance juxtaposition of those two trains, and none had known how. Here was a way.

The music of the roar which rose now from the cabined hundreds of both trains was something to penetrate the [soul] of a Briton…Those wonderful rising and falling waves of sound I shall never forget. It was only when the two trains were divided by a gap of fully 200 yards that the music of it died away slowly in the soft summer air. The Kings and Generals have been answered from the very bottoms of the hearts of brave men strung to tense feeling by the sudden pressure of emotion that not one among the many hundreds of them could analyse or explain. Pride, modesty, eager curiosity, deep-seated determination, pity, respect, wonder, admiration, satisfaction, reassurance, aspiration, high ambition, and heartfelt good wishes and comradeship – all were there for ears that could catch their different notes in the thrilling ringing successive waves of 'No!' 'No!' 'No!' 'No!'

This cleverly crafted piece of narrative appears to be clear propaganda designed to obscure the true cost of the Battle of the Somme from the public. And yet it is dangerous to read it with too jaundiced an eye, as it is not difficult to imagine such an event taking place. Perhaps less well known is the fact that the authorities regularly screened off platforms at London railway stations to allow the wounded to be transferred to ambulances hidden from general view. Morale-boosting stories of new recruits cheering their injured comrades at the dockside was one thing, but the harsh truth of countless battered and broken bodies being brought home day after day, and night after night, was quite another. The citizens of Britain, Ireland and the wider Empire needed only to check the Casualty Returns in their local and national newspapers on a daily basis to gain some idea of what was really happening to their menfolk across the English Channel.

21

THE LEGACIES OF
1 JULY 1916
AND THE REST OF THE WAR

With all of the analysis, discussion of tactics, and the benefit of hindsight which the ensuing decades rendered in relation to the military strategies employed on 1 July 1916, it was the observations of men who took part in the attack which perhaps contain the most telling indictments of all. Written just hours later under the heading 'Suggestions & Criticisms', the War Diary of the 12th York and Lancaster Regiment – the Sheffield Battalion which had suffered heavy losses in front of Serre – noted:

(A) The wait in the Assembly trenches was too long.

(B) The first wave should not have occupied the front line. Owing to the Trench Mortars being in position in the front line, it became a death trap when the enemy retaliated against them.

(C) More bombardment slits should have been dug. It was found that men occupying these suffered very slightly compared with those in Assembly trenches; those that were dug should have been deeper.

(D) More men should have been trained in the use of the Bangalore torpedo. It was found that all trained men had become casualties by the time the torpedoes were actually required.

(E) Smoke bombs would have been useful to conceal our efforts to cut the enemy's wire. As it was, anyone attempting to cut the wire was immediately sniped.

Tactics

(i) The assault should have been made at dawn or soon after. As it was the enemy had 4.5 hours to prepare for an attack, as our intention was undoubtedly given away by the gaps cut in our wire and the tapes laid out in front. Men who reached the German wire state that on looking towards our own lines, they could see almost every movement. This being so any attack by day was scarcely likely to succeed.

(ii) The attack should have been in double time.

(iii) The waves were too far apart, the distance between them allowing the enemy to pay attention to each wave before the next came up.

Miscellaneous

Assaulting bombers state that they think they could have carried their bombs better in jackets than in the buckets.

The general opinion was that Officers, N.C.O's and Machine gunners were marked men.[1]

On a more expansive level, it has since been argued that the gains in the south – around Montauban and Mametz – should have been exploited by the cavalry, which had been held in reserve for just such a breakthrough. The terrain, however, was not suited to a swift charge across shell-holes, barbed wire and the debris of warfare, whilst the tank had yet to deployed on the Western Front. But the German reinforcements were stretched to the limit here, and this question remains one of the major 'if-only' scenarios of 1 July. Elsewhere along the line it was clear the attack had stalled and casualties were mounting, so maybe consolidation in the sectors where ground had been gained was the only sensible option. By the time the Germans had shored up their defences and introduced more manpower, the British finally launched the next stage of their offensive against an ever-more resilient enemy.

So the campaign dragged on, through the summer and into autumn. The Divisions were 'rotated' to allow periods of recuperation, whereas the most severely shattered remnants of county regiments were withdrawn altogether. The focus of the attack narrowed around the original main thrust along the Albert–Bapaume Road and battlefields around Serre and Gommecourt were shut down, although the fighting remained just as fierce. Mametz Wood, Trones Wood, Pozieres Ridge, and many other blood-soaked place-names became horrific reminders of the carnage associated with the First World War, and in late November the *Stroud News* declared, 'Special services of thanksgiving in celebration of the British victory at Beaumont Hamel were held at the Holy Trinity Church, Stroud, on the previous Sunday, the preacher being the Vicar.'

With the weather worsening and both sides utterly exhausted, the Battle of the Somme had finally ended. Whether it really was a 'victory' for the Allies has been hotly debated ever since, although the British and Commonwealth forces had at least partially achieved their initial targets; they had relieved the pressure on the French at Verdun, its armies had fully engaged the Germans in total warfare for over four months, and the line had moved forwards by approximately six miles at its furthest point. But after 140 days of bloodshed the first day target of Bapaume was still four miles away, and the British/Commonwealth casualties have been placed at anywhere between 400,000 and 600,000 men, with the French and Germans suffering similar losses. The volunteer army, made up entirely of men who had chosen to fight for their country, was crushed, and those sent to replace them were the conscripts who were now drafted into the army in stages according to their age, marital status and occupation.

If 1916 marked a year of brutal changes then 1917 was bleaker still. The Germans tactically withdrew from a number of key positions on the Somme in the first few months, and despite gradual advances in Allied military techniques and approaches the horrors of 'Passchendaele' (July–November) plunged hundreds of thousands of troops into an unbelievable quagmire of carnage and suffering. (At Tower Hamlets Spur, east of Ypres, on 4 October eight men were in a shell-hole when one of them attempted to throw a bomb at the enemy, but was shot in the process, causing the grenade to roll back amongst his comrades. Devon-born Pte Thomas Sage immediately flung himself on the explosive to smother the blast, severely wounding himself in the process, but saving the lives of his fellow soldiers. Pte Sage was awarded the Victoria Cross, and the small group all belonged to the 8th Somerset Light Infantry, which had attacked with the 21st Division on the Somme on 1 July 1916.) The collapse of the Eastern Front was now imminent, and large numbers of battle-hardened German veterans soon crossed Europe to join their comrades in the west for one final thrust to break the deadlock before the Americans joined the fray. After so nearly achieving their goal, the attack finally petered out, allowing the combined forces of the British, French, Commonwealth and now the United States to drive home their superior advantage in manpower, equipment and supplies. It was, however, a close run affair, and losses were dangerously high, especially for the British Army, but with the eventual smashing of the trench systems, the more modern and mechanised style of warfare we know today came to the fore, leading to the cessation of hostilities on 11 November 1918.

As this momentous day approached, one Old Boy of Wycliffe College ventured:

Would it not be well at the 'After the War' Gathering of O.W.s to hold a Front Trench supper? Grub – H²O, port and plum and bully and staff of life; utensils – mess tins stolen from someone else, jack knife found before it was lost, one spoon ditto; location of trench – a stretch of canal past the Bathing House, emptied the night before so that there will be enough room to [drench] the troops. This can be called 'Sunken Road a la Somme', or 'Somewhere in Glos.'[2]

Gloucestershire-born Col W.W. Foster, DSO & Two Bars, served with a Canadian Infantry unit throughout the war, and received his first DSO for gallantry at Mouquet Farm, near Thiepval on the Somme, in mid-September 1916. Known as 'Mucky Farm' by the British, it was nearly captured by the 36th (Ulster) Division on 1 July, but the supports were too thin on the ground to effect a final push towards this strategic position, which was situated close to the Schwaben Redoubt. Two and a half years later Col Foster reflected:

> The last month of the war, in spite of a lot of hard fighting, was one great triumphant procession, culminating, as far as we were concerned, in the taking of Mons a few hours before the Armistice. I was lucky enough to command the detachment from our Brigade which made the official entry. Amidst all the satisfaction and rejoicing one cannot help feeling what a pity it is that men who have done the real work, and whose sacrifice helped to bring about this accomplishment, are in so many instances not able to share it with us.[3]

There is a huge irony in the capture of Mons, as it was the site of the first major battle of the BEF way back in August 1914. These 'Old Contemptibles' of the professional, pre-war army were virtually wiped out by Christmas, leading to the introduction of the New Armies throughout 1915 and into 1916. 1 July of the latter year marked a watershed in the First World War, and it has even been stated that this one date ushered in the entire modern era. The nature of the battalions also changed after the opening day of the Somme campaign. New recruits from all parts of the country were sent to fill the gaps once occupied by men from predominantly the same town or county as their comrades. A proportion of the 1 July wounded did not wish to return to their old units, as they knew most of the familiar faces had gone forever, and so preferred anonymity amongst the ranks of a neutral regiment. In deed and reality, but not in thought and spirit, the Pals ethos was no more.

The following narrative was written by a correspondent of the *Gloucestershire Echo*, who watched the soldiers making their way to the Front in the final days of June 1916:

WHISTLING ON THE WAY TO DEATH

As we stood, in the shadow of some trees 20 yards from a road which led directly down to the trenches, detachments of our troops could be seen swinging across country in half-companies, companies, and battalions. Long before they came close one heard the steady roar of their feet – tramp-*tramp,* tramp-*tramp*! And always as they passed they whistled softly in unison. Some whistled 'Tipperary', some 'Come back, my Bonny, to me', and some, best of all in the place and surroundings, 'La Marseillaise'. As we came back along that road, far behind the front, we saw more companies, more battalions. On the tree-shaded road it was too dark to see them, save only as vague, dark masses against the light background of the highway. One felt their presence…always the steady tramp-*tramp*, tramp-*tramp* as they shouldered by, and they were always whistling.

COMMEMORATION
ON THE SOMME

The onus of ensuring each and every casualty of the Somme campaign – and the wider war – was properly recorded fell to Clifton-born Major-General Sir Fabian Ware, whose colossal task of remembering the dead began even whilst the conflict was ongoing. (Ware spent his final years in the Gloucestershire village of Amberley, and lies buried in the parish churchyard.) As has been established in the biographies of certain officers in this text, the bodies of a proportion of them were exhumed from the site of their original interments and brought to larger, purpose-built burial grounds after the Armistice. Designed by prominent architects, each Commonwealth War Cemetery has been sympathetically laid out, and all of the gravestones are of the familiar white granite, prompting some to suggest they resemble ranks of soldiers standing to attention on parade, waiting for the order to 'dismiss' which will never come.

For those 1916 Somme casualties whose remains were never found, the vast majority are remembered on the Thiepval Memorial to the Missing, which contains the names of almost 73,000 British, Irish and South African servicemen who fell in the area and have no recognised final resting place. The memorial is 150 feet high, stands on a ridge overlooking the battlefields, and was unveiled by the Prince of Wales in 1932, revealing the 'Piers' – or panels – upon which the individuals are commemorated alphabetically by regiment. The Somerset Light Infantry, for example, has a total of 580 from all ranks, whilst the number for combined battalions of the Glosters tops 1,000. It was once believed that fourteen-year-old Pte Reginald Giles, of the 1st Glosters, was the youngest Somme casualty, losing his life in action on 20 August 1916. A look at the 1901 Census, however, reveals that Cirencester-born Reginald Giles is aged five in this year, which would have made him nineteen or twenty in 1916. There is no indication of the birth of another person with this name around the year 1902.

Annually, on 1 July, a memorial service is held at Thiepval, with all nationalities represented. Similar events are organised along the entire Somme Front, attended by descendants of those who had a particular affiliation to specific areas of the line, as well as those who simply have an interest in military history. At La Boisselle, the Friends of Lochnagar now hold an emotive ceremony at the site of the huge mine which was blown at 7.28 a.m. on this date back in 1916, launching the attack of the 34th Division. At this exact time every year, a firework is lit, followed by a piper walking slowly round the rim of the crater playing a sad lament – a reminder of the brave pipers of the Tyneside Brigades and all those who went 'over the top' into such a maelstrom of bullets and bombs. The event – which is exceptionally moving – encompasses those of all backgrounds, and one incident which occurred during the 2001 commemorations still sticks in my mind as clear as Mr Campbell's oration on the same subject twenty-one years previously. At around 7.30 a.m. on the morning of 1 July, on a warm, clear, calm summer's morning in France, four lines of birds flew from the direction of the 34th Division's assault and crossed

The Lochnagar Crater at 7.30 a.m. on 1 July 2006 – the exact time of the attack ninety years earlier. The village of La Boiselle is in the mist in the distance. There was birdsong and the church bells were ringing.

Mash Valley today. The 8th and 34th Divisions attacked up the hill towards the camera, suffering dreadful casualties from machine guns to the front and on the flanks. The German defences ran along the back edge of the houses to the left (La Boiselle) and curved round to where this image was taken.

Massed graves at Serre Road, 2006. This image, taken by Terry Carter between 7.30 and 8.00 a.m. on 1 July, shows the site of the advance of the 4th and 31st Divisions ninety years before. A number of Bristol men serving with the 1st Somersets lie buried here.

over the crater, disappearing into the distance beyond the peaceful village of La Boisselle. It was startling and unexpected, prompting obvious comparisons with the proud battalions setting off in four waves of perfect formation. Romantics and cynics formed their own opinions, and whilst a rational view was taken by most, there was still a spectre of doubt to haunt even the most sceptical of souls. In a world where we think we know it all, Nature still has the ability to shake our perception of knowledge and understanding to its core.

I also attended the ninetieth commemoration ceremonies at Lochnagar and Thiepval, taking photographs which are included in this book. Having researched the men of Gloucestershire and North Bristol who fell along the entire Front, this second journey was a much more personal experience, allowing me to briefly put a few faces to carved names on gravestones and memorials. Ninety years on, some were still officially 'missing presumed dead', having last been seen going 'over the top' on 1 July 1916. Their loss haunts me to this very day.

CONCLUSION

Whilst I was writing this book, I happened across an original card sent by a soldier from the Front, presumably to his loved ones back home. Dated January 1916, it has the verse:

> Adown the paths of life may gladness greet you;
> Dame Fortune guide, protect, and good luck meet you.

Followed by:

> The Season's Greetings and all Good Wishes through 1916 is the Sincere Wish of...

And it is signed in ink, '...your old boy Herb'. Underneath is printed, 'Somerset Light Infantry'. The whereabouts of 'Herb' at the time is deliberately vague, due to the war-time censorship of precise military locations, and his ultimate fate is equally unknown. However, seventy-nine men named 'Herbert' in the ranks of the SLI lost their lives between the beginning of 1916 and the end of the conflict – four even on 1 July 1916, while serving with the 1st or 8th Battalions. (SDGW.) The human cost of the First World War is incalculable.

Two accounts of military funerals on the Somme form the conclusion to this tribute to the men of Gloucestershire who fell on this one date in history. The first focuses upon the high-profile death of Brig.-Gen. C.B. Prowse, DSO, the CO of the 11th Infantry Brigade and former officer with the Somersets. (His family links with Gloucestershire, as well as a short biography, are revealed in Chapter Thirteen.) There is a file[4] kept at the Somerset Record Office which contains eyewitness testimonies, as well as heartfelt sympathies (in the form of type-written letters), which were sent to Brig.-Gen. Prowse's widow in the days following the tragic event, and amidst all of the carnage on such a blood-soaked day, the sincerity and shock expressed by men of all ranks at the loss of their Commanding Officer is palpable.

W.R. Bailey, Prowse's servant (or 'batman'), informed Mrs Prowse that her husband had been going round the front line following the attack when heavy German shelling commenced in the vicinity, and soon afterwards the Brigadier-General was hit in the left side of his back by a 'rifle bullet'. His first thoughts were for his wife and children back home, and the second for the progress of his men in the advance. Taken back to Divisional HQ on a stretcher, the casualty succumbed to his wounds a short while later with Bailey faithfully at his side. The CO's servant admitted that he was grief-stricken, and would write again when the turmoil of 1 July had receded, allowing him to think more clearly.

Geoffrey Prideaux, a Staff Captain with the 11th Brigade, told Violet Prowse that at around 10.00 a.m. on 1 July, the CO had taken the greater part of his HQ Staff up to the captured front line, and just as he moved over the parapet of the British forward trench he was struck by a bullet from a German machine-gun. 'This seemed to paralise [sic] his lower limbs,' noted Prideaux, who added: 'He is an irretrievable loss both to his regiment and to the Army as a whole.' Major E.G. Elger of the Somersets concurred: 'The poor Regiment has suffered very severely. Col Thicknesse and many others have gone and as yet we do not know our losses.' The Major went on: '…the grave is in a little garden by the side of a small country lane off the main high road.'

The Commander of VIII Corps, Lt-Gen. Sir A.G. Hunter-Weston, expanded upon the burial service:

> I attended his funeral, a simple and very impressive ceremony. The coffin being borne on the shoulders of six N.C.O.s and attended by his Corps and Divisional Generals,★ and their and his Staff officers, by his old friend, Major Elgar, and several other officers and many men. Revd Laurie, Chaplain to the Forces, conducted the ceremony. He was laid to rest in a charmingly pretty, peaceful plot of ground under a cloudless blue sky, while the thunder of heavy artillery in the battle line formed an appropriate last salute to a great soldier and a gallant gentleman. I am having an oak cross and kerb and iron railing put round his grave, and will cover his body's resting place with growing flowers.

On 3 July, W.R. Bailey wrote to Mrs Prowse again, revealing that '…the General looked into my eyes and smiled sweetly before he became unconscious.' Referring to the grave itself, the Chaplain to the 11th Infantry Brigade, Revd A.E. Laurie, told Violet that it was '…unlikely the place will ever be disturbed', and would serve as a:

> …reminder, witness and inspiration to our men as they pass up to press on the advantage so gallantly initiated by your husband…The grave was filled in by men of his old Regiment, the Somersets.

Everyone present at the graveside knew the Brigadier-General personally, and were described as 'sincere mourners'. Revd Laurie recalled how the former had showed him photographs of his wife and children a short while before, and concluded: 'He was one of the simplest and kindest of men I have ever met…He died a hero's death. [He] was not merely a General, but a very dear friend…'

Nine days on from the death, Gen. Hunter-Weston contacted Mrs Prowse once more, telling her: 'The grave of my dear friend, your husband, looks so peaceful, pretty and happy with its carpet of growing flowers and its background of green…He was a man. A gentleman and a soldier. I am proud to have had the friendship of such a hero.'

An unnamed church minister from Bristol passed on his impressions of a multiple burial of fallen soldiers to the *Western Daily Press* upon his return to England:

> Summer sun was glowing as we wended our way along the dusty main road, which was thronged with lorries and motor cars, and with pedestrians, military and civilians. A touch of the picturesque [was provided] by the nursing sisters with the red facings and long flowing white caps. Our objective was the English cemetery by the roadside [which] contained some hundreds of our brave lads who had made the supreme sacrifice for King and Country. We saw the crowd of little grave mounds, all symmetrically laid out, and with two wooden crosses at the head of each, for each grave contains the bodies of two soldiers. In the golden sunshine away from the dusty roadside, the resting places of those heroes was one blaze of soft and blended colour…

★One was Gen. Lambton, the CO of the 4th Division, which included the 11th Brigade and the Somersets. Lt-Gen. Sir T D'Oyly Snow referred to Brig.-Gen. Prowse as '…one of the bravest men I have ever known.'

Above left: A section of the graves in Ovillers Military Cemetery, at the head of Mash Valley. Many of those at rest here are casualties of the attacks on 1 July 1916.

Above right: Fricourt British Cemetery contains a memorial to the men of the 7th Yorkshires (Green Howards) who fell trying to storm the village on 1 July 1916.

A British General then stepped forward and spoke of 'the boys who slept their long sleep – duty well done…', whilst at the head of each interment stood a serviceman, holding a wreath made out of either roses or carnations. At a given moment, these floral tokens of respect were placed on top of each cross, whereupon the minister recalled:

> Then I noticed that all the graves faced, not east, but west, towards home, 'dear old Blighty', as the soldiers say. Are not all the boys' thoughts at the last of home? A dear Bristol lad, the nurse told me, spoke with his last breath of his mother.

NOTES AND REFERENCES

(NB: 'NA' stands for 'National Archives')

CHAPTER ONE – THE WESTERN FRONT

1 *Wycliffe & The War* (published by the College during the 1920s)
2 *Wycliffe & The War*
3 *Wycliffe & The War*
4 *Wycliffe & The War*

CHAPTER TWO – THE FINAL SEVEN DAYS

1	War Diary, NA	1st Glos. Btty. (3/1st S.Mid. Bde	WO95/2749
2	War Diary, NA	46th Trench Mortar Btty. (Z46)	WO95/2675
3	War Diary, NA	1st Somerset Light Infantry	WO95/1499
4	War Diary, NA	1st Somerset Light Infantry	WO95/1499
5	War Diary, NA	1st Somerset Light Infantry	WO95/1499
6	War Diary, NA	1st Somerset Light Infantry	WO95/1499
7	*Wycliffe & The War*		
8	War Diary, NA	6th Northamptonshire Regt	WO95/2044
9	War Diary, NA	10th King's Own Yorkshire Light Infantry	WO95/2162
10	War Diary, NA	6th Northamptonshire Regt	WO95/2044
11	War Diary, NA	10th KOYLI	WO95/2162
12	War Diary, NA	6th Northants.	WO95/2044
13	*Dursley Gazette*	July 1916	
14	War Diary, NA	8th Somerset Light Infantry	WO95/2158
15	War Diary, NA	8th Somerset Light Infantry	WO95/2158
16	War Diary, NA	13th King's Royal Rifle Corps	WO95/2533
17	War Diary, NA	13th King's Royal Rifle Corps	WO95/2533
18	War Diary, NA	2nd Wiltshires	WO95/2329
19	War Diary, NA	2nd Wiltshires	WO95/2329
20	War Diary, NA	1st Somerset Light Infantry	WO95/1499
21	War Diary, NA	1st Somerset Light Infantry	WO95/1499
22	*Wycliffe & The War*		
2	*Wycliffe & The War*		

Chapter Four – 30th Division

1	*Wycliffe & The War*		
2	War Diary, NA	19th Manchesters	WO95/2329
3	War Diary, NA	18th King's Liverpool Regt	WO95/2330
4	War Diary, NA	18th King's Liverpool Regt	WO95/2330
5	War Diary, NA	18th Manchesters	WO95/2339

Chapter Five – 18th (Eastern) Division

1	W/D, NA	8th East Surrey Regt	WO95/2050
2	W/D, NA	8th East Surrey Regt	WO95/2050
3	W/D, NA	8th East Surrey Regt	WO95/2050
4	W/D, NA	8th East Surrey Regt	WO95/2050
5	W/D, NA	8th East Surrey Regt	WO95/2050
6	W/D, NA	8th East Surrey Regt	WO95/2050
7	W/D, NA	8th East Surrey Regt	WO95/2050
8	Service Record, NA	Lt E.H.A. Goss	WO339/20784
9	*Bristol Times & Mirror*		
10	Service Record, NA	Lt E.H.A. Goss	WO339/20784
11	Service Record, NA	Lt E.H.A. Goss	WO339/20784
12	W/D, NA	7th Bedfords	WO95/2043
13	W/D, NA	7th Bedfords	WO95/2043
14.	W/D, NA	7th Bedfords	WO95/2043
15	W/D, NA	6th Northants.	WO95/2044
16	W/D, NA	6th Northants.	WO95/2044
17	W/D, NA	6th Northants.	WO95/2044
18	Service Record, NA	Pte W.R. Savage	WO363/1311

Chapter Six – 7th Division

1	W/D, NA	22nd Manchesters	WO95/1669
2	W/D, NA	2nd Queen's (Royal West Surrey)	WO95/1670
3	W/D, NA	2nd Queen's (Royal West Surrey)	WO95/1670
4	W/D, NA	2nd Queen's (Royal West Surrey)	WO95/1670
5	W/D, NA	2nd Queen's (Royal West Surrey)	WO95/1670
6	Service Record, NA	T/Capt. E.C. Thorneycroft	WO339/451
7	S/R, NA	Cpl H.R. Gething	WO363/G257
8	W/D, NA	2nd Gordon Highlanders	WO95/1656
9	W/D, NA	9th Devons	WO95/1656
10	W/D, NA	9th Devons	WO95/1656
11	W/D, NA	9th Devons	WO95/1656
12	W/D, NA	8th Devons	WO95/1655
13	W/D, NA	8th Devons	WO95/1655
14	W/D, NA	8th Devons	WO95/1655
15	S/R, NA	Capt. G. Tregelles	WO339/11523
16	S/R, NA	2nd Lt R.B. Holcroft	WO339/18678
17	S/R, NA	2nd Lt R.B. Holcroft	WO339/18678
18	S/R, NA	2nd Lt R.B. Holcroft	WO339/18678
19	W/D, NA	8th Devons	WO95/1655

20 W/D, NA   2nd Borders   WO95/1655
21. S/R, NA   2nd Lt D.H.H. Logan   WO339/240

CHAPTER SEVEN – 17TH DIVISION, 50TH BRIGADE

1 W/D, NA   10th West Yorkshire Regt   WO95/2004
2 W/D, NA   7th East Yorkshire Regt   WO95/2002
3 W/D, NA   5th Special Brigade, Royal Engineers   WO95/122
4 W/D, NA   5th Special Brigade, Royal Engineers   WO95/122
5 S/R, NA   Sapper Richard St John   WO363/2138

CHAPTER EIGHT – 21ST DIVISION

1 W/D, NA   8th Somerset Light Infantry   WO95/2158
2 W/D, NA   8th Somerset Light Infantry   WO95/2158
3 S/R, NA   Capt. W.G. Warden   WO339/38491
4 S/R, NA   Capt. W.G. Warden   WO339/38491
5 *Western Daily Press*
6 S/R, NA   Major G.B. Bosanquet   WO339/6698
7 W/D, NA   9th King's Own Yorkshire Light Infantry   WO95/2162
8 S/R, NA   2nd Lt F.A. Golding   WO339/47645
9 S/R, NA   2nd Lt F.A. Golding   WO339/47645
10 S/R, NA   2nd Lt F.A. Golding   WO339/47645
11 S/R, NA   2nd Lt F.A. Golding   WO339/47645

CHAPTER NINE – 34TH DIVISION

1 W/D, NA   15th Royal Scots   WO95/2457
2 W/D, NA   10th Lincolnshire Regt   WO95/2457
3 W/D, NA   10th Lincolnshire Regt   WO95/2457
4 S/R, NA   L/Sgt K.R. Brotherton   WO363/354
5 S/R, NA   T/Lt. R.Q. Gilson   WO339/29720
6 W/D, NA   101st Co., Machine Gun Corps   WO95/2458
7 W/D, NA   101st Co., Machine Gun Corps   WO95/2458
8 W/D, NA   207th Field Co., RE   WO95/2449
9 W/D, NA   207th Field Co., RE   WO95/2449
10 Military Cross Citation (Lt. Wilding), *London Gazette* 26/9/1916
11 S/R, NA   Lt H.D. Wilding   WO339/71906
12 W/D, NA   1st Tyneside Scottish (Northumberland Fusiliers) WO95/2462
13 W/D, NA   4th Tyneside Scottish   WO95/2463
14 W/D, NA   3rd Tyneside Scottish   WO95/2463
15 W/D, NA   4th Tyneside Scottish   WO95/2463
16 W/D, NA   103rd Co., MGC   WO95/2467
17 W/D, NA   103rd Co., MGC   WO95/2467
18 S/R, NA   2nd Lt W.C. Hickman   WO339/5871
19 S/R, NA   2nd Lt W.C. Hickman   WO339/5871
20 W/D, NA   10th Lincolnshire Regt   WO95/2457
21 *Wycliffe & The War*

CHAPTER TEN – 8TH DIVISION

1	W/D, NA	2nd Middlesex Regt	WO95/1713
2	DSO citation (Lt-Col E.T.F. Sandys), *London Gazette* 22/9/1916		
3	W/D, NA	2nd Royal Berkshire Regt	WO95/1729
4	DCM citation (Sgt Trimmer), *London Gazette* 3/6/1916		
5	S/R, NA	Rifm. Harry Skinner	WO363/2324
6	W/D, NA	8th King's Own Yorkshire Light Infantry	WO95/2187
7	W/D, NA	8th King's Own Yorkshire Light Infantry	WO95/2187
8	S/R, NA	Lt E.M.B. Cambie	WO339/20197
9	S/R, NA	Lt E.M.B. Cambie	WO339/20197
10	W/D, NA	8th York & Lancaster Regt	WO95/2188

CHAPTER ELEVEN – 32ND DIVISION

1	S/R, NA	2nd Lt FM Ransom	WO339/44818
2	W/D, NA	1st Dorset Regt	WO95/2392
3	W/D, NA	1st Dorset Regt	WO95/2392
4	W/D, NA	1st Dorset Regt	WO95/2392
5	W/D, NA	1st Dorset Regt	WO95/2392
6	S/R, NA	L/Cpl W.E. May	WO363/1405
7	W/D, NA	2nd King's Own Yorkshire Light Infantry	WO95/2402

CHAPTER TWELVE – 29TH DIVISION

1	W/D, NA	1st King's Own Scottish Borderers	WO95/2304
2	W/D, NA	2nd South Wales Borderers	WO95/2304
3	S/R, NA	Capt. A.A. Hughes	WO339/6895
4	S/R, NA	Capt. A.A. Hughes	WO339/6895
5	W/D, NA	1st Border Regt	WO95/2305
6	W/D, NA	1st Lancashire Fusiliers	WO95/2300
7	W/D, NA	1st Lancashire Fusiliers	WO95/2300
8	W/D, NA	1st Lancashire Fusiliers	WO95/2300
9	W/D, NA	1st Lancashire Fusiliers	WO95/2300
10	W/D, NA	2nd Royal Fusiliers	WO95/2301
11	W/D, NA	16th Middlesex Regt	WO95/2302
12	S/R, NA	Pte M.P.H. Blumer	WO363/1871
13	W/D, NA	86th Co. Machine Gun Corps	WO95/2302
14	W/D, NA	2nd Monmouth Regt	WO95/2295

CHAPTER THIRTEEN – 4TH DIVISION

1	W/D, NA	1st Hampshire Regt	WO95/1495
2	S/R, NA	Lt H.I. Adams	WO339/39849
3	S/R, NA	Lt H.I. Adams	WO339/39849
4	W/D, NA	1st Somerset Light Infantry	WO95/1499
5	W/D, NA	1st Somerset Light Infantry	WO95/1499
6	S/R, NA	Lt E.C. MacBryan	WO339/17275
7	S/R, NA	Lt E.C. MacBryan	WO339/17275

8	S/R, NA	Lt E.C. MacBryan	WO339/17275
9	S/R, NA	2nd Lt W.H. Treasure	WO339/56263
10	S/R, NA	2nd Lt W.H. Treasure	WO339/56263
11	S/R, NA	2nd Lt W.H. Treasure	WO339/56263
12	S/R, NA	2nd Lt W.H. Treasure	WO339/56263
13	S/R, NA	2nd Lt W.H. Treasure	WO339/56263
14	W/D, NA	1st Somerset Light Infantry	WO95/1499
15	W/D, NA	1st Somerset Light Infantry	WO95/1499
16	S/R, NA	Capt. K. Herne	WO374/32938

Chapter Fourteen – 31st Division

1	W/D, NA	15th West Yorkshire Regt	WO95/2361
2	*Wycliffe & The War*		
3	S/R, NA	2nd Lt A. Beacall	WO339/47323
4	W/D, NA	11th East Lancashire Regt	WO95/2366
5	S/R, NA	2nd Lt A. Beacall	WO339/47323
6	W/D, NA	12th York & Lancaster Regt	WO95/2365
7	W/D, NA	12th York & Lancaster Regt	WO95/2365
8	S/R, NA	Cpl F.E. Watkins	WO363/714
9	W/D, NA	12th York & Lancaster Regt	WO95/2365
10	*Wycliffe & The War*		
11	W/D, NA	92nd Co. Machine Gun Corps	WO95/2358
12	S/R, NA	2nd Lt A.M. Herapath	WO339/48303
13	S/R, NA	2nd Lt A.M. Herapath	WO339/48303
14	S/R, NA	2nd Lt A.M. Herapath	WO339/48303

Chapter Fifteen – 48th Division

1	W/D, NA	1st Glos. Battn., 3/1 South Midland Bde.	WO95/2749
2	W/D, NA	1st Glos. Battn., 3/1 South Midland Bde.	WO95/2749
3	W/D, NA	1/5th Gloucestershire Regt	WO95/2763
4	W/D, NA	1/6th Gloucestershire Regt	WO95/2758
5	W/D, NA	1/4th Gloucestershire Regt	WO95/2758

Chapter Sixteen – 56th (London) Division

1	W/D, NA	1/16th Westminster Rifles (London Regt)	WO95/2963
2	W/D, NA	1/16th Westminster Rifles (London Regt)	WO95/2963
3	W/D, NA	1/16th Westminster Rifles (London Regt)	WO95/2963
4	W/D, NA	5th London Rifle Bde. (London Regt)	WO95/2961
5	W/D, NA	5th London Rifle Bde. (London Regt)	WO95/2961
6	W/D, NA	5th London Rifle Bde. (London Regt)	WO95/2961
7	W/D, NA	5th London Rifle Bde. (London Regt)	WO95/2961

CHAPTER SEVENTEEN – 46TH AND 37TH DIVISIONS

1	W/D, NA	11th Royal Warwickshire Regt	WO95/2538
2	W/D, NA	11th Royal Warwickshire Regt	WO95/2538
3	*Wycliffe & The War*		
4	W/D, NA	1/7th Sherwood Foresters	WO95/2694
5	W/D, NA	1/7th Sherwood Foresters	WO95/2694
6	W/D, NA	46th Co. Machine Gun Corps	WO95/1954
7	S/R, NA	Pte A.W.E. Willey	WO363/1068
8	W/D, NA	154th Co., RE	WO95/2523
9	W/D, NA	13th King's Royal Rifle Corps	WO95/2533
10	S/R, NA	Sapper W. Paxton	WO363/647–8
11	W/D, NA	11th Royal Warwickshire Regt	WO95/2538

CHAPTER EIGHTEEN – 19TH (WESTERN) DIVISION

1	*Stroud News*, July 1916		
2	W/D, NA	9th Welch Regt	WO95/2092

CHAPTER NINETEEN – THE LOSSES

1	S/R, NA	2nd Lt A.J. Maybrey	WO339/34597

CHAPTER TWENTY – THE VCs AND THE WOUNDED

1	W/D, NA	4th Tyneside Scottish	WO95/2463
2	W/D, NA	10th Lincolnshire Regt	WO95/2457
3	W/D, NA	18th King's Liverpool Regt	WO95/2330
4	W/D, NA	1/16th Queen's Westminster Rifles (London Regt)	WO95/2963
5	*Wycliffe & The War*		
6	W/D, NA	5th London Rifle Bde. (London Regt)	WO95/2961
7	W/D, NA	24th Field Ambulance	WO95/1703

CHAPTER TWENTY-ONE – THE LEGACIES

1	W/D, NA	12th York & Lancaster Regt	WO95/2365
2	*Wycliffe & The War*		
3	*Wycliffe & The War*		
4	Somerset Record Office	DD/SLI/17/3/142	

BIBLIOGRAPHY

The First Day On The Somme (Martin Middlebrook, Penguin Books)

The Imperial War Museum Book of the Somme, (Malcolm Brown, Pan Books in association with the IWM)

The Somme Day-By-Day Account (Chris McCarthy, Brockhampton Press, London)

A Military Atlas of the First World War (Arthur Banks, Leo Cooper)

The V.C. & D.S.O. Book, Volumes I–III (reprint, Naval & Military Press)

British Regiments 1914–18 (Brig. E.A. James, reprint Naval & Military Press)

The Gloucestershire Regiment in the War 1914–1918 (Everard Wyrall, reprint Naval & Military Press)

Kelly's Directories (Glos. Record Office)

INDEX

If you are interested in purchasing other books published by Tempus,
or in case you have difficulty finding any Tempus books in your local bookshop,
you can also place orders directly through our website

www.tempus-publishing.com